Bound with an
Iron Chain

Bound with an Iron Chain

The Untold Story of How the British Transported 50,000 Convicts to Colonial America

Anthony Vaver

PICKPOCKET
PUBLISHING

Westborough, MA
www.PickpocketPublishing.com

ISBN 978-0-9836744-0-5

Library of Congress Control Number: 2011908764

Pickpocket Publishing

41 Piccadilly Way, Suite 202

Westborough, MA 01581

http://www.PickpocketPublishing.com

Although the author and publisher have made every effort to ensure the accuracy and completeness of information contained in this book, we assume no responsibility for errors, inaccuracies, omissions, or any inconsistency herein. Any slights of people, places, or organizations are unintentional

For

Martha, Madeleine, and Audrey,

who are everything to me

Down to the harbour I was took again,
On board of ship bound with an iron chain,
Which I was forc'd to wear both night and day,
For fear I from the sloop should run away.

—James Revel, *The Poor Unhappy Transported Felon's Sorrowful Account of His Fourteen Years Transportation, at Virginia, in America.*

Table of Contents

Preface

The seed for my interest in convict transportation to colonial America was planted in 1996 while writing my doctoral dissertation on 18th-century British crime literature. As I was researching the history of crime for this project I came across references to convict transportation to America and thought that this peculiar form of punishment deserved more exploration. I did not follow through on this thought, because such an investigation would have pulled me away from my task at hand, so I tucked the topic away as something to pursue at a later time and place.

Ten years later, I began investigating crime in early America, and convict transportation popped into my head as a subject that could form a perfect bridge between my old knowledge of 18th-century British crime and my new research interest. But when I discovered that more than 50,000 convicted felons were forcibly shipped across the ocean and that they played a significant role in performing needed work in colonial America, I was shocked. How could I not have known more about this form of punishment and the people who were subjected to it? Apparently, I was not the only one who had such a gap in my knowledge of American history. When I mentioned my budding interest in convict transportation to family and friends, their immediate response was almost always, "Right,

Australia," not realizing that our own American shores had served as the first major destination for British convicts.

I decided that I needed to learn more. As I set out to research convict transportation to America in earnest, I fully expected that Georgia would be the main focus of my investigation. I had a distinct memory from grade school of a map of colonial America with the words "penal colony" in parentheses under the label for Georgia. Other people I talked with seemed to have a similar memory, because whenever I pointed out that convict transportation started in America and not in Australia, they would then say, "Oh, that's right, Georgia. Weren't the convicts all sent to Georgia?" I soon learned that we were all mistaken. Georgia never served as a penal colony—in fact, none of the American colonies ever did—and the only group of transported criminals ever to land in Georgia was a shipment of 40 Irish convicts in the mid-1730s after they were refused entry to Jamaica.[1]

How is it that 50,000 convicts were sent to the American colonies by the British, yet we as Americans remain so misinformed about the history of this massive migration? Clearly, I thought to myself, this story needed to be told.

What is the real story behind the transportation of 50,000 British criminals to the American colonies? Why would someone in England risk committing a crime knowing that he or she could be forcibly transplanted to a foreign land if caught? And what happened to these convicts once they arrived in America? Did they prosper under conditions of unlimited opportunity, as Daniel Defoe claimed in *Moll Flanders*, or were they ostracized by American colonists and doomed to personal failure? And why did Britain stop sending their convicts across the Atlantic and start shipping them east to Australia?

Bound with an Iron Chain tells the story of British convict transportation to America by focusing on the personalities and experiences of the various people who were involved in it at every level: the government officials who invented this new form of institutionalized punishment; the merchants who amassed fortunes transporting criminals across the Atlantic; the plantation owners in America who put the convicts to work after they arrived; and, of course, the convicts who found themselves bound together with iron chains on a ship heading towards a new land and a new way of life. Convict transportation forces America to re-examine its roots and recognize the significant role that convicts played in establishing and populating colonial America, and *Bound with an Iron Chain* is my attempt to bring this fascinating and important chapter of American and British history to light.

A Note about Conventions

When quoting from primary sources, I have kept the original spelling and grammar to retain the true character of the passages. The exception is the appearance of the long-s, which looks more like an "f" and has no modern typographical equivalent. In these cases, I have resorted to using our common "s."

Up until 1752, Britain, with the exception of Scotland, used March 25 as the legal start of the New Year, which means dates that fell between January 1 and March 24 before this time were recorded as one year behind current calendar conventions.

When citing dates that fell within this period, I have followed the common convention used by historians of adjusting the year up in order to conform to the current practice of counting January 1 as the start of the year.

Under English coinage values in the eighteenth century, 12 pence (abbreviated d.) equals one shilling (abbreviated s.); 5 shillings equals a crown; 20 shillings equals one pound (£); and 21 shillings equals one guinea. Currency issued by individual colonies in America generally followed the same conventions, but they had less value than their British equivalent and were not equal in value to currency issued by other colonies. The designation "sterling," which specifically refers to British currency, indicates a value higher than money issued by the colonies. To confuse matters even more, currencies from other countries, like Spain, also circulated in the American colonies.

Acknowledgements

When I began listing the institutions and people I needed to thank for helping me write this book, I had no idea the list would become as long as it is. Even so, I am sure I have forgotten to include many people who deserve to be on it, and I apologize to them in advance for my neglect.

I am indebted to the following institutions for giving me access to crucial research materials: The Brandeis University Library, The Boston Public Library, The Westborough Public Library, the Proceedings of the Old Bailey Online website, The Maryland State Archives, The Colonial Williamsburg Foundation, The Salem State University Library, The American Antiquarian Society, and The Library of Congress.

I have had amazing mentors over the years, and their influence on me will never fade. Stephen Lacey at Cornell College was responsible for drawing me into the humanities and English literature, and Michael Sprinker at SUNY at Stony Brook sharpened my mind, as did the rest of my dissertation committee—Clifford Siskin, Rose Zimbardo, and Lisa Low. I always say that I was dumb before I started writing my dissertation, but was smart by the time I finished it. David Carr, who mentored me at Rutgers University, continues to fill me with wisdom about libraries, learning, and life.

I unfortunately cannot list and thank all of my friends from graduate school at SUNY at Stony Brook, but a few stand out. I credit Linda Frost with saving my graduate school career by showing me how to write sophisticated papers. Eric Hoffman, Chip Rhodes, Patti Sakurai, Sandra Sprows, Paula Haines, and Peter Naccarato also deserve special mention. Devoney Looser has always been particularly supportive, and I will forever be grateful to her for introducing me to my wife.

I got the idea to write a book about crime in early America just before I left working at the Brandeis University Library. Again, I cannot list everyone from Brandeis who helped me create excitement for this project, but standouts include Robert Evensen, Karen Adler Abramson, Mark Alpert, Sherry Keen, Leslie Reicher, Leslie Homzie, Ralph Szymczak, and Jim Rosenbloom.

My friends in life have also been important to the writing of this book. David Syring and Bret Ammons were my intellectual partners at Cornell, and I continue to value my discussions with them. Susan Edwards helped me become both a librarian and a Red Sox fan and gave me great research advice. Judson Potter, Lisa Anastasio Potter, Shyamala Reddy, Elizabeth Algieri, Andrew McKuin, and the rest of the "Rocktober" crowd filled me with energy for the project with their questions and periodic gatherings. Jim Turner and Mindy Blodgett have provided the same, although more regularly since they live locally. I also thank the members of the Natick Shakespeare Club, the Westborough Library Board of Trustees, and my softball team, the Spiders, for providing much needed distractions. A special thank you goes out to Dave "Grad Man"

Gradijan for copy-editing this book, and, more importantly, for organizing the Spiders softball season every year.

The seclusion of researching and writing this book prompted me to start a blog called EarlyAmericanCrime.com, and through it I have met some wonderful colleagues, albeit only virtually. Brian Swann generously shared his extensive knowledge of convict transportation with me. David Loiterstein at Readex, Jason Zanon of ExecutedToday.com, and Robert Wilhelm of MurderByGaslight.com have all cheered me on. I had the good fortune of meeting Lucy Inglis for tea while I was in London. Her blog, GeorgianLondon.com, makes blog history writing appear effortless. I also thank Karen J. Hatzigeorgiou of USHistoryImages.com for providing some of the illustrations for my book. She probably does not know I exist, but she represents a large group of people who provide free online sources out of the goodness of their heart for people like me to use.

My recently deceased grandmother, Gertrude Riffel, lived to be 100 years old. She sincerely marveled at my accomplishments no matter how small, and the hours we spent together poring over old family photographs and discussing family history fostered my interest in the lives of common people. My mother-in-law, Carolyn Heller, provided similar enthusiasm for my projects, and I wish she were still alive to see the completion of this one.

My father-in-law, Mark Heller, continually challenges me intellectually and is my model for someone who pursues his interests with passion, values his family, and simply loves life. The same can be said of my other in-laws, Cynthia Heller, Steven

Bound with an Iron Chain

Weinreb, Justin Heller, Ruth Heller, Jason Heller, Alison Heller, and, of course, all of their children.

I would not be who I am today without my parents, Gerald Vaver and Jeanne Vaver. They bent over backwards to give me opportunities to pursue my many interests, and I am a happy, intellectually curious adult as a result. My brother, Jon Vaver, and my sister, Maria Vaver Zike, were necessary partners in these pursuits, and I highly value the time we spent together during all of our activities. I only wish that I lived closer to my two siblings, my two other in-laws—Kristin Vaver and Stephen Zike—and my three nephews.

And finally, this book would have been inconceivable without the support of the love of my life, Martha Heller, and of my two daughters, Madeleine Vaver and Audrey Vaver. They have put up with me disappearing into our upstairs library for long stretches of time to write, endured being dragged to obscure historical crime sites, and listened to me talk incessantly about transported convicts. For all of this, and more, I dedicate this book to them.

Introduction: The Beginning of an Epic Journey

James Bell most likely had no idea when he started running down the street with a book in his hand that he was embarking on an epic journey that would take him across the ocean to a new and strange land. But on a winter's day in 1723, this tailor of only 20 years of age had been wandering the narrow London streets not far from where the notoriously rank Fleet Ditch emptied out into the River Thames. At one point, Bell paused in front of a bookstall near the gateway in Whitefriars and picked up a book entitled *Origenis contra Celsum*, a defense of Christianity by a third-century theologian. He was either overly excited about adding to his knowledge of religion or, more likely, in desperate need of money, because he dashed off with the book without paying. Now, sensing that he was being pursued as he ran down the street, he attempted to hide, but he was soon discovered holed up in a dog kennel with the pilfered book in his hands. At his court trial on January 16, Bell denied ever having been at the bookstall or in the dog kennel, but the jury did not believe him. He was found guilty of grand larceny and sentenced to transportation to the American colonies for seven years.[1]

The picture of James Bell huddled in a dog house, clutching the stolen book, and praying that his pursuers will not discover him is a pathetic image, but what happened to him next is truly pitiful. One month after his trial, Bell and 35 other convicted felons were paraded through the London streets in chains from Newgate Prison down to the banks of the Thames at Blackfriars, only a few short blocks from Whitefriars where Bell originally committed his theft. There, the prisoners were loaded on a former slave ship, the *Jonathan*, which set sail for America the following day. Conditions on board the ship were harsh. Bell spent the entire voyage below deck in cramped quarters with little light, no fresh air, and chained to a group of five other felons. The ship that transported him was owned by Jonathan Forward, and its journey was long and traumatic. At least two of Bell's shipmates died during the voyage.

Bell was one of more than 50,000 convicted felons who were similarly uprooted from their families and friends in Great Britain between 1718 and 1775 and forced to travel overseas to begin new lives as indentured servants in the American colonies. The number of convicts who made this trip was not insignificant. During these years, one out of every four British immigrants who landed in America was a convict. To put the 50,000 number in even more perspective, when Britain regularly started sending convicts to the American colonies in 1718, the white population of Maryland was around 50,000. And in 1765—10 years before convict transportation to America came to an end—the entire population of Boston was only 15,520. All told, British convicts constituted one of the largest groups of people ever to be forced to immigrate to America, second only to African slaves.[2]

The Untold Story

Despite the fact that so many people were sent to America, relatively few documents that chronicle their experiences survive. This short supply of records is partly due to the nature of convict transportation. The felons were generally illiterate and did not have the skill or desire to write about their experiences. If anything, they wanted to hide their criminal past, not record it for posterity. Merchants involved in transporting convicts did not leave behind much evidence of their business practices either. They tended to keep a low profile and were careful to shield their methods and profits from both the government and their competitors. Only a handful of published accounts about the experiences of convicts in America exist, mostly because once the convicts left British shores, the public seemed uninterested in what happened to them. Media accounts that did appear tend to record unusual events or focus on notorious criminals, and while these sensational stories provide crucial insight into the practice of convict transportation, they are not representative of the experiences of most convicts. Thanks to the work of genealogists, however, more information about transported felons is beginning to emerge every day. But tracing the full journey of an individual convict from Great Britain to America often hits dead ends.

The dearth of documentation about convict transportation may be one reason Americans generally do not know much about it. But given the number of convicts involved, it is still amazing that the subject is practically ignored when the story of the founding of the United States is told. Almost as soon as convict transportation to America came to an end, Americans began to downplay the number and significance of criminals sent to the colonies. In 1786, Thomas Jefferson led the way by claiming:

The Malefactors sent to America were not sufficient in number to merit enumeration as one class out of three which peopled America. It was at a late period of their history that the practice began. I have no book by me which enables me to point out the date of its commencement. But I do not think the whole number sent would amount to 2000 & being principally men eaten up with disease, they married seldom & propagated little. I do not suppose that themselves & their descendants are at present 4000, which is little more than one thousandth part of the whole inhabitants.[3]

If Jefferson truly believed what he wrote, he should have known better. In the period leading up to when he wrote the Declaration of Independence, the British were sending nearly 1,000 convicts to America every year, and about half of them ended up in his home colony of Virginia.

Historians participated in this cover-up as well. Through the 19th century, most historians simply ignored the institution, and those who did recognize it usually claimed that nearly all of the people who were transported were political prisoners.[4] In 1896, J. D. Butler finally began to question these claims in an article that appeared in the *American Historical Review*. Butler cited evidence that the majority of convicts shipped to America during the colonial period were decidedly not political prisoners, and he speculated that the number sent was higher than previously reported.[5] But even after Butler made his argument, historians continued to resist conducting a true count of the convicts sent overseas and were unwilling to acknowledge their impact on colonial America.[6] Only in the latter part of the 20th century did historians finally begin to research convict transportation to America in a serious and systematic way. Today, historians generally agree on the 50,000 number, one that is higher than Jefferson, 19th-century historians, or even Butler ever imagined.[7]

Convicts were transported from all over Great Britain. More than 30,000 felons from practically every county within England were transported between 1718 and 1775, and almost 18,600 of them were from London and its nearby counties alone. Wales accounted for 5,000 convicts and Ireland for more than 16,000. Only 700 to 800 criminals from Scotland were officially transported during this same time period, mostly because the punishment was generally reserved for more serious offenders. In the hope of avoiding a death sentence, criminals coming up for trial in Scotland could ask to be banished before their trial even began. Those who were granted such a request had to make their own arrangements out of the country, so unless they happened to be wealthy and could pay for their own trip to America, they were forced to become bound to a ship captain as an indentured servant. This decentralized system greatly reduced the number of convicts transported from Scotland when compared to the other parts of Great Britain. All told, though, convicts made up the most diverse group of people who emigrated from Great Britain to America.[8]

An American Institution

The transportation system that brought convicts to the colonies was uniquely American. It was an inventive form of institutionalized criminal punishment born out of new types and unprecedented levels of crime in England. In passing the Transportation Act of 1718, England for the first time hired independent contractors to oversee the punishment of their convicted criminals, and merchants eagerly lined up to profit from the physical removal of felons from British society. In many respects, convict transportation successfully employed free enterprise to achieve social and governmental ends, an arrangement that was largely absent when Great Britain later turned to Australia as a place to send its unwanted criminals.

Convict transportation also reshaped the way people thought about the American colonies. When the British began expelling criminals from their country and sending them overseas, they not only cut ties with their unruly citizens and abdicated responsibility for punishing their behavior, but they also displaced the criminality that was a product of their own society on to the American colonies. America became recast as a destination for British convicts, and its reputation became tarnished as a result. In addition, convict transportation reinforced the subordinate position of the American colonies to Great Britain. If England was willing to dump its criminals on America, then what did that say about how it perceived the relationship between the two countries? Convict transportation may not have been a direct cause of the American Revolution, but it certainly helped create the conditions that gave rise to it.

In the process of being sent to America, convicts had to change the way they thought about themselves. In addition to losing their freedom, they were forced to renegotiate both their national identity and their position in society. They suddenly found themselves bound to a fellow Englishman who claimed ownership over everything they did. They worked alongside indentured servants and African slaves, and their status fell somewhere in between these two servant groups. If convicts were lucky, they were treated more like indentured servants and asked to perform a specific trade. If not, they were sent out into the fields along with the African slaves. In the end, their social rank in America hinged on the skills they brought with them from England, the needs of the plantation where they ended up, and the temperament of their owner.

Convict transportation adds new dimensions to popular notions of immigration to early America that go beyond Pilgrims and brave men crossing the Atlantic in search of religious freedom and unlimited opportunity in a new, untamed land. Most of the people transported to America were like James Bell, petty criminals who came out of the ranks of the destitute poor. In fact, most people who came to America during this time arrived under similar circumstances as Bell's, whether they were a convict or not. Between 1700 and 1775, a total of 585,800 immigrants arrived in the 13 colonies from all over the world. About 52,200 of these immigrants were convicts and prisoners (9%). Slaves by far constituted the largest group (278,400; 47%), followed by people arriving with their freedom (151,600; 26%) and indentured servants (96,600; 18%).[9] Note that almost three-quarters of all the people arriving in the American colonies during this time period did so without their freedom. The aim of this book is not to diminish the accomplishments of those who founded America and ultimately fought in the Revolution, but it does ask us to change the way we commonly think about early immigration to America.

Bound with an Iron Chain connects the history of English crime and criminals with American colonial history. It begins by describing the kingpins and professional criminals who made up England's changing criminal underworld, as well as the petty thieves who took increasing advantage of growing urban centers, where long lines of shops offered a dizzying array of goods to people from all stations in life. It then chronicles how an anxious British government, in an effort to solve the country's growing crime problem, devised a new institutionalized form of punishment by enlisting the help of well-connected and greedy merchants. The book then follows the convicts as they crossed the Atlantic in conditions on board ships that were considerably worse than the prisons that held them before they started their journey. Once they landed, the convicts were sold to a plantation owner, who generally had the good fortune to start a new life in America through his own means. Some convicts adjusted to their new surroundings and became planters themselves. Others continued their criminal ways.

England struggled with the question of how to turn convicted criminals into productive citizens, just as we do today, and convict transportation was viewed as a possible means to this end. By taking the radical step of partnering with private merchants, England created a new form of criminal punishment that was surprisingly efficient in its administration. But was the ultimate decision to send convicts to the colonies a genuine attempt to reform the criminals, or was it simply an expedient means on Britain's part to empty its jails and wash its hands of its criminal problem? Either way, convict transportation asks Americans to re-examine their colonial roots and to recognize the significant contributions that convicts like James Bell made to the development of early America.

Chapter One: England's Criminal Underworld

A buzz filled the air as people stood on their toes and filled every window in an attempt to get a glimpse of the great Jonathan Wild as he was paraded through the London streets on Monday, May 24, 1725. Wild had long enjoyed his celebrity status, but press coverage of recent events had generated even more interest in him. Phony tickets had been printed and circulated to help advertise Wild's public appearance, a broadsheet containing a ballad about Wild was hawked on the streets, and pamphlets chronicling his life were sold for one shilling. People had suddenly become fascinated with this man, and all of London seemed to have come out on this day to see him.

Despite the festive atmosphere surrounding the procession, Wild appeared to be unmoved by the shouts of the crowd, his attention focused instead on a book he held open in his hands. He wore a calamanco nightgown and a head-cloth, and he was accompanied in the open cart that carried him through the streets by three men—William Sperry, Robert Sandford, and Robert Harpham—although few paid attention to them. After traveling about a third of the way to his destination, the procession stopped at the Griffin Tavern near Gray's Inn on

High Holborn Street across from Chancery Lane, so that Wild could drink a glass of wine. Over his drink, he was heard to mutter about the crowd, "What a strange rig* they run upon me!" After he finished his refreshment, the parade continued, but it was slowed by the coaches belonging to the gentry and wealthy merchants that crammed the city streets.[1]

Not long after leaving the Griffin Tavern, a rock thrown from a window hit Wild in the head, and blood began to pour down his face. The crowd roared with approval and people started to hurl insults at him, along with more stones and dirt. Sperry and Sandford, who sat on each side of Wild, were also injured by rocks that missed their mark. The cart stopped twice more before reaching its destination: first at the White Lion across the street from St. Giles Church, where Wild handed money to a friend to pay for another glass of wine, and once again at the Oxford Arms on Oxford Street, home of the bare-knuckle boxing champion James Figg, where Wild drank a tankard of beer and even more wine.[2] His next and final stop was Tyburn Hill, where he was scheduled to be executed.

---

* rig: "Sport, banter, ridicule. Chiefly in phr. *to run* (one's) *rig(s) upon* (another), to make sport or game of, to banter unsparingly." (*Oxford English Dictionary*)

"Ticket" to the execution of Jonathan Wild at Tyburn.
(Source: Wikipedia Commons, http://commons.wikimedia.org)

Convicts often stopped for drinks at various taverns during their march from Newgate Prison to Tyburn to be executed, so the fact that Wild stopped at three along the way to his execution was not unusual. What was unusual was the fact that he was able to hold down the alcohol he consumed, given that at 2 a.m. he had tried to kill himself in his jail cell by drinking a large dose of laudanum (i.e., a concoction of opium dissolved in alcohol). After taking the drug, Wild had become so drowsy that he could not keep his head up or his eyes open for prayers. Two of Wild's fellow prisoners noticed that something was wrong with him, and they quickly stood Wild up and helped him walk around a bit to wake him up. While being held up by the prisoners, Wild became pale, sweated profusely, and then began to vomit. He had not eaten anything for four days, so the dosage of laudanum he took on top of his empty stomach was far too large to have its intended effect. He threw up most of the drug soon after taking it, which in the end saved his life. Partly from the laudanum he took the night before, and partly from his disbelief that he was actually going to be executed, Wild was already in a half-stupefied state before his slow journey to the gallows and his wine drinking even began.[3]

Perhaps for the first time in his life, Wild appeared to be penitent as he was pulled through the streets in the open cart. Witnesses saw him crying as he feverishly read the Bible, even though he had avoided attending church services while he was being held in Newgate Prison by claiming that he was too sick. Wild suffered from gout, which made standing up on his own nearly impossible, and he complained that the two fractures on his head, which had been covered with silver plates, were also bothering him.[4] His absence at church troubled more than the Ordinary of Newgate, who was responsible for attending to the spiritual well-being of the prisoners. On the Sunday before he was paraded through the streets, between 300 and 400 people paid eight pence to witness Wild say his prayers in Newgate Chapel. They waited from 9 a.m. until noon before realizing that Wild was not going to show up. The group grew so angry that they had not seen anything for their admission fee that they forced the turnkeys to drag out three different prisoners, so that they could gawk at them and satisfy their curiosity.[5]

Detail from *The Funeral Procession of the Celebrated Mr. Jonathan Wild*
(Source: Prints and Photographs Online Catalog, Library of Congress)

When Wild finally reached the gallows at Tyburn, the noise from the crowd was so loud that the Ordinary of Newgate found it almost impossible to say his prayers with the four criminals scheduled to die. The hangman, Richard Arnet, who years before had been a guest at Wild's wedding, tried to give Wild as much time as he needed before preparing him for execution. The crowd, however, grew restless and threatened to tear Arnet to pieces if he did not proceed in carrying out his duties immediately. Reluctantly, Arnet placed a noose around Wild's neck.[6]

A great shout went up from the crowd as the cart drove away, leaving the convicts dangling from the ropes tied around their necks. After the drop, Wild desperately used his legs to grab on to Robert Harpham, who was being executed for coining, in an attempt to lift himself up and slacken the rope around his neck. Arnet intervened and separated the two, and after a few minutes, the life of Jonathan Wild came to an end at the age of about 42.[7]

The scene of Jonathan Wild's execution, while perhaps more spirited than most due to his heightened notoriety, was repeated about every six weeks throughout the year in London. English laborers, who only received a few standard holidays like Christmas or Easter off each year, also received nine "hanging days," where they were encouraged to take the day off to witness the spectacle. On those days, convicted felons were paraded at a leisurely two-hour pace through the London streets to meet their final end at the Tyburn Tree, and the government authorities hoped that their example would deter crime.[8] But author Henry Fielding doubted that these public executions produced such an effect. In *An Enquiry into the Causes of the Late Increase of Robbers* (1751), Fielding characterizes executions as a "Day of Glory" for the criminals, since the atmosphere surrounding them was more celebratory than solemn. He goes on to assert that the frequency of hangings actually taught felons to approach their executions as moments of triumph, and he advocates making executions private in order to increase their terror.[9]

Fielding had a point. The heavy reliance on using punishment as a deterrent proved ineffective in meeting the challenges presented by the rising crime rate during the early 18th century. Through this period the government continued to rely on outdated modes of law enforcement and sentencing laws, despite societal changes that were diminishing the effectiveness of these approaches. As a result, even though executions continued to rise in number, they seemed to have little effect on reducing crime.

Wild's dramatic execution marked a precipitous fall for a man who was perhaps the most influential person in England's criminal justice system, even though he never held an official government position. As the self-proclaimed "Thief-Taker General of Great Britain and Ireland," Wild was instrumental in capturing and bringing to justice scores of petty thieves that plagued the London streets. He even consulted the government on passing laws meant to encourage the capture of criminals. But he also oversaw a vast criminal empire, the likes of which has never been duplicated.

London in the 18th Century

By 1700, the legacies of England's medieval state were rapidly beginning to disappear. England was in the midst of deep social changes that set the foundations for the Industrial Revolution and the emergence of modern society. Only 12 years earlier in 1688, the Glorious Revolution dissolved any notion of the divine right of kings when the British Parliament deposed Charles II and handed the royal throne to the Dutch outsiders, William and Mary. The Financial Revolution, brought about by the founding of the Bank of England in 1692, magically seemed to fill government coffers when the state took on an unprecedented amount of debt that only theoretically would be paid back at some point in the distant future. This massive government debt was backed by wealthy merchants, and a new breed of moneyed men now began to seize political and financial power away from an aristocracy that had always inherited such power through lineage. In addition, England's dominance in world trade made it the most powerful state in Europe, and the country's appetite for creating colonies overseas was just beginning to take hold. [10]

At the center of all this new activity was London. With a population of about 675,000 at the beginning of the 18th century, London claimed about one-tenth of the entire population of England and was by far the largest city in Western Europe, a title it had already achieved when it surpassed Paris in the previous century. The London beast gobbled up the countryside, using its ever-growing tentacles of streets to claim the open space that immediately surrounded the city. The growth was so rapid that there was little of the transition in population density between the city and the country that we usually experience today with our suburbs. Anyone traveling on a road that led outside of the city would find an abrupt end to the urban landscape and almost immediately be in full view of open fields. [11]

The sudden realization that one had left the urban environment of London when traveling out of the city ran counter to the experience of heading toward it. As one approached London, the sweet smell of the countryside would gradually be replaced by the stench emanating from the city and the open fields that surrounded it. These open fields were hardly pastoral. Refuse heaps sprinkled the area, and large numbers of hogs raised to feed the inhabitants of London fed on the garbage produced by the city. Ditches filled with foul-smelling muck and mud caused travelers to hold their noses as they passed by. London was also surrounded by smoking brick kilns, and vagrants tended to loiter around them in order to cook food and keep warm on cold nights. This vagrant population, along with footpads who preyed on travelers going to and from the city, could make traveling through this surrounding area of London a harrowing experience.[12]

As one continued on towards the city, the stench of the open fields would gradually be replaced by smells emanating from burning coal, manure-laden streets, and open sewers that only half-successfully carried away the waste of London proper. The odor of the city was so overwhelming to newcomers that it was hard to think that they could ever get used to it. The smoke emanating from houses during the winter and from blacksmiths, glass blowers, and earthenware factories throughout the year resulted in a gray smog that continually hung over the city and could be seen from miles away. The sounds of the city—the shouts of people, the groans of livestock being shuffled through the streets, the beating of horses' hooves on cobble-stones— would also become louder as travelers neared.[13]

Most new visitors to 18th-century London were amazed by the number of shops that lined the streets. Signs announcing the name and nature of businesses hung out and over the pedestrian walkways and perpendicular to the street, and their long rows emphasized the number of shops and businesses that were available to a newly formed consumer base.[14] With business names like the Bull and Gate, the Golden Bottle, and the Magpie, the inventiveness and occasional elaborateness of these signs helped give London its particular character. The signs also had a functional value that went beyond announcing the location of a particular business. Buildings lacked a formal numbering system, so one's address was often a description of its proximity to a well-known sign or place of business along a particular street. The addresses given for the publishers of *Select Trials for Murders, Robberies, Rapes, Sodomy, Coining, Frauds, and Other Offenses* is typical: "Printed for L. Gilliver at *Homer's-Head*, over against St. *Dunstan's* Church, in *Fleet-Street*; and J. Huggonson in *Sword-and-Buckler-Court*, opposite the *Crown-Tavern*, on *Ludgate-Hill*."

The bustle of horses, carriages, and human-powered sedan chairs along the city streets created a pace that would have been faster than anyone coming from the country could have imagined. Pedestrians determinedly moved from place to place and ignored anyone who passed by or stood in their way. Traffic jams were so common that it was customary for pedestrians to walk in between, or even through, the carriages that clogged the street if they needed to cross to the other side. But crossing the street provided more challenges than simply weaving through coaches. The streets themselves were a mire of mud, horse manure, dead animals, and standing puddles of rain and urine. People emptied their chamber pots out into the streets, and butchers emptied their offal into them as well. The risk of ruining one's shoes was constant, although elevated footpaths along the side of the streets provided some relief to pedestrians trying to avoid the mess. Rain washed some of the filth into the kennels that ran down the middle of the streets, but a lot of this runoff found its way into the Thames, the city's main source of drinking water.[15]

With little urban planning guiding its growth, London was a complicated maze of narrow streets, lanes, and courts that sprung off of winding thoroughfares of connecting streets. Buildings could rise as high as three to four stories above the ground, and they were packed with inhabitants. The tall buildings contributed to the stuffiness of the city, and the only place where one could receive fresh air was to walk out across one of the bridges over the Thames. The labyrinth of streets served the criminal element well by providing ample nooks and corners in which to hide before ambushing their victims, as well as offering easy means for disappearing after committing the crime. A lack of public lighting facilitated robberies, burglaries, and other forms of street crime as well. Lighting was the responsibility of individual inhabitants, who were required by law to illuminate the street in front of their houses. Londoners were supposed to hang out lights during the winter months from 6 to 11 p.m. on 18 "dark nights" when the moon was at its lowest illumination. Street lighting did not become a requirement throughout the entire year until 1736, but even so, adherence to all of these rules was spotty at best.[16]

During a time when traditional hierarchies were beginning to be overturned in favor of modern ones, social status was of great concern, and clothing was an important indicator of one's place in society. Almost everyone except for the poor wore wigs, since short hair made it easier to control lice. But wigs were expensive. Women of the upper classes wore elaborate wigs and had them re-powdered daily. Used wigs could be purchased at a lower cost, although affordability often meant a less accurate fit. The kind of fabric used to make clothes also signaled one's place in society. Silk, satin, velvet, and damask were worn by the upper classes, while wool and cotton clothed the lower ones. Clothing in general was extremely expensive, since mechanized weaving of cloth had yet to be invented. Poorer people wore used clothing, not having money to buy new, and they generally purchased such clothing on Monmouth Street or at Rag Fair.[17] Clothes, linens, and other textiles were often targets of theft, and anyone caught stealing them could be in big trouble. The case of John Flint, a 23-year-old weaver, is a classic example. He was found guilty in 1723 of stealing some linen clothing that was hanging on a hedge to dry and was sentenced to transportation for seven years.[18]

The petty act of theft committed by Flint was part of a larger trend in the 18th century. The nature of crime was changing radically in England, and a sharp rise in property crime was its most prominent feature. Indeed, property crime became so prevalent that when those in the 18th century referred to "crime," they generally meant violence and theft, and particularly offenses that combined the two, such as burglary or robbery. Expanding urbanization was partly responsible for this rise in property crime. Before the growth of cities, property crime was rare, and most criminal offenses could be dealt with by summary justice or informal sanctions. But the crowded streets of London and other cities provided more temptations for theft and greater anonymity. The large number of stores and shop stalls also provided easy targets for thieves, and since people no longer lived in more or less self-contained communities, criminals could easily disappear into the crowd.[19]

Overcrowding in the cities significantly added to the increase in crime. London's growth mainly came from people who were being forced out of the countryside and into the city to look for work. When the gentry and new moneyed men started claiming more and more of the open countryside for their exclusive use through land acquisition and the enactment of enclosure laws, it created hardship for the common people who had lived on or near these lands and had enjoyed unrestricted hunting and fishing. By cutting off access to a major source of their food, the laws forced people to abandon their familiar mode of living and move to the cities.[20] Other people came to the city to seek their fortune on their own accord in the exciting metropolis. But no matter how or why they arrived, success in London was hard to come by.

Industrialization was only beginning to take hold at this time, and it had yet to create the large number of factory jobs in the cities that it would later in the century. Most of those who came to the city from the country ended up in domestic service, which had the potential advantage of offering shelter, but also involved low wages and long hours that made moving up the social ladder difficult. Others arrived in London only to fall immediately into a life of prostitution or crime, either by necessity or through bad influences, much like Moll Hackabout in William Hogarth's *A Harlot's Progress*. Many of the people coming to the city failed to earn a living and then were recruited into the army, pressed into the navy, or ended up in indentured servitude on overseas plantations in the colonies.[21]

In Plate One of William Hogarth's *A Harlot's Progress*, Moll Hackabout arrives in London from the country and is immediately recruited into prostitution by Elizabeth Needham, a notorious procuress and brothel-keeper.

(Source: Wikipedia Commons, http://commons.wikimedia.org)

Yet despite the lack of jobs, people continued to pour into the city. Even the passage of poor laws and vagrancy laws, which attempted to restrict the movement of people away from their original place of settlement, failed to stem the influx of people to

London. Further complicating job prospects and contributing to the overcrowding of city streets were the periodic return of soldiers and sailors from oversea wars. Hardened from brutal fighting in the field, these men arrived with few skills and connections, and crime became a natural outlet for those seeking to profit from the aggression they practiced out on the battlefield.[22]

Mary Young, a.k.a. "Jenny Diver"

Mary Young came to London in the belief that she could buck the odds and make her mark. Young was born in Ireland, although she later denied the fact and claimed that she was English. Her parents were poor and both of them died when she was an infant, so Young was raised by an older woman who taught her to read, write, and perform needlework, for which she showed great talent. At 15, Young quarreled with her caretaker and decided that she could do better on her own. She headed to London with a suitor, who stole a great deal of money and a gold watch from his master to fund their trip. As soon as the two arrived in Liverpool, they were seized and held in custody for the theft. During questioning, the boyfriend concealed Young's role in the affair, so she was allowed to continue on her way to London. He, however, was returned to Ireland and was sentenced to death for his crime—although he later received a reprieve in exchange for being transported to America.[23]

Young planned to earn a living by performing needlework, but like most women who arrived in London with similar ambitions, her business soon failed. Poverty was widespread in London, and women tended to feel its effects the most. A woman's economic well-being often depended heavily on having a male companion. Widows, deserted wives, and unmarried mothers who had to fend for themselves found few opportunities for work, and the jobs that were available to them were low-paying, taxing, and unpleasant. Women filled the poor houses, and newspaper stories of people who were found starved to death almost always involved women. Young was unable to find work, so her landlord, Anne Murphy, sensing Young's growing desperation, stepped in to help her out. She introduced Young to a gang of thieves and suggested she join them.[24]

Young began her criminal career by targeting places where there were large groups of people, such as a theater when a play had just let out, and using the distraction of the crowd to move about and pick the pockets of unsuspecting victims. With the hands of a needle worker, Young proved so dexterous and proficient in the art of picking pockets that she earned the nickname "Jenny Diver," after the character in John Gay's *The Beggar's Opera*. She was also a quick learner, and she soon became the leader of the gang on the strength of her ability to come up with new and clever ways to empty purses and pockets. She created a fake set of arms folded piously over a similarly fictitious pregnant belly and then, wearing the costume, began attending church. With her hands hidden away in the recesses of her disguise, she was free to steal money and watches from those who sat down next to her, with the victims unaware that this seemingly devout woman was emptying their pockets. Young was not the first to employ this method of theft, but her reputation solidified her association with it.[25]

Young continued to find other ways to use her fake belly. Donning her disguise, she would wander through a park and then pretend to fall down. As a crowd gathered around her, she would claim to be too hurt and frightened from the fall to get up, and while she milked the drama for all it was worth, her companions moved through the concerned spectators and stole watches, snuff boxes, and purses. In another scheme involving the disguise, Young and an accomplice posing as her servant knocked on a door and asked the mistress of the house if she would allow Young to come inside for a moment to recover from a sudden spell of illness. While the lady of the house left to retrieve smelling salts, Young emptied the drawers in the room and stashed the goods in her fake belly. Her pretend footman, who was usually conveyed to the servant quarters to wait, also took the opportunity to steal silverware and salt-and-pepper shakers. Once Young was satisfied that she had procured as many stolen goods as she could, she would proclaim that she had recovered from her supposed illness. As she boarded a coach outside, she then invited the lady of the house to visit her and named the home of an eminent merchant as her place of residence. As soon as the coach turned the corner and was out of sight, Young told the coachman that she was too sick to continue and made off with her stolen goods on foot. Young performed this trick several times, until the newspapers reported her scheme and made it impossible for her to continue.[26]

Young represented a new breed of criminal who continually invented new and industrious ways to extract money from unsuspecting victims. And the number of criminals like her, along with the more petty variety, was growing. But crime was not only changing qualitatively and quantitatively; it was also changing geographically. The locus of crime moved from the countryside—where large expanses of land and unmonitored roads provided easy escape routes for highwaymen—to the cities, where the crowded, winding streets provided cover for petty thieves. Daniel Defoe, a prolific commentator on 18th-century society at the time, observes:

> Violence and Plunder is no longer confin'd to the
> High-ways, where the Robbers have lurking Places
> to hide and numberless Turnings, to avoid and
> escape the Pursuit of the Country, and the Force of
> a Hue and Cry.
>
> The Scene is quite chang'd, the Field of Action is
> remov'd; and the Actors themselves are likewise
> chang'd. The Scene, I say, is chang'd: The Streets of
> the City are now the Places of Danger; Men are
> knock'd down and robb'd, nay, sometimes
> murther'd at their own Doors, and in passing and
> repassing but from House to House, or from Shop
> to Shop.[27]

Defoe was not alone in expressing anxiety over the changing nature of crime. A dramatic increase in the amount writing about criminals went hand in hand with rising concerns about crime. Criminal writing—in the form of broadsides, pamphlets, newspaper and magazine articles, prose literature, and even plays—saturated the reading market. Criminals and their actions were one of the most popular topics for printed works, which recorded the acts of even the most common criminal. Some criminals, like Jonathan Wild, became celebrities as a result of this attention by the press, and prison turnkeys tried to capitalize on the new celebrity status of criminals by charging polite society money to view them in their jail cells. The large number of printed works detailing the activities of known or executed criminals certainly helped contribute to the commonly held notion that crime had reached epidemic proportions.[28] People believed that something had to be done to stop the recent crime wave, but unfortunately England's law enforcement and criminal justice system, as they were currently constituted, were ill-equipped to handle the new criminal underworld that was developing.

Jonathan Wild Arrives in London

Jonathan Wild first came to London in 1704 from his hometown of Wolverhampton, which lies northwest of London near Birmingham. He had agreed to become a servant for a lawyer who was moving to the big city, but after they arrived in London, Wild was either let go by the lawyer for disobedience or he simply ran away. Wild then became a "setter" (i.e., a bounty hunter for debtors) before going back to Wolverhampton to resume his original trade of buckle-making. In 1709, he returned to London for good, this time abandoning his first of many wives and two children. Wild spent only a short time in the city before William Smith, a professional burglar, took legal action against him and had him thrown into the Wood Street Compter for debt.[29]

With no friends or family members to help him out, Wild languished in prison. He was first confined in the Common Ward of the jail, because he lacked the resources to pay for better living quarters from his jailers. Prison keepers and turnkeys in the 18th century bought their positions, so in an attempt to profit from their investment they tried to extort as much money from inmates as they could through fees. Prisoners were responsible for paying these often exorbitant fees, which were especially devastating to debtors who already brought financial difficulties with them to prison. Those without money or resources could easily descend down the layers of privileges until they found themselves in the "Hole"—a cold, damp, and dark cellar where three or four prisoners slept together on wooden shelving built out from the walls—which is where Wild soon found himself. While locked in the Hole, Wild must have been willing to perform jobs that few others were willing to do, such as cleaning out cesspits and jail cells. Either that or he was able to use his willingness to interact with criminals to his advantage, because Wild was eventually able to move out of the Hole and then even out of the Common Ward. Despite his improved circumstances, Wild might have stayed in the Compter for the rest of his life if Parliament had not passed an act for the relief of debtors in September 1712. Wild was released shortly thereafter on December 16.[30]

While he was confined in the Wood Street Compter, Wild met Mary Milliner, and now that the two of them were out on the streets, they set up a small brothel on Lewkenor's Lane, a short narrow street off of Drury Lane in Covent Garden.* At the time, this area was known for dangerous gangs, prostitutes, and rats. Gambling dens were everywhere. Fights often broke out in the

---

* Today, Lewkenor's Lane is called Macklin Street.

taverns and gin shops that lined the street. One had to be fearless to walk through this tough neighborhood, let alone live there.[31]

London neighborhoods were often defined by the city's numerous parishes, and each had its own character and reputation. London during the 18th century mainly grew to the west, with the wealthy building planned communities—such as Cavendish Square, Hanover Square, and Grosvenor Square—in an attempt to escape both the fumes created by industry and the poor in the east. In addition to Covent Garden, where Wild and Milliner set up their business, Whitefriars, Blackfriars, and St. Giles in the Fields were areas of particular ill-repute. The precinct of Blackfriars had a reputation for harboring thieves and prostitutes, mainly due to its proximity to Fleet, Ludgate, and Newgate prisons, as well as to the noxious Fleet Ditch. St. Giles housed many of the Irish who came to London seeking work, because the parish had gained a reputation in Ireland as being generous with its poor relief. As a magnet for the Irish poor, St. Giles became a center for beggars and thieves, and it owned the record of being the parish with the largest number of crimes prosecuted at the Old Bailey, which is where criminals from London and Middlesex County were brought to trial. Estimates in 1750 claimed that at least one out of every four houses in St. Giles was a gin shop. People in rags roamed the street, many without shoes or stockings, and stray dogs sniffed the ground, seeking food among the decayed vegetables and filth that littered the streets.[32]

The lower classes from these parishes lived in dilapidated houses that always seemed on the verge of collapse. Such housing was classified into tenements, common lodging houses, or brothels. Most of these dwellings were windowless, due to a tax on the number of windows a house possessed. To avoid paying the tax, original windows were boarded up, which created dark and suffocating interiors. Working-class families lived in one room, and the very poor lived in either the cellar or the garret of a house. Three to eight people could share a bed together, and sheets were rarely replaced with clean ones. A large number of the poor lived in furnished rooms that were rented by the week, and lodgers desperate for money were sometimes caught pawning the contents of these dwellings.[33]

Mary Milliner was well-versed in the art of thieving, and Wild benefited from her experience. In addition to running their brothel on Lewkenor's Lane, the two of them practiced "Buttock and Twang," also known as the "Whore and Bully." This not entirely clever scheme involves a street prostitute luring an unsuspecting "cull"—or "John" as we commonly say today—into a dark alley. As soon as she is able to pick his pocket, she gives a signal to her male accomplice to attack the victim, who at this point presumably has his pants down around his knees, and the scuffle gives the prostitute enough time to run away with the stolen goods. The term "Buttock and Twang" can also refer to a slightly more sophisticated version of this scheme, where the female brings the victim up to her room, and after she is able to secure the contents of his pockets, the male accomplice bursts in claiming to be the husband and displaying shock at what is going on. The victim at this point eagerly flees the scene for his life—his wallet and watch being the least of his worries.[34]

Once Wild and Milliner secured stolen goods through these or other methods, they then faced the problem of how to dispose of their booty. Their best option was to sell the goods to a fence, or middle man, although doing so could be risky and would cut into their potential profit. Wild soon learned, however, that if Milliner could steal a diary or other personal object from a client, he could then subtly blackmail the owner, who would be anxious to cover up where and how he originally lost the object. By using blackmail, Wild found that the owner would pay far more than what he could normally get by disposing of such an object through normal means, and he cut out the middle man to boot. This method of realizing the value of stolen goods proved to be so profitable that Wild moved away from Lewkenor's Lane in the summer of 1713 and rented a small brandy shop on Cock Alley directly across from St. Giles's Church in Cripplegate to practice this form of trade in stolen goods full-time.35

Wild's Growing Business

Even though urbanization was rapidly changing the complexion of London and other English cities, law enforcement in the early 18th century continued to function under the logic of a small-scale community. Cities lacked a central, organized police force due to British fears of supporting a standing army, which, it was believed, could potentially be used by the government to curtail the rights of individuals. Instead, night watchmen, who were often ridiculed for their incompetence, patrolled the streets. Amazingly, the creation of an official police force was over a century away in England.36

With the exception of assistance offered by constables and the generally ineffectual Night Watch, crime victims were basically responsible for apprehending and convicting offenders on their own. As a result, few people pursued prosecuting criminals, since bringing an offender to trial was difficult and expensive. The victim of a crime was expected to obtain an arrest warrant, summon the constable, and gather friends and acquaintances to help find and arrest the criminal. Once the victim caught the perpetrator, he or she was responsible for covering the costs of prosecution. This expense could be considerable, especially since most anyone in the legal system had bought his position and therefore had to be paid for his services. Furthermore, if the offender belonged to a gang, the threat of retaliation by a fellow member would be enough to discourage victims from pursuing legal action. The difficulty of bringing criminals to trial meant that most crime went unprosecuted.[37]

The inability of law enforcement to police the streets effectively provided Wild with the perfect conditions in which to build his new business. Victims of theft generally had little chance of getting back what was stolen from them, let alone catching the thief. Through Wild's new service, however, owners of lost or stolen property could apply to him for help in recovering their possessions for a fee that fell below what it would cost them to replace the objects. Wild would then use his connections in the criminal underworld, which he began developing during the time he spent in the Wood Street Compter, to recover the goods and return them to the owner. He appealed to the public for help by placing hundreds of advertisements in newspapers that asked for assistance in the recovery of specific lost or stolen objects. Wild also grew his business by proactively contacting owners of lost and stolen property. After catching wind of the whereabouts of a lost or stolen object, Wild would approach the owner, offer his services, and claim that he could broker a deal with the person in current possession of it. His business proved to be extremely popular. Owners were grateful to get their property back at a price below full replacement cost, and Wild received a fee for recovering the object.[38]

In addition to recovering lost and stolen property, Wild was particularly adept at catching and prosecuting criminals, a public service that enhanced his general reputation and made him popular with the authorities. In the absence of a true police force, the government relied on rewards to encourage citizens to police the streets themselves. Anyone who could capture a thief and convict him or her with evidence received a reward of 40 pounds, far more than what most people in England could earn in a year.[39] Wild benefited from this policy by collecting a fee every time he was able to prosecute a criminal. His office, then, essentially served as the de facto "Scotland Yard" of the day.[40]

Amazingly, Wild was not only able to catch and bring to trial petty criminals, but he was also able to break up some of the most notorious gangs in the country. His major coup was breaking up the Whitehall gang, which got its name from a series of burglaries the group committed in and around Whitehall. Using his connections, Wild quickly obtained intelligence about three members of the gang—Robert Parrot, William Parker, and John Chance—who had burglarized the house of the Lord Bishop of Norwich by stealing a pair of diamond earrings, a gold watch and chain, some plate, and clothes on August 18, 1714. Employing techniques that he would use throughout his career, he pressured one of the members of the gang to snitch on the others and consequently was able to convict at least five members of the gang within three months. These five convictions netted him an award of at least 200 pounds.[41]

On the heels of his success with the Whitehall gang, Wild moved again sometime late in 1714. He rented a tavern called the "Blue Boar" not far from the Old Bailey and set up an Office for the Recovery of Lost and Stolen Property. By now, his reputation both as an aid in locating lost and stolen property and as a thief-taker was growing, and the location of his residence near the Old Bailey and Newgate Prison only helped to solidify his standing. Wild no longer needed to approach people who had been robbed; they came to him. He began to charge an up-front search fee of five shillings, and as he searched for the lost or stolen goods, he strung their original owner along until he was certain that he had reached the maximum amount of reward money that the victim was willing to pay. Wild's incredible success at catching and prosecuting criminals continued as well. He captured the highwayman James Goodman, who had grabbed headlines by scaling the spiked fence and railings of the bail-dock at the Old Bailey while bound in irons after he was convicted of stealing a horse. He broke Obadiah Lemon's gang, which specialized in the "Rattling Lay," where members of the gang would jump on the back of coaches, cut through the leather, and then grab hats, wigs, and jewelry from passengers. And he captured and prosecuted about 50 street robbers and burglars during this time.[42]

In order to accommodate the tremendous growth of his business, Wild made his final move in the fall of 1719 and purchased a large house on the west side of Great Old Bailey just north of Ludgate Hill. At this point in his career, Wild boldly used spectacle to promote his role as the central authority in controlling England's criminal underworld. He proclaimed himself "Thief-Taker General of Great Britain and Ireland," even though no such government position officially existed, and he walked through the streets holding a long silver staff to help validate his unofficial title. Through his wealth he purchased a coach-and-six to drive him around London in high style. In one of the rooms of his new house, he created a museum of artifacts relating to crime—bits of hangman's ropes, knives, guns, and pieces of cloth stained with blood—and gave tours to impress clients before sitting down to negotiate the return of a piece of property. His name regularly appeared in newspapers, which reported on his exploits in capturing thieves and reserved special sections for him to advertise for the return of stolen goods for his clients.[43]

Wild's knack for catching criminals brought him great renown. He often appeared at trials to give evidence against the criminals he helped to capture. He got to know the bailiffs of the prisons and could be seen socializing in the local taverns with Justices of the Peace. He entertained government officials in his house. With his newfound success and popularity, Wild expanded his enterprise beyond the city of London by hiring agents all over England to provide him with information about criminals that he could use in returning stolen items.[44]

Wild had created a profitable business—albeit one with a seedy side to it—by systematically hunting down thieves, extracting stolen goods from them, and occasionally prosecuting them. He was willing to interact with the criminal underworld when few others were willing to do so. His service appeared to be so valuable that questions about how Wild developed such close connections with the criminal underworld, and possessed such an in-depth knowledge of how it operated, simply were not asked. As long as Wild was able to recover stolen property and make London that much safer by clearing the streets of at least one more thief, the people and the government were happy. But behind the public mask of Jonathan Wild was a dark and sinister face.

The Private Face of Jonathan Wild

Jonathan Wild, the man supposedly responsible for clearing the streets of criminals, was in point of fact the head of a vast criminal empire and a well-oiled criminal machine. Wild's Lost Property Office was actually a clearinghouse for stolen goods that members of his own organized gang had themselves acquired. The thieves he apprehended, supposedly for the good of the community, were fall guys; they either belonged to rival gangs, or were members of his own gang who had tried to double-cross him, quit his business, or ceased to be more valuable than the 40-pound reward given by the government for capturing and convicting a criminal. Wild sent many of these criminals to the gallows by appearing in court to give evidence— real or false—against them. The unofficial head of crime prevention turned out to be the leading perpetrator of crime and organizer of criminals in London and throughout Great Britain.[45]

Wild engaged in and facilitated many types of crime, including coining, forging, smuggling, and protection rackets for brothels and gambling houses. He even purchased a boat in order to trade his stolen goods in Holland and Flanders. Wild keenly understood the profit that could be made by organizing and inter-relating various criminal activities under one umbrella operation. His system allowed him to expand the notion of what constituted profitable stolen merchandise: diaries, letters, pocketbooks, and even scraps of paper could become valuable objects if their recovery were advertised with the proper hint of blackmail. If a personal item were found or taken near a brothel, Wild would advertise it so as to imply that not only did he know who owned it, but that if the owner did not meet Wild's price, he would reveal the place where the item was found to the owner's wife or mother. Wild's newspaper advertisements and his proactive attempts to return stolen merchandise to their owners were in point of fact instruments of blackmail.[46]

Wild was a master at manipulating the law in order to keep those working in his criminal empire under his tight control. Public officials had long suspected that Wild's activities were not above-board, but they were reluctant to draw up charges against him. Not only was he the most effective crime-stopper in the city, but he also had bought off most of the government authorities, which in turn gave him the means to indict them for accepting bribes if they ever did try to bring him to trial.[47]

Just as merchants kept detailed ledgers of their business and financial dealings, so did Wild of his criminal dealings. He maintained extensive lists of criminals in his gang and carefully chronicled how much money each of them brought into his organization. When Wild was able to confirm the details of a robbery, he placed a cross next to the name of the person who committed it in his ledger book. The cross identified the thief as someone who could easily be turned over to the authorities in case Wild quickly needed a fall guy to protect a more valuable member of his organization or if he simply desired the 40-pound reward for giving evidence against the criminal in court. Once the offender was secured by the authorities or hanged, Wild added another cross next to his name, giving us the expression "double-cross," to indicate the betrayal of someone within the same organization.[48]

The power that Wild wielded in the courts, law enforcement, and the criminal underworld is difficult to overestimate. Wild raised crime to a new level by organizing it into a highly structured business, and his success pointed out just how much England's criminal justice system was in need of reform. The old methods for capturing, convicting, and punishing criminals that functioned when the population tended to live in smaller, self-contained communities were no longer working. The rapid growth of the cities, where people could exist next to each other in anonymity, changed both the nature of crime and the number of crimes committed. New approaches for controlling England's crime problem needed to be developed.

Chapter Two: The Need for a New Punishment

In the early part of the 18th century, the British criminal justice system was in disarray as it faced a growing crime rate with little official means of policing its streets. But rather than reform the system itself, the government tried instead to reverse rising crime trends by passing laws to add and reclassify more and more criminal offenses as capital. The theory behind this course of action was that the harsher penalty of execution would be enough to dissuade potential offenders from committing crime. Property crime in particular was an acute problem, so Parliament tended to focus on protecting property owners by passing laws such as the Waltham Black Act of 1723, which created more than 50 new capital offenses aimed at protecting land owners. These steps led to what would become known as the Bloody Code, a short reference to the high number of classified offenses punishable by death, a number that reached 160 by 1765.[1] Under the Bloody Code, criminals found guilty of even the pettiest of crimes could now face execution. No wonder England held so many hanging days throughout the year.

Similar Crimes, Different Sentences

On February 11, 1718, Richard Wood wandered through the Newgate Market at 10 o'clock at night, carefully studying the people around him. The often-crowded market was located between the notorious Newgate Prison and St. Paul's Cathedral, and it served as a central supplier of meat for the population of London. Market activity at this late hour would have been slower than during the day but still significant, as markets were beginning to stay open later and well past nightfall to accommodate the new consumerism that was emerging with the onset of the Industrial Revolution.[2]

Through the crowd, Wood spotted a woman who was in the middle of making a purchase. He casually walked up beside her and in a flash, grabbed her small purse and ran. The woman cried out for help, and Wood was immediately pursued. He ran down the line of market stalls and headed towards London's twisting streets where he could potentially disappear, but he was not fast enough. Just as he was about to fall into the clutches of his pursuers, Wood quickly dropped the purse in a feeble attempt to ditch the evidence of his crime, but both he and the purse were gathered up and taken into custody.[3]

Two weeks later on February 27, Wood was brought to trial at the Old Bailey. He was indicted for pickpocketing, a capital offense defined as stealing goods worth over one shilling without the owner's knowledge, although proving in court that the owner was unaware of the theft was often difficult, since such knowledge was essentially a precondition of bringing the offender to court in the first place.[4] Unfortunately for Wood, the purse he stole contained two handkerchiefs and nine shillings—

with a total value of one guinea and two pence—and there were plenty of witnesses willing to give evidence against him. Even though Wood denied having stolen the purse, the jury found him guilty, and he was sentenced to death.[5]

* * *

During the same court session in which Richard Wood was tried, Edward Higgins of St. Giles's in the Fields was brought before the judge and jury for feloniously stealing two coach cushions. On January 23, 1718, Higgins and an accomplice removed the cushions from a coach that was standing on Russell Street, not far from the Covent Garden Market, which served as London's fruit and vegetable market. The coach belonged to Sir Philip Jackson, who three years later would become a director of the Bank of England. Jackson was possibly visiting one of the area's many coffee houses, which increasingly served as both intellectual and business centers for England's elite. Luckily for Jackson, several witnesses saw Higgins and his accomplice take the cushions, and they started to chase the two thieves. Once Higgins and his accomplice realized that they were being pursued, they threw down the cushions to give themselves a better chance for escape and a pretext for denying their crime. Higgins was eventually caught, but his accomplice managed to get away.[6]

At his trial, Higgins claimed that he merely found the cushions in the street, but the jury did not believe that "he had been honestly so lucky" and convicted him of simple grand larceny—i.e., the theft of goods valued over one shilling without any aggravating circumstances, such as assault or stealing without the knowledge of the owner. The jury was not without some sympathy for Higgins, because they only found him part guilty of his crime and reduced the value of the cushions to 4s. 10d. In doing so, the jury avoided handing down a verdict that brought a mandatory death sentence for stealing goods valued at over five shillings, which the two cushions surely were. As punishment, Higgins was branded with a "T" for theft on his thumb and released.[7]

* * *

The difference between the two crimes that Richard Wood and Edward Higgins committed was not great. Both stole goods that had relatively high value; both ran away from their pursuers and tried to dump the goods they took as they were being chased; and both denied having committed the act in court. Neither criminal had presumably appeared for trial at the Old Bailey before this time.

But the penalty that each one received could not have been more different. Wood earned a death sentence for his impulsive act, whereas Higgins got away with merely a burn on his hand. Higgins received a lighter sentence because the cushions he stole were deemed by the court to have a lower value than the contents of the purse taken by Wood. But the jury purposely undervalued the cushions that Higgins stole, so that he would not receive a death sentence. This same jury did not extend a similar show of mercy to Wood. Given the fact that Higgins had stolen items of value from someone as important as Sir Philip Jackson, one might assume that he would have received a harsher sentence than Wood, but this did not turn out to be the case. Furthermore, whereas Wood probably had no foreknowledge of exactly what was contained in the purse he stole, Higgins had full knowledge of the potential worth of the items he took.

Why did Higgins receive what appeared to be preferential treatment, whereas Wood did not? Did Wood appear more reticent to reform? Were Wood's protestations of innocence perceived to be more insulting to the court in the face of his guilt than Higgins's? The trial accounts do not offer any clues in answer to these questions. But the stark difference between the punishments received by Wood and Higgins dramatizes how arbitrary sentencing in the early part of the 18th century could be.

Rewards and Punishments

Since England lacked an official police force, its criminal justice system relied on a system of rewards to encourage people to capture and convict criminals. But with a growing crime rate, this approach was increasingly not up to the task. So in response to a surprising increase in highway robberies in 1720, the Privy Council turned to Jonathan Wild for help in finding solutions to this serious problem. Wild suggested raising the reward for catching highway robbers and argued that 100 pounds would serve as a greater incentive for people to capture them. The Council agreed with Wild, although when the policy finally went into effect, a question arose as to whether 100 pounds should be the total award or whether it should be added to the original 40-pound reward. In the end, the Council decided that the increase should be added to the original amount—thereby raising the reward for capturing a highway robber to 140 pounds—and in the process inadvertently awarded Wild a hefty pay increase for every bandit he captured and prosecuted. Such a reward was both enormous and unprecedented, it being the equivalent of three-year's income for an experienced worker in a trade.[8]

Outdated sentencing laws also contributed to the failure of the criminal justice system. Convicted felons generally faced one of only two possible sentencing options: If they were first-time offenders, they could be set free after receiving a minor punishment; but if they had committed a second offense, they could be put to death. In many cases, neither punishment seemed to match the severity of the crime.

First-time offenders of minor infractions were generally sent back on the street after claiming "benefit of clergy" and reading the first verse of the 51st Psalm, which begins, "Have mercy upon me, O God, according to thy loving kindness." Benefit of clergy was a legal relic from medieval times. Defendants who could read were judged to be from the holy orders—since few people outside of the clergy could read—and therefore they technically fell outside the jurisdiction of the civil courts and instead were subject to the authority of the ecclesiastical courts. This sentencing loophole was often misused, to say the least. Even illiterate criminals memorized the verse in case they were ever called upon to recite it in court, and most judges overlooked the obvious fact that many of the offenders who came before them could not read. This legal farce came to an end in 1706 when the requirement of having to read scripture was eliminated through legislation, although the practice of claiming benefit of clergy remained intact. Even though benefit of clergy no longer served its original purpose, it was kept in place because it helped counteract the harsh death sentences called for by the Bloody Code.[9]

Those who received benefit of clergy were branded on the thumb, usually with a "T" for theft, although the temperature of the branding iron could be adjusted according to the circumstance of the crime or to the size of the bribe given to the person carrying out the sentence. First-time offenders could also receive some other form of corporal punishment, usually whipping, in addition to or in lieu of branding. Once offenders claimed benefit of clergy, though, they were then subject to execution if they appeared before the courts a second time and were found guilty. Sentencing under England's criminal justice system essentially followed a "two strikes and you're out" policy, albeit with higher stakes than the similar "three strikes and you're out" policy that exists in the United States today.

Despite these strict sentencing provisions, judges and juries had great latitude in handing out sentences and could reclassify the crime committed by an offender to a lesser charge so as to avoid creating a state-sanctioned bloodbath at the hanging tree. But this latitude also gave an arbitrary appearance to the criminal justice system. As in the cases of Wood and Higgins, some criminals could be let off with little punishment, while others could be hanged for committing basically the same crime.

The modern penitentiary was originally born out of the idea that criminals could be turned into productive citizens through the use of long-term incarceration. But sentencing criminals to long-term stays in prison to atone for their crimes and to receive rehabilitation was a concept that was still decades away for a variety of reasons. For one, prisons in the 18th century were crowded, filthy, and disease-ridden, so the thought of intentionally locking someone away in such conditions was practically unimaginable; on the other hand, some people thought that imprisonment in general was not a harsh enough punishment. The belief that jails and prisons had a detrimental effect on those who inhabited them was also common. People worried that when petty thieves and debtors came into contact with professional criminals in prison—much like Jonathan Wild did when he served time in the Wood Street Compter for debt— there was a danger of turning them into hardened criminals. And finally, prisons were already overcrowded and expensive to run, and the government was unwilling to commit resources to building more in order to facilitate long-term confinement.[10]

Crime in early 18th-century England was out of control, yet current laws and punishments did not seem to have any effect on reducing it. Something had to be done.

Finally, in 1718 the British criminal justice system underwent a radical change. The set of trials involving Wood and Higgins that took place on February 27 of that year turned out to be the last Old Bailey session that was held before the British Parliament passed the Transportation Act, which transformed sentencing practices in Great Britain. Had Richard Wood been tried one court session later than he was, he would have received a much different punishment for stealing the purse than the death sentence that he received.

The Origins of Convict Transportation

Before 1718, the British criminal justice system did not provide an official sentencing alternative for convicted felons that fell somewhere in between branding them on the thumb or the death penalty. There was, however, a third, unofficial sentencing option, namely transportation, although it technically fell outside the control of both judges and juries. Under this provision, convicted felons could petition for and receive royal pardons from the Crown on the condition that they remove themselves from the realm for a defined period of time.

Back in the 15th and 16th centuries, Portugal, Spain, and France had all used criminals and vagrants to help populate their colonies, but Elizabethan explorer and geographer Richard Hakluyt was probably the first Englishman to come up with the idea of transporting English criminals to America and putting them to work on extracting resources from the land. In *A Discourse Concerning Western Planting* written in 1584, Hakluyt observes:

> many thousandes of idle persons are within this realme, which, havinge no way to be sett on worke, be either mutinous and seeke alteration in the state, or at leaste very burdensome to the common-wealthe, and often fall to pilferinge and thevinge and other lewdnes, whereby all the prisons of the lande are daily pestred and stuffed full of them, where either they pitifully pyne awaye, or els at lengthe are miserably hanged.

48

He proposes that:

> these pety theves mighte be condempned for certen
> yeres in the westerne partes, especially in
> Newefounde lande, in sawinge and fellinge of
> tymber for mastes of shippes, and deale boordes; in
> burninge of the firres and pine trees to make pitche,
> tarr, rosen, and sope ashes; in beatinge and
> workinge of hempe for cordage; and, in the more
> southerne partes, in settinge them to worke in
> mynes of golde, silver, copper, leade, and yron; in
> draggine for perles and currall; in plantinge of suger
> canes, as the Portingales have done in Madera ...[11]

The government did not act upon Hakluyt's idea, but in 1597 under Queen Elizabeth I, it did pass the first official act that sanctioned the transportation of rogues and vagabonds to the English colonies. This statute did not institute a system of forced labor in the colonies—merely deportation—so even though it made the act of reprieving felons in order to send them to work in the fields of Virginia possible, the use of convict labor for colonization ultimately failed to take hold, since there was no official place to send them.[12]

But in 1611, the colony of Virginia was desperately struggling. Disappointed with the original crew that came over with him to help build the colony, Governor Thomas Dale asked King James I to send across the Atlantic all of the convicts who were both being held in prisons and sentenced to die in order to furnish his colony with able men. The British government was slow to act on Dale's request, but on January 23, 1615, the Privy Council finally issued a warrant that enacted forced labor in the colonies. As punishment for idleness or misdemeanors, the Council created a system for transporting convicts by granting reprieves on condition that the felons remove themselves to one of the colonies.[13]

According to common law and the Habeas Corpus Act, judges were not allowed to sentence convicts to transportation directly, but under the new provision passed under James I, the king or queen could pardon felons on condition that they leave the country for a specified amount of time. Convict transportation could now be used as a means of granting leniency to those who would otherwise be executed. But felons first had to be sentenced to death before they could be pardoned. Those who subsequently received a pardon from the Crown were essentially free, just as long as they remained abroad for the required term, which could even amount to banishment for life. One of the benefits of this system was that the Crown could now show mercy to those who might otherwise have been executed, yet at the same time purge this criminal element from the realm.[14]

In the 1660s, judges discovered a way to use this system of conditional pardon for first-time offenders who ordinarily would have been sent back on the street under benefit of clergy. Basically, once a judge heard a series of trials, he would identify those criminals whom he thought deserved transportation and then force them into failing the literacy test that was required to receive benefit of clergy. Rather than sentence this group to death, the judge sent the criminals back to jail, where they waited for the possibility of receiving a conditional pardon from the king. Criminals who refused the pardon were hanged. But this practice began to fall out of use in the 1690s, and a third, middle-ground sentencing alternative continued to elude the authorities.[15]

Throughout the late 17th and early 18th centuries, the British government considered various proposals to put in place an official system of convict transportation as a way to give judges more flexibility in sentencing, but nothing ever came of them. The press also weighed the possible merits of sending convicts to the colonies. In the sensationalist pamphlet *Hanging, Not Punishment Enough, For Murtherers, High-way Men, and House-Breakers* written in 1701, the author weighs whether transportation has enough teeth as a punishment to deter criminals:

> It may be, that the condemning them for Life, to the
> same condition with the *Negro's*, in our *West*
> *Indian* Plantations, first marking them in the Face,
> to distinguish them from Honest Men, may be a
> Proposal lyable to as few Exceptions, as any other.

The author worries, however, that the planters might allow the criminals to return to England if they are not forced to give some kind of security to prevent such an occurrence. In the end, the author concludes that such an idea is not feasible: "I fear they [i.e., the planters] will hardly take them on *such* Conditions, they beginning already, as I hear, to grow weary of *Those* they have."[16]

One of the reasons a formal system of convict transportation was never established up until this point was that Parliament had long resisted the idea of giving judges direct decision-making power over sending convicts to the colonies. But convict transportation had a strong advocate in the criminal justice system waiting in the wings. William Thomson was a prominent lawyer who had long seen the flaws of Britain's sentencing system and had sought more flexible provisions for judges in handing down sentences. He believed transportation could be an effective means of dealing with persistent offenders who were unable or unwilling to support themselves and who would likely return to crime again and again.

With the support of Robert Walpole, Thomson became Recorder of London on March 3, 1715. The Recorder served as the principal sentencing officer at the Old Bailey and was responsible for reporting to the Cabinet on all of the cases involving offenders who were capitally convicted. Thomson was elected to this position during a time when there was deep concern over theft and robbery in London, and he brought enthusiasm and new ideas for combating crime with him to the job. He believed that the new character of crime that was emerging required new approaches for policing the city and necessitated a new category of punishment.[17]

By most accounts, Thomson was not popular. Even though commentator Daniel Defoe characterized him as someone with a notable sense of humanity and justice, Thomson was repeatedly accused of corruption during his tenure, and his early biographies accused him of greed in acquiring government positions and consolidating power. After becoming Recorder, Thomson was appointed to several other offices, which normally would have called for his resignation from the current position he held as he rose up the career ladder. Instead, Thomson held on to his various offices—and the salaries and perquisites that each brought with them—and served as Recorder for 24 years up until his death.[18] Some of the negative perceptions of him were no doubt fueled by the intense partisan politics of the time. Whether he held on to his positions because of greed or because he believed he could handle the extra workload, he appears to have been dedicated to his jobs and to his vision for improving England's criminal justice system.

Thomson bided his time as Recorder until 1717, when he became Solicitor-General and was knighted by George I. At this point, Sir William Thomson held the offices of Recorder, Solicitor-General, and Member of Parliament. Now was the perfect time for him to turn his vision for transforming England's criminal justice system into reality. One of his first steps was to create a mechanism for maintaining an alphabetical record of all the offenders who had appeared before the city courts, updated annually, to make it easier to identify repeat offenders. Another was to draft a bill, which he introduced in the House of Commons on December 23, that would add convict transportation to the list of possible sentencing options for judges.[19]

Thomson staked his career on passing his convict transportation bill, and he oversaw almost every step of its passage through Parliament. He chaired the committee that considered the bill in the House of Commons, and after the bill passed through this chamber, Thomson steered it through the House of Lords. He then took the lead in mediating the differences between the two passed versions.[20]

After years of discussion and experimentation, a formal system of convict transportation finally became law. Citing the fact that current punishments had failed to deter people from committing crimes such as robbery, burglary, and larceny, and that there was a great need for labor in the American colonies, the British Parliament passed "An Act (4 Geo. I, Cap. XI) For the Further Preventing of Robbery, Burglary and Other Felonies, and For the More Effectual Transportation of Felons, and Unlawful Exporters of Wool; and For the Declaring the Law upon Some Points Relating to Pirates," better known as the Transportation Act of 1718.

Criminals who were banished from the British Isles during the 16th and 17th centuries were mostly serious or repeat offenders. They were responsible for removing themselves from the country's borders, which they often neglected to do, and the government provided no oversight in making sure that the convict followed up on the stipulations of his or her pardon. But passage of the Transportation Act now formally institutionalized convict transportation as a punishment and made the British government responsible for actively transporting convicts out of the country.

Under the old system of convict transportation, which went from the time of the first settlement in North America until 1718, around 5,000 or 6,000 convicts were banished from Great Britain.[21] This number was about to grow exponentially. With the passage of the Transportation Act, judges could now sentence convicted felons to transportation overseas to a British colony. This new Act gave judges the option of removing felons from the streets and jails without having to take away their lives in the process. As a side benefit, the Act seemed to offer help with the American colonies' desperate need for cheap labor. Settlers in America faced the problem of securing labor at a cheap enough price for them to grow their businesses, mainly because anyone who had sufficient means to make the trip overseas from Great Britain to start a new business in America had no intention of working for anyone else. Transported convicts could help fill this labor vacuum. In the eyes of the British government, convict transportation killed two birds with one stone: It rid the Isles of unwanted criminals and provided cheap labor for the American colonies.

The Transportation Act applied to two categories of crimes. For offenses where criminals would normally have received benefit of clergy, the judge could now directly sentence the guilty party to transportation for seven years in lieu of branding or whipping. The second category covered by the Act was non-clergyable offenses—i.e., more serious felonies where execution was the normal punishment. After being handed a formal sentence of death, the offender could receive mercy from the Crown and be pardoned on condition of transportation for 14 years or even life. Convicts who had been sentenced to transportation in either category and then returned to Britain before finishing out their term were liable to an automatic death sentence.[22]

The Transportation Act had an immediate effect on sentencing. At the Old Bailey session on April 23, 1718—the one directly following the Act's passage—27 of the 51 people convicted of crimes were sentenced to transportation. Banishment proved to be so popular among judges that it quickly became their preferred sentence. The punishment of transportation to the colonies was mostly used in cases of petty theft, but even offenses that normally called for the death penalty, such as murder or the theft of anything valued over 2 pounds, were often commuted to transportation as well.[23] Between 1718 and 1775, more than two-thirds of all convicted felons at the Old Bailey in London were sentenced to transportation, while only one-sixth received the death penalty during the same time span.[24]

Even after the Transportation Act was passed, Thomson remained a strong advocate for this new form of punishment and made sure that its provisions would not weaken through practice. Thomson obsessively supervised all of the details in implementing the Transportation Act in London and once claimed that he read "the names in every bond that is given by the merchant for transportation, and see with my own eyes, that everything is right."[25] At another time, he objected to the possible pardon of a convict sentenced to transportation by arguing that when such persistent minor offenders "are set at liberty, they very seldom if ever, leave off that ill habit, and persons of credit will not venture to employ 'em, and so they are generally observed to follow the same course of life." A pardon, he continued, would go against the intent of the Act, which was to "prevent their doing further misschiefe."[26]

Thomson's advocacy was one reason why transportation became the most common non-capital punishment handed down in London, with its use far surpassing any other jurisdiction in England.[27] Thomson's achievements were monumental. Within the span of a year, he both created a registry to help identify repeat offenders and succeeded in pushing through legislation that added a brand-new form of punishment to the criminal justice system. But Thomson had his eye on one more problem:

Tucked away in the Transportation Act was a provision aimed at curtailing the activities of Jonathan Wild.

William Thomson and Jonathan Wild

The authorities had a vague idea of how Jonathan Wild operated all along, but they were hesitant to toy with a system that appeared to yield such good results in capturing criminals. Thomson nonetheless included a provision in the draft of his Transportation Act aimed specifically at curtailing Wild's organized criminal activities. This provision made it a crime for anyone to take a reward for returning stolen goods to their owner without at the same time capturing and giving evidence against the thief. Failure to turn in the criminal could subject the person taking the reward to the same punishment as the thief, assuming the latter was ever caught. This provision was so clearly aimed at Wild that the Transportation Act also became known as "The Jonathan Wild Act."[28]

Despite this obvious attempt to curtail his illicit activities, Wild continued his trade for many years afterward. He knew that if he carefully covered his tracks and received payment indirectly from his clients, it was virtually impossible to secure a conviction against him.[29] Even more, the Transportation Act had the unintended consequence of actually helping to strengthen Wild's hold on the members of his criminal empire. Under the Act, returning before one's term of transportation had expired was punishable by death, and convicts who did so made ideal candidates for Wild's criminal network. Once Wild got wind of transported convicts who had returned early to England, he could quickly and easily bring them into his fold by threatening to reveal their identity to the authorities. Since the Transportation Act made it a crime to collect a reward for returning stolen goods without turning in the perpetrator as well, Wild shielded himself by using transported convicts to return stolen goods and collect the reward from their owners. Returned convicts not only provided Wild with protection from the provision in the Transportation Act aimed directly at him, but if they ever tried to betray him, he could easily turn them in for a large reward, and they would receive an automatic death sentence.[30]

Wild was a master at manipulating the law to benefit his criminal enterprise, but eventually the law caught up with him. In 1725, he was arrested for theft and receiving stolen goods. After Wild's arrest, William Thomson drew up a "Warrant of Detainer" to keep Wild in custody. The warrant included 11 articles that provided details about the operation of Wild's criminal empire, and people were flabbergasted when the warrant became public. The warrant also gave the impression that Thomson had just discovered Wild's activities during the inquiry after his arrest. Most likely, however, Thomson knew about Wild's methods all along and only acted when it became clear that other magistrates were building a case against him.[31] After Wild was found guilty of receiving stolen goods, Thomson pronounced the sentence of death on him.[32]

Wild headed the largest and most complex criminal organization England had seen to date—and perhaps has ever seen to this very day. He transformed the nature of crime by organizing it into an efficient, multi-layered business that brought a large number of London's criminals and gangs under his direct control. Yet by hiding behind a veil of respectability, he maintained the public's favor and support up until his trial and execution. Wild's ability to manipulate both the laws and public opinion for his own criminal purposes exposed the contradictory nature of law and crime in 18th-century England. Indeed, after he was executed, the number of criminals apprehended and convicted fell sharply.[33]

The Fate of Wood and Higgins

Even though Richard Wood and Edward Higgins were tried and sentenced at the Old Bailey session that took place just before passage of the Transportation Act, they both felt the Act's effect. At their original trials, Higgins was convicted of stealing two coach cushions, pleaded benefit of clergy, and was sent back on the street after being branded on the thumb with a "T" for theft; Wood, on the other hand, was sentenced to death for pickpocketing. But the Transportation Act allowed the punishment of transportation to be retroactively applied to those who were sentenced before the Act's passage. Under this provision, Wood's death sentence was changed to transportation to the American colonies for 14 years. So on August 28, 1718, Wood boarded the *Eagle*, a ship originally used in the slave trade, and along with 106 other convicts became the first to be transported to America under the Transportation Act. The ship's initial destination was Maryland or Virginia, but after a run-in with a pirate, the ship was rerouted to Charlestown, South Carolina.[34] And with its arrival in the American colonies, Wood completed his narrow escape from execution.

Higgins, on the other hand, confirmed the fears that helped push through passage of the Transportation Act in the first place. He evidently did not learn his lesson from his first brush with the law, for two years later he was once again caught stealing three coach seats. This time the court was not so lenient and sentenced him to transportation.[35] Higgins was turned over to Captain Darby Lux and placed on board the *Gilbert*, which set off for Annapolis, Maryland in October 1720. But Higgins did not appear on the *Gilbert*'s landing certificate, so it is quite possible that the man who initially received benefit of clergy for his first offense died during his passage to America for his second offense.[36]

* * *

With the passage of the Transportation Act in 1718, Britain became the only European country after 1700 to transport convicts as part of a major governmental policy.[37] Transportation was so popular among judges and quickly became their preferred punishment for lesser felonies because mass executions were considered too barbaric, long-term imprisonment was too expensive, and transportation was seen as a more effective deterrent to recidivism than corporal punishment. Transportation no longer involved simply banishing a criminal offender from England's borders: It now became an institutionalized practice that emptied the jails and systematically purged criminal elements from the ranks of the destitute poor. Convict transportation also turned out to be big business.

Chapter Three: The Business of Convict Transportation

Before Parliament passed the Transportation Act of 1718, the British government conducted an experiment in transporting convicts. On December 7, 1716, Francis March, a West Indies merchant, received a government contract to transfer a number of convicts to the colonies. He received 40 shillings per head to cover freight costs, with the Treasury supplying one pair of iron handcuffs and one pair of feet irons for every felon. About one week later, March loaded three ships with 54 felons, all of whom had been pardoned on condition that they serve eight years on plantations overseas, and set sail for Jamaica.[1]

The Treasury not only paid March a total of 108 pounds for his service, but it also paid William Pitt, the Keeper of Newgate Prison, 170.1.3 pounds for the cost of "passing a Pardon"—i.e., removing the irons from the convicts, preparing them for their journey, and transferring the felons to the ship.[2] Pitt's itemized expenses for readying the convicts included the following:

- £4.1.0. for bread, beef, beer, brandy, cheese, etc. sent with 30 of the prisoners and their guard.
- £0.10.0. given to those prisoners who were almost naked.

- £32.8.0. for 54 hand and feet irons @ 12s. a head.
- £36.0.0. fees to the Clerk of the Peace for 54 persons @ 13s.4d. each.
- £40.1.0. fees to the Keeper @ 14s.10d. each.
- £10.15.0. for my own trouble and attendance four days in passing the pardon and 2 days and 2 nights in passing the prisoners.[3]

The experiment had a high price tag, with both March and Pitt realizing huge profits.

One year after March unloaded the convicts in Jamaica, the Governor updated the Lordships of Trade and Plantations on the fate of the transported felons:

> These people have been so far from altering their evil courses and way of living and becoming an advantage to us that the greatest part of them are gone and have induced others to go with them a pyrating, and have inveigled and encouraged several negroes to desert from their masters and go to the Spaniards in Cuba. The few that remains proves a wicked, lazy and indolent people that I could heartily wish this country might be troubled with no more.[4]

The failed plan to turn the convicts into productive laborers was not the only mishap of the experiment. The episode affected the future development of the convict transportation business and ultimately cost the British government much more than the 278 pounds it shelled out to remove these 54 convicts from the country's borders.

The First "Contractor for Transports to the Government"

After the British Parliament passed the Transportation Act, the government faced the problem of how to administer the transportation of convicts to the colonies. William Thomson, the main author of the Act, originally proposed that the government sign official contracts with private merchants to ship the convicts overseas, but the House of Lords resisted the idea. Its members were evidently unsatisfied with the results of Francis March's voyage and did not want to use government funds to support the new system of punishment. Unable to find a suitable solution for financing convict transportation, Thomson simply left this crucial detail out of the legislation in order to get it passed.

The failure to finance the measure properly through legislation meant that each jurisdiction throughout England was individually responsible for making arrangements to transport its own convicted felons. Without financing or a standard mechanism in place for carrying out this new form of punishment, the London jails quickly filled up with convicts awaiting transportation. Thomson saw that the situation had become a crisis and intervened. He formally recommended to the Treasury that a 33-year-old tobacco and slave merchant, Jonathan Forward, be granted an exclusive government contract to oversee convict transportation. Forward was a perfect fit for the job. He commanded a small fleet of ships, which made regular trips to London, Africa, and the American colonies as part of his tobacco and slave trade. Through these ventures, Forward had gained valuable experience in transporting human cargo and had developed the necessary connections with plantation owners in the colonies who could buy the convicts' labor.[5]

Another advantage working in Forward's favor for securing the contract was that he had already transported a couple shiploads of convicts to Maryland for the government. Either Forward's keen business foresight or his connection with Thomson convinced him even before passage of the 1718 act that convict transportation would eventually become big business. In the hope that a more permanent contract would come his way, Forward decided not to charge the government for these first voyages and instead relied solely on the profits taken from the sale of the convicts into servitude in America to fund the trips.

In 1717, while Parliament debated the Transportation Act, Forward sent his first convict ship to Maryland with 134 transports on board. Forward contracted the *Dolphin*, which was owned and commanded by Gilbert Powlson, to take the convicts to America and then load up the ship with cargo, most likely tobacco, for its return trip to London. The total cost to outfit the ship was 375 pounds, and Forward was to pay Powlson upon his return a set rate per month for the time the ship spent outside of London. The *Dolphin* arrived in the Patuxent River in early 1718 with seven felons having died before the trip's end. The remaining convicts were sold off to plantation owners, but before Powlson could return to London, he was arrested for debts he had incurred in the province. While being held in jail, Powlson sent a petition to the Governor of Maryland stating that Forward owed him 470 pounds and asking him to enforce payment to secure his release. The Governor was not pleased with the fact that convicts were now arriving in his colony, so he passed the matter on to his Attorney General, Thomas Bordley, who froze 2,000 pounds of Forward's assets in Maryland and impounded the ship. The litigation went on for 12 years, and before it came to an end, Powlson had long left the colony and Bordley had died in England while pursuing the case. In the meantime, due to a cabin window that was inadvertently left open, the *Dolphin* sank while sitting in the harbor. Its main deck and quarter-deck had to be reconstructed in order for it to sail again, but despite efforts to fix these problems, examiners in the end declared the ship unfit to carry cargo.[6]

Even though Forward's first venture into convict transportation ended in a legal fiasco, he took another shipload of convicts to America at another discounted rate in the spring of 1718. Forward shrewdly sensed that these initial forays would help him lure the government into signing a lucrative long-term contract with him, and with the London jails already filled beyond capacity, he was now in a position to take advantage of the situation. Forward no doubt knew about the Treasury's earlier arrangement with Francis March, so he offered to transport prisoners on a regular basis in exchange for three pounds for every convict from London and five pounds per head for those from the rest of the country. Forward justified the fees by arguing that they were necessary for covering his expenses, since death, sickness, and other accidents severely cut into his potential profit.

On July 9, 1718, Thomson appeared before Treasury officials and testified that Forward's proposed contract was a bargain. He claimed that no one else could transport convicts as cheaply and pointed out that Forward's flat rate included all fees to officials, the cost of leg irons, and the hiring of guards to accompany the convicts to the ship. Thomson also argued that an effective convict transportation system would actually save the government money, because the net effect of the new punishment would lower the number of rewards the government would have to hand out for the capture of highwaymen and housebreakers. At last, the Treasury accepted Thomson's arguments, and one month later Jonathan Forward became the first Contractor for Transports to the Government.[7]

Contracting out the punishment of convicted felons to private enterprise was a radical step for the British government, which never before had hired outside firms for this purpose.[8] Forward's new position essentially granted him a monopoly on the convict trade, and he held the position until 1739. In this role, Forward became one of the most important figures in criminal punishment, and he set precedents for the North American convict trade that would last until the practice ended.

Business Models

Before passage of the Transportation Act in 1718, British convict transportation was a haphazard process, mainly because prisoners were generally responsible for making their own arrangements for leaving the country. Once convicts were sentenced to banishment from the country, there was little follow-up by the government and no measures were put in place to ensure that offenders did not return before the specified time ran out. After passage of the Act, convict transportation became an official business, and the British government supervised the mechanisms of removing banished convicts. The transportation practice was now codified with standard rules and procedures that needed to be followed in order to ensure the removal of convicts from the country.

When the British government developed the legal and procedural structures for transporting convicts to America under the Transportation Act, it used the indentured servant trade as a model. In order to become an indentured servant, all one had to do was sign a binding contract that obligated that person to become a servant in America for a specified amount of time, and in exchange he or she received free passage across the Atlantic. Anyone in England could become an indentured servant, but those who did tended to be people who could not find work and found themselves in debt or some other form of trouble. Others simply wanted to start a new life in the American colonies but lacked the money to make the trip.[9]

**An indentured servant contract signed by Henry Mayer
with an "X" in 1738.**

(Source: Wikipedia Commons, http://commons.wikimedia.org)

Potential servants could sign a contract directly with an agent of a planter in America before departure, but most planters did not want to risk acquiring a servant sight unseen. More commonly, a merchant, an emigrant agent, or a ship captain took those who wanted to become indentured servants on consignment. Once the servants arrived in America, the agent or captain auctioned each of them off and used the money he received from the sale to cover the cost of their passage. If the sale of a servant brought in more than 4 pounds, which is about what it cost to travel across the Atlantic, then the agent would realize a profit.[10] The demand for labor in the colonies was so great that profits were practically guaranteed for servants who possessed even minimal skills, so there was a lot of money to be made in the indentured servant trade. And the high profits naturally led to abuses in the system. Some agents used coercive tactics and false advertising to trick people who were looking for easy money or opportunities to improve their station in life into signing contracts.[11]

When convicts arrived in America, they were sold off to plantation owners just like indentured servants, and since indentured servitude served as a model for administering convict transportation, there were many similarities between the two trades. Both set fixed terms for servitude before the future servants left port. Indentured servants generally served for a period of four years, while convicts who were sentenced to transportation generally served seven-year terms. In both trades, the government utilized the private sector to carry out the transport of these future servants across the ocean. Once in America, both types of servant were sold to the highest bidder, with the proceeds helping to offset the associated costs of carrying them overseas. The labor that each servant performed in America, as well as their legal rights, was fairly similar as well. The main difference between the two was that the term of contract and the subsidy paid out for transporting convicts were set by the government, whereas both the length of service and the cost of passage were negotiated by the indentured servants themselves. And because the two trades were similarly structured, many of the merchants who traded in indentured servants also took up the convict trade, which meant that criminals were often transported alongside indentured servants.[12]

Indentured servitude in the 17th century was an attractive option for those who could not find work in England, especially during times of falling wages and bad harvests. Up until 1660, a young man who was able to complete his servitude in America had a good chance of creating a comfortable life for himself. But as land became scarcer and more expensive, servants had an increasingly difficult time making something of their lives once they became free. Severe poverty was often the driving force behind both those who entered indentured servitude and those who committed crime. In many respects, people who were hungry and lacked shelter in 18th-century England were destined to find themselves in America, either as an indentured servant for four years or as a transported convict for seven.[13]

The Preferred Destination for Convicts

One of the most common misconceptions about convict transportation is that the British set up Georgia as a penal colony to receive their transported felons. The truth is Georgia never served as a primary destination for British convicts, nor did it ever function as a penal colony. So how did Georgia come to receive this reputation?

James Edward Oglethorpe, founder of the colony of Georgia

(Source: Wikipedia Commons, http://commons.wikimedia.org)

The colony of Georgia was originally the brainchild of James Edward Oglethorpe, who was moved to action when he witnessed the abuses carried out on inmates by the keepers and jailers of debtor prisons. Oglethorpe came up with the idea of founding a colony in America where the poor and destitute could start anew and at the same time help England by producing

71

wines, silks, and spices that normally were imported from foreign countries. In 1732, Oglethorpe secured a charter to found what would eventually become Georgia (named after George II, who granted the charter). One year later Oglethorpe brought his first group of settlers across the Atlantic with him and founded Savannah.[14]

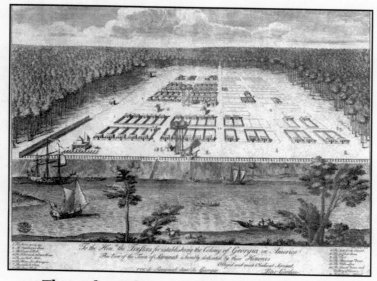

The early settlement of Savannah, Georgia.
(Source: Wikipedia Commons, http://commons.wikimedia.org)

Unfortunately, the people who originally came with Oglethorpe did not supply the kind of industrious work needed to start a colony, and the trustees of the colony quickly agreed in 1734 to abandon the idea of populating the colony with debtors, contending that "as many of the poor who had been useless in England were inclined to be useless likewise in Georgia." The second wave of settlers to Georgia came from the Jewish community in London, including 20 families of Portuguese Jews and 12 families of German Jews. While the former group quickly became independent, the latter group continued to rely on Oglethorpe's charity in America, which again greatly displeased the trustees of the colony.[15]

Georgia never ended up serving as a penal colony, nor did any of the other American colonies. Most likely, confusion over Oglethorpe's original intention to set up Georgia as a debtor's colony for those who were serving time in prison for their financial mismanagement eventually led to the misplaced popular belief that it was originally an American penal colony. So if Britain's transported convicts were not sent to Georgia, then where did they end up? Much like the indentured servant trade, the vast majority of transported convicts were sent to Maryland and Virginia, with the remaining few going to Pennsylvania, South Carolina, and the West Indies. Between 1718 and 1744, 7,010 convicts were transported from London to America, and of those, 6,815 (97.2 percent) were sent to Maryland or Virginia. In all, 80 percent of the total number of convicts transported to America from Great Britain, or about 40,000, ended up in Maryland or Virginia.[16]

In Maryland specifically, more than one-quarter of all immigrants who arrived between 1746 and 1776 were convicts, and most of them ended up on Maryland's Western shore. In 1755, convicts accounted for 12 percent of all productive adult laborers in the counties of Baltimore, Charles, Queen Anne's, and Anne Arundel. In fact, the number of convicts and indentured servants was so great in these four counties that white strangers traveling through these areas had to be careful so as not to be mistakenly identified as bound servants who had run away from their masters.[17]

Why were so many convicts sent to Maryland and Virginia and not to other colonies? The short answer to this question is tobacco.

The Chesapeake region did not initially start out as a center for tobacco cultivation when the British first settled the area. The main purpose for founding the colonies of Maryland and Virginia was to grow crops that England normally had to import from foreign countries. The theory was that if England could grow these crops in the colonies for use at home, it could improve its balance of trade and increase the country's overall wealth. Early settlements in Virginia struggled, however, since the crops and goods that were produced there could not be supplied on a scale sufficiently large enough to make the colony profitable. But once it was discovered that tobacco could be grown in great quantities and that there was a large market for it back in England, planters started growing tobacco anywhere and everywhere they could. Tobacco in Maryland and Virginia quickly became king.[18]

One of the main reasons the tobacco industry thrived in these two colonies was geography. Tobacco could be grown in other climates, but the ease of transportation provided by the area's waterways, more than soil and climate, was responsible for tobacco's growth in Maryland and Virginia. The numerous natural rivers and tributaries that flowed into the Chesapeake Bay allowed for both large-scale production of tobacco and rapid settlement of the region. In addition, tobacco is particularly susceptible to damage when transported, especially over land, but the vast water network in the area made it the perfect place to grow tobacco and smoothly ship it across water with less potential damage.[19]

Most convicts transported overseas ended up working on tobacco plantations in Maryland and Virginia, due to the intensive labor needed to cultivate this crop. Tobacco cultivation is not physically taxing, but it does require constant attention throughout the year, with at least 36 separate steps needed to produce one crop. Every step in the process was considered crucial to the overall success of the crop, and many of the more complicated ones were only carried out by skilled workers. Given the ease with which tobacco could be damaged during transport, cooperage was also an important part of the whole operation, although, unlike the cultivation of tobacco itself, it was generally carried out by unskilled workers.[20]

The complexity involved in cultivating tobacco meant that large-scale operations did not offer special advantages over smaller ones. The main difference between the large plantations and the smaller ones was simply the amount of land owned by the planter and the number of people he employed. Tobacco planters who wanted to grow their businesses could only do so by increasing their land holdings and employing more people at a dear price.[21]

The intensive care needed to cultivate tobacco was one reason the need for labor was so great, but there were others. The great planters of tobacco insisted on maintaining an independent existence, which came at a high cost. In order to preserve their autonomy as much as possible, the great plantations became self-contained communities, where every need—cooperage, blacksmithing, carpentry, shoemaking, etc.—was carried out by those who lived on the plantation, and so they required a vast labor supply. Eventually, planters began to diversify their crops by adding wheat and corn to their staple of tobacco, and this move called for even more unskilled laborers.[22]

Over the course of the 18th century, Maryland and Virginia also experienced growth in manufacturing. The need for skilled labor for non-plantation work—which generally could not be performed by slaves given cultural and language barriers—was particularly acute during the first part of the century. And as wages and working conditions improved back in England with the rise of industrialization, the demand for skilled labor in the American colonies only increased, because fewer indentured servants crossed the ocean to fill the need for skilled and semi-skilled workers in the colonies. Over time, convict labor became one of the few viable solutions for this labor shortage, so many transported felons also ended up working in manufacturing industries, most notably in iron works.[23]

The Chesapeake was the only one of the three major staple-producing regions in America—South Carolina and the West Indies being the other two—whose economies were based on an immigrant labor force made up of both black slave labor and white servants.[24] Because of the high demand for cheap labor, the already accepted use of white indentured servants, and the ability of convict merchants to fill up their ships with tobacco and grains to take back to England after selling off their human cargo, Maryland and Virginia became the preferred destination for transported felons.

Theoretically, Georgia or even North Carolina could have received convict servants to work on their plantations just as easily as Maryland or Virginia. But these two states did not become a primary destination for convicts due to their nascent economies. The wealthier plantations and the high demand for labor in Maryland and Virginia meant higher auction prices for felons. Convict merchants could also realize an even greater profit by filling their empty ships with the valuable tobacco and grains that were available in these two colonies for the trip back to England, which in turn put Maryland and Virginia in a better position to purchase the labor of future convicts. Georgia and the Carolinas simply could not offer merchants the same kind of profits that could be had farther north.[25] Another reason the Chesapeake received the vast majority of convicts was that Jonathan Forward had most of his American business connections there.

Jonathan Forward's Business

Jonathan Forward ran his new business out of his house on Philpot Lane off of Fenchurch Street in Cheapside, London.[26] Now that he had been appointed to the position of Contractor for Transports to the Government, he deployed a fleet of slave and merchant ships—with some of them named after himself—to carry the growing number of convicted criminals who were sentenced to transportation to the American colonies. Over the course of the first year, Forward transported more than 400 felons to Maryland and Virginia on four ships.[27] He sold them all, collected his fees from the Treasury, and pocketed the profits.

Not long afterward, Forward discovered a surefire way to increase his revenue. In March 1719, he returned to the Treasury and demanded a higher fee structure. He claimed that the low price of tobacco, which was essentially used in exchange for convicts in America, made it financially impossible for him to continue under the present terms. This time, Forward sought 5 pounds a head for felons from English county jails and beyond, while maintaining the 3 pounds per person for shipping convicts from Newgate Prison in London. The need to clear the jails was so great that the Treasury caved in to Forward's demands and granted him a new long-term contract. In 1727, Forward returned to the Treasury to secure yet another raise, which made 5 pounds the standard fee for transporting all convicts, including those from London.[28]

Forward fiercely protected his lucrative business interests. His name frequently appears in court cases involving bankrupt tobacco farmers, and he used his connections in the British government to challenge any attempts by the American colonies to limit his trade. In 1723, both Maryland and Virginia grew concerned over the number of convicts arriving on their shores. Knowing that it did not have the power to ban importing convicts into its colony outright, the Virginia assembly passed a law containing several measures designed to make the practice more difficult to carry out. Under the new law, ship-masters had to provide the names of all the convicts they were carrying upon arrival along with a 50-pound bond to ensure that none of them would leave the ship before they were sold. They also had to supply a 100-pound bond to guarantee the good behavior of the convicts for two months after the sale. In addition, anyone who purchased the felons was required to appear before the local court to register their names and the crimes that led to their transportation and to surrender 10 pounds to guarantee their good behavior. Forward immediately complained to the Board of Trade in England and argued that these provisions would effectively prevent him from carrying out his contract with the government. The law was quickly overturned. Maryland's attempt to pass a similar law that same year was also disallowed.[29]

At times, Forward had to defend his own actions before the government. In November 1735, 139 convicts from five previous sessions at the Old Bailey were still waiting to be transported, so Forward was brought before the Lord Mayor of London to account for the delay. Forward argued that the number of convicts being sentenced to transportation was too great for the number of ships in his fleet. Unimpressed by his argument, the Lord Mayor forced Forward into agreeing to clear all convicts waiting to be shipped from Newgate Prison three times a year: in March, August, and December. Despite this agreement, the problem persisted, and Forward was once again brought in to face the same charges one year later.[30]

Much like other elements of Britain's criminal justice system in the 18th century, the business of transportation was riddled with scandals and shady dealings. Forward had strong ties with Jonathan Wild, and the two of them worked together to capture convicts who returned early from transportation. Forward needed to maintain the integrity of his business, and he could face steep penalties if his organization were ever shown to have helped a transported convict return early. Whenever

Forward learned through inside information about the early return of a convict, he would tip off Wild about his or her presence. Wild would then locate the returned convict and either recruit him or her into his criminal empire or turn the felon over to the authorities and collect a handsome reward.[31]

One time, Forward fell victim to illicit dealings within his own organization. William Loney, one of Forward's senior captains, commanded 10 convict voyages over the course of 10 years starting in 1727. After Loney had long retired to Hatton Garden in London, Forward discovered that Loney had been swindling him back when he was his employee. Loney, it turned out, had been systematically switching marks on hogsheads of tobacco, so that he received quality leaf as compensation for his services while Forward was left with inferior leaf to sell back in England. Loney also manipulated account ledgers so that the payment of debts owed to Forward instead fell to himself. In the end, Forward estimated that the losses incurred by Loney's actions totaled 1,400 pounds.[32] Needless to say, Forward took Loney to court to recoup his losses.

Bristol and Other Firms

Even though Jonathan Forward held the official position of Contractor for Transports to the Government, his monopoly did not extend throughout England and the rest of the British Isles. From 1718 to 1773, the British government paid a flat fee for every convict transported from London, Middlesex, and the surrounding Home Counties to a single contractor. But localities outside of the London radius that needed to transport convicts from their jails were not entitled to the central government subsidy and had to strike deals with convict transporters on their own. Any shipping firm or independent contractor throughout the kingdom could place a bid to transport convicts for localities, including London, but that firm would not be entitled to receive a government subsidy for fulfilling its contract.[33] For the most part, the profit for these other firms came solely from the proceeds generated during the sale of the convicts' labor in America, unless the firms could convince a locality to pay a subsidy as part of the contract.

Competition among unsubsidized shippers of convicts drove down profit margins to nearly zero. To help increase their profits, unsubsidized shippers tended to fill their empty cargo space with indentured servants, whereas subsidized shippers almost exclusively reserved their cargo space for convicts.[34] But while firms that held an exclusive government contract enjoyed significant advantages over those that did not, there were drawbacks. Subsidized firms were required to transport all convicted criminals from the prisons in and around London, no matter what their physical condition was. Women, the elderly, and the physically challenged all brought lower prices when they were sold off in America, so transporting them was less profitable. If convict merchants had their druthers, they would pick the convicts they wanted to ship in order to keep their profits high, but such selectivity would have run counter to the government's goal of clearing out the jails. Smaller firms that also dealt in slaves and indentured servants were used to the freedom of deciding who they would carry overseas, and so they tended to be more selective in the convicts they agreed to transport as part of their direct negotiation with local authorities.

But merchants who struck exclusive deals with local governments or jails generally had less control over the condition of their human cargo.[35]

For the most part, convict transportation was organized by only a few merchant firms. After London, Bristol was the next largest center for convict transportation in England, although it did not begin to thrive in this trade until the 1750s. Bristol served as the launching point for most of the convicts transported from the western part of the country, including Wales, and only two firms dominated the trade from this city: Sedgely & Co. (1749-1768) and Stevenson, Randolph, & Cheston (1768-1775). These two firms transported 2,954 convicts during their existence and accounted for about 90 percent of the total trade in Bristol.[36]

Sedgley & Co. was founded by Samuel Sedgely, who was a wealthy subcontractor for both the convict and slave trades in Bristol, and his success helped him land the position of Sheriff of Bristol in 1739.[37] Stevenson, Randolph, & Cheston was formed after Sedgely & Co. (then, Sedgley, Hilhouse & Randolph) went bankrupt in 1768. The new firm started out with just two partners, William Stevenson and James Cheston. But William Randolph, with his added stock contribution and experience from the former bankrupt firm, joined them one year later. Stevenson and Randolph ran the operations in Bristol, where they acquired convicts and cargo, while Cheston supervised the business in Maryland. Cheston was in charge of gathering tobacco, wheat, corn, and pig iron for the trip back to Bristol after the convicts were unloaded. He also set up a store to sell some of the European goods that were also carried on the convict ships. Cheston initially arranged for the convicts to be sold by the merchant firm Smyth & Sudler at Chestertown off the Eastern Shore of Maryland, but he later moved the operations directly across the Bay to Baltimore Town, which he considered a better location for selling prisoners.[38]

Even though Stevenson, Randolph, & Cheston dabbled in transporting other goods to America, the firm quickly realized that the key to their business was convicts. They concentrated their efforts on monopolizing the convict trade in Bristol and grew to the point where they were sending two full ships of convicts to Maryland per year. The voyages were timed to leave soon after the spring and fall sessions of the assize courts, so they arrived in America in June or July and in October or November.[39] The firm did not receive a government subsidy, but it did make exclusive arrangements with jailers. These arrangements minimized the jail fees associated with releasing the convicts, which most contractors were normally responsible for covering as part of their business agreements. While these arrangements helped the bottom line, the firm's profits were more modest than those that received a government subsidy. They averaged a profit of 1.45 pounds per convict, or a 17 percent profit per freight space.[40] Still, such a profit margin was considered enormous. By comparison, merchants in the British slave trade during this same period could expect to earn profits of less than 10 percent, which shows how much money could be had in transporting convicts.

The efforts of Stevenson, Randolph & Cheston to corner the Bristol convict market apparently worked, because the firm shipped 93 percent of the 1,577 convicts sent to Maryland during its existence.[41] With its heavy reliance on convicts, though, the firm dissolved soon after the American convict trade came to an end. And during bankruptcy proceedings, it was revealed that one of the partners, William Stevenson, had been appropriating large sums of money from the firm.[42]

Jonathan Forward's Successors

Over the course of the century, a tight network of convict transporters filled the position of Contractor for Transports to the Government, and they dominated the industry up until the practice of shipping convicts to America ended. In 1739, Jonathan Forward mysteriously lost his exclusive government contract to Andrew Reid, who was one of Forward's agents in Port Tobacco, Maryland. Reid was friends with the Secretary to the Treasury, and he struck a deal with the Treasury for the exact same terms that were enjoyed by Forward, so he must have used this connection to help secure the position.[43] But despite losing his government contract and subsidy, Forward continued in the convict trade until he retired from the business in 1747. Spurning Reid, Forward turned over all of his American agencies and trade networks to John Sydenham, who was Forward's agent in Virginia, and to Thomas Hodgson, one of Forward's former clerks.[44]

Jonathan Forward died a wealthy man at the age of 80 in 1760 and left much of his personal property to his grandson, Edward Stephenson. He gave his West Country estates to his daughter, Elizabeth, who was married to Robert Byng. Byng would later become Paymaster of the Navy and then Governor of Barbados. At the time of her marriage in 1734, Elizabeth was worth an estimated 10,000 pounds. Such a large dowry gives some indication of the vast wealth accumulated by Forward in the convict trade.[45]

Sydenham & Hodgson became one of the leading black slave firms in the country. Based in Bristol and London, it also became the dominant firm in transporting convicts outside of London and the Home Counties. But when the company added tobacco and other merchandising ventures to its enterprises, the moves eventually doomed the company when numerous suits and financial disputes dragged it into bankruptcy in 1763. Sydenham's son, Jonathan Forward Sydenham, saw the flaw in his father's business model and rebuilt the company by focusing solely on the convict trade. By 1768, he could boast being "the Contractor with the greatest Part of the Counties in England for the Transportation of their Felons."[46]

Under Andrew Reid's watch, the convict trade reached its low point. Voyages conducted by his firm were characterized by a high death rate among the prisoners, despite an apparent financial incentive to keep them healthy so as to increase profits during their sale in America. Even though Reid would occasionally express compassion for those convicts who died during voyages, he did little to improve conditions on board his ships throughout his term.[47]

Reid was not an efficient transporter of convicts either. In 1749, he was accused of neglecting his responsibility for clearing the London jails of criminals waiting transportation. He gave the same excuse as Forward did back when he faced similar charges: that he lacked the resources to handle the vast numbers of convicts being sentenced to transportation. On March 26, 1751, the Secretary of the Treasury complained to the Lord Mayor that

Reid was still not meeting the terms of his contract and that he should be held more strictly accountable to those terms, especially in light of the late increase in robberies. Again, despite the Treasury's complaints, conditions did not improve. So in 1752, James Armour, acting as Reid's agent, was forced to pay £14.17s.6d. to compensate the city for housing prisoners beyond the time that they should have been transported by Reid.[48]

John Stewart, a Scotsman, joined Reid as a partner in 1748, and in March 1757, Steward succeeded Reid as the Contractor for Transports, with James and Andrew Armour as his partners. Stewart was a much more efficient transporter than Reid, and during the time he held the position both the timeline for emptying jails and the death rate on ships improved. In 1763, Stewart pitched a proposal to the Treasury to become the first contractor with an exclusive nationwide franchise. He cited both his efficiency in removing convicts and the improved mortality rate under his watch, and then argued that other parts of the country could benefit from his methods, since no rules or standards governed the practice outside of the London radius. He also asked for a 21-year contract. But Stewart's arguments fell short. The Treasury granted him only a seven-year contract and did not extend the geographic reach of his franchise.[49]

* * *

Convict transportation was a lucrative business, especially for those lucky enough to land an official government contract, and when transportation to America came to an end in 1775, convict merchants were enjoying record profits. For these merchants, convicts were simply another form of cargo to add to tobacco and slaves. But there was also a human element to the business of convict transportation, and the stories of how these mostly petty offenders went from prison, to ship, and across the ocean could be heart-wrenching.

Chapter Four: From Prison to Convict Ship

On May 5, 1727, two watchmen stopped and searched John Wilson, alias Smith, of St. Mary Walbrook on suspicion that he and another man stole a padlock from a warehouse door. The accomplice managed to get away, but the watchmen found eight picklock keys on Wilson, and the padlock was later found in the Channel where Wilson threw it as part of his attempt to get rid of the evidence of his crime.[1]

This brush with the law was not Wilson's first. In 1705 under the name of Smith, Wilson was found guilty of robbery and sentenced to execution. Miraculously, he survived his hanging when, after being cut down, he was taken to a nearby house where he was somehow resuscitated. Smith was subsequently granted his freedom for having outlived his execution, and from that point on he was known as "Half-Hanged Smith."[2]

In the case of the stolen padlock, the court agreed that Wilson had intended to rob the warehouse, which could have earned him a death sentence. But the jury only found him guilty of stealing the padlock, which they valued at two shillings, so he was sentenced to transportation. Still, Wilson appealed his sentence to Sir John Eyles, the Lord Mayor of London, in an attempt to avoid being transported:

> That your petitioner is now in the sixty sixth year of his age his eyesight much decay'd and wounded in both his hands in her late Majestie's service at Vigo, being then a Soldier in the Lord Cutts his Regiment in Colonel Bissetts Company, hath now a poor wife and two children.
>
> Therefore your lordships poor petitioner most humbly prays your Lordship that in consideration of his great age, his wounds and bodily infirmities together with the smallness of the crime laid to his charge, that your Lordship will be pleas'd to inflict such corporal punishment in lieu of transportation as your Lordship and the Honourable court shall think meet.

Wilson's petition was denied. He was placed on board the *Susannah* and sent to Virginia in July 1727 despite his disability and his family's circumstances.[3]

Stories about how people like John Wilson came to the American colonies are not often told. Instead, popular characterizations of early immigration to America give the impression that most of the people who made the trip across the Atlantic in the colonial period either belonged to religious groups looking for a place where members could freely practice their beliefs, such as the Pilgrims, or were brave and ambitious men seeking unlimited opportunity in a new, untamed land. Such notions fall far short of the truth. From the time when the first European settlers put foot on America and up until the American

Revolution, close to three-quarters of all immigrants to the 13 American colonies arrived as a slave, a convict, or an indentured servant. Even during the 17th century, when Europeans were just beginning to populate America, only a third of all immigrants arrived in a state of freedom.[4]

Depending on the severity of their crimes, transported convicts could receive one of three sentencing terms: seven years, 14 years, or banishment for life.[5] Given that most of them were sentenced to seven-year terms, transported convicts became colloquially known as "His Majesty's Seven-Year Passengers." Almost all of them were from the lower orders of society and around 80 percent of them were male.[6] Even though murderers, highwaymen, and professional thieves were certainly among those sent overseas, the most prevalent offense for which a criminal was transported was by far the theft of a handkerchief, an act most likely committed out of economic desperation.[7] From this perspective, transportation was indeed harsh punishment. It involved a lengthy wait in jail before being transferred to the convict ship, a long journey to America in crowded and suffocating conditions, and sale to a planter, who could subject the convict to harsh treatment and back-breaking work for seven years.

Starting the Journey in Newgate Prison

In December 1728, Elizabeth Howard of St. Bride's parish was found guilty of stealing three yards of ribbon and a piece of silk lace from Thomas Worsley. The stolen items were valued at 3s. 2d., but the jury reduced the value of the goods to 10 pence, so that she could receive a reduced sentence of transportation to the colonies. The fact that Howard was only 12 years old at the time must have entered into the jury's decision to lighten her sentence.[8] After sentencing, Howard was committed to Newgate Prison to wait for a ship that would take her to America.

Most of the people who were transported to America for their crimes were petty criminals like Howard who came out of the ranks of the destitute poor. The terrible economic situation in England during the 18th century generally offered the unemployed two choices: They could either sell themselves into indentured servitude in America or steal for their subsistence and risk being transported to America anyway. Many chose to gamble with their futures by taking up a life of crime in a desperate attempt to maintain their freedom in England as long as possible—and lost.

Convicted criminals who were tried at the Old Bailey in London and received a sentence of transportation began their journey to the American colonies in the notorious Newgate Prison. Like those who were sentenced to transportation in other cities and towns, they waited in prison for the next convict ship to leave port, which sometimes could be several months after sentencing. Prisons in 18th-century England mainly functioned as holding places for those moving through the criminal justice system—much like our modern-day jails today—with debtors generally being the only long-term inhabitants.[9] Given the rampant diseases that often ran through the prisons, it was not unusual for convicts waiting to be transported to die before they even boarded a ship.

Perhaps the most striking characteristic of 18th-century English prisons was their smell. The stench coming from

Bound with an Iron Chain

Newgate Prison permeated the surrounding neighborhood. In 1750, the odor got so bad that 11 men were hired to wash down the walls of the prison with vinegar and install a ventilation system. During the process, seven of the men working on the project came down with "gaol fever"—i.e., typhus. Only five years after the cleaning, the horrible smell from the prison was still so strong that nobody in the neighborhood could bear standing in their doorways.[10] John Howard, who published a study of English prisons in 1777, describes the intense odor he encountered at practically every prison he visited:

> Air which has been breathed, is made poisonous to a more intense degree by the effluvia from the sick; and what else in prisons is offensive. My reader will judge of its malignity, when I assure him, that my cloaths were in my first journeys so offensive, that in a post-chaise I could not bear the windows drawn up: and was therefore often obliged to travel on horseback. The leaves of my memorandum-book were often so tainted, that I could not use it till after spreading it an hour or two before the fire: and even my antidote, a vial of vinegar, has after using it in a few prisons, become intolerably disagreeable. I did not wonder that in those journies many gaolers made excuses; and did not go with me into the felons wards.[11]

John Howard
(Source: Wikipedia Commons, http://commons.wikimedia.org)

Prisoners generally received a meager diet of food, although better fare could be purchased. In addition, almost every English prison had a tap-room that sold alcohol to its prisoners, so they were often scenes of drunkenness and riot. One contemporary observer said of the tap-room in Newgate Prison, "Felons are permitted to converse and drink with the Debtors; by which Means, such Wickedness abounds therein, that that Place seems to have the exact Aspect of Hell itself."[12] Some prisons and jails were even situated inside public houses. The sale of alcohol was so profitable for prison-keepers that when a 1751 act banning the sale of spirits in prisons was passed, they basically ignored it. Felons who had access to an opening to the street were allowed to beg for food or money, which could then be used either to supplement their diet or to spend in the tap-room.[13]

When prisoners first arrived at Newgate Prison, they were placed in irons and led through the prison gate. The keeper's house was on the left, and below it was the Stone Hold, where newly arrived prisoners and convicted felons awaiting execution were kept. The Hold was described as "a most terrible stinking, dark and dismal Place, situated under Ground, in which no Daylight can come." Prisoners entered the Hold through a hatch, and the chamber was entirely constructed of stone, with hooks and chains fastened into the floor to restrain unruly prisoners. An open sewer ran down the middle of the room, emitting a stench that filled the space. The Hold had no beds, so prisoners were forced to sleep on the stone floor.[14]

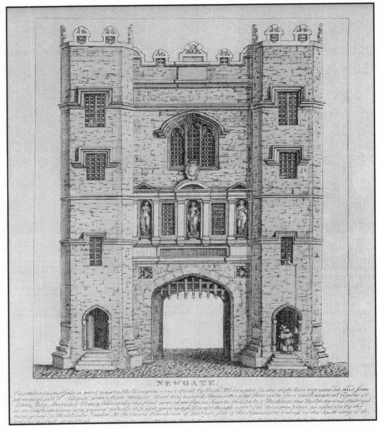

The entrance to Newgate Prison

(Source: Wikipedia Commons, http://commons.wikimedia.org)

A contributing factor to the general abuse that characterized all English prisons was that jailers bought their positions and then used fees to recoup and profit from their investment. Jailers even extracted fees from those being held on mere suspicion of committing a crime, and they charged set fees for the release of any prisoner, whether he or she was found guilty or not. Those who could not pay the fees were not allowed

95

to leave until they could somehow come up with the money to free themselves.[15] Prisoners who entered Newgate with money could pay to have the weight of their irons reduced or removed entirely. If they had any money left over, they could then pay for entry to either the Master's Side or the Press Yard. The Steward of the Ward, generally the senior prisoner who was entrusted to oversee the daily care of the prisoners, then collected from the prisoner a "garnish," which was a fee that went toward the purchase of brooms, candles, coal for heat, and drinks for the other prisoners. Those who could not pay a garnish were subjected to intense abuse by fellow inmates.[16]

Prisoners who lacked sufficient funds to pay for the privilege of better accommodations were put in the Common Felons Side, which was divided into five wards—three for men and two for women. Each ward had varying degrees of comfort, relatively speaking, and once again felons were placed in them according to how much money they could pay. Those who could not pay the entrance fees remained in the Stone Hold. Felons who could pay dues would be placed in the Middle Ward, which was not as dark or cold as the Hold, and while these prisoners still did not receive beds, they slept on oak flooring instead of stone.[17]

In 1724, a contemporary observed that most of the prisoners who inhabited the Common Felons Side were:

> generally those that lie for Transportation; and they
> knowing their Time to be short here, rather than
> bestow one Minute towards cleaning the same,
> suffer themselves to live far worse than Swine; and,

to speak the Truth, the *Augean* Stable* could bear no Comparison to it, for they are almost poisoned with their own Filth, and their Conversation is nothing but one continued Course of Swearing, Cursing and Debauchery, insomuch that it surpasses all Description and Belief.[18]

The beginning of a transported convict's journey to the American colonies was inauspicious, to say the least.

Convict Attitudes toward Transportation

Convict transportation was conceived as an easy means of emptying British prisons and of punishing petty criminals without having to resort to a death sentence, although it was generally regarded as less humanitarian and more severe than corporal punishment. Even though transportation was supposed to serve as a more lenient sentence in cases that would normally call for execution, those caught committing petty crimes were no doubt stunned to learn that their minor acts of theft earned them enforced banishment from the country and servitude in a far-off land.

Some convicts tried to appeal their sentences while they waited in prison to be transported in a desperate attempt to avoid being shipped overseas. While languishing in Newgate Prison after her trial for stealing three yards of ribbon and some lace, 12-year-old Elizabeth Howard petitioned to have her sentence reduced from transportation to some form of corporal

---

* A reference to the filthy Aegean stable that Hercules had to clean out as one of his 12 labors.

punishment. She anxiously wrote to Sir Robert Bayly, the Lord Mayor of the City of London, and asked him to change her sentence:

> The humble petition of Elizabeth Howard
>
> That your petitioner being disguis'd in liquor was guilty of committing a crime which she never before did and hopes by the grace of God never to do the like again. Your petitioner since her unhappy confinement in goal has lost the use of her limbs.
>
> Most humbly prays on the account of her tender age not yet thirteen years and only cast to the value of single tenpence that your Honour out of your extensive goodness will be pleas'd to let her receive corporal punishment here for the heinousness of her crime and not to transport her out of her native isle.
>
> And your petitioner as in duty bound will ever pray etc.

The petition worked, because Howard was ordered to be discharged on account of her age. But unfortunately she died in prison before she could be released.[19]

Most convicted criminals facing potential execution were probably relieved to receive a reprieve from death in exchange for servitude in the American colonies. There are a few cases, however, where felons refused to be transported and preferred death instead. Mary Standford, who was convicted of privately stealing a shagreen pocketbook, a silk handkerchief, and four guineas from William Smith on July 11, 1726, was one such case.

After her conviction, she rejected pursuing a petition to change her sentence to transportation in lieu of execution.

Standford was raised just outside of London by good parents who sent her to school and educated her in the principles of Christian values. But Standford showed more interest in the "Company of *Young Men*," so she was sent to London to become a servant, where she lost several positions on account of her insolent behavior. In her final position as a servant she was seduced by a footman, which resulted in the loss of her job and forced her into prostitution.[20]

Standford quickly fell in with Mary Rawlins, "a Woman of notorious ill fame," and the two of them walked the streets between Temple Bar and Ludgate-Hill with the aim of emptying the pockets of gullible men. They had considerable success targeting sailors who, after receiving their salary upon returning from their voyages, had money to spend for their favors. Standford eventually married a man with the last name of Herbert, but after a year and a half she left him or, by her account, he abandoned her. Soon afterward, she had a child out of wedlock from another man, who was a servant.[21]

With two mouths to feed, Standford now set out to practice prostitution on her own, and it was then that she was arrested for theft. William Smith, who brought her to trial, was surprisingly frank in his testimony against her. He related that he was walking along Shoe Lane after one o'clock in the morning when he was approached by Standford, who asked him if he would like to "take a Lodging with her." He spent two or three hours with her, all the while ordering drinks to be brought up for them from downstairs. He eventually realized that he was missing his money, and when he confronted Standford, she bolted from the room.[22]

A constable caught Standford in the street as she was running away from Smith. The officer picked up one of Smith's guineas off the ground after Standford had dropped it, and he found another one in her hand and two in her mouth. He also discovered Smith's handkerchief and pocketbook on her. In his testimony at the trial, the constable called Smith a "Country Man" and described him as very drunk at the time.[23]

Standford's version of the event was quite different. She claimed that Smith was drunk when she met him, and that he forced himself up to her room. There, he placed the four guineas one by one in her bosom and then threw her on the bed. She speculated that in the struggle, his pocketbook must have fallen out of his pocket, and when she discovered it after he left, she ran after him to return it. Not believing her story, the jury found her guilty, and she was sentenced to death.[24]

After receiving her sentence, Standford's friends pleaded with her to request a pardon in exchange for transportation, but Standford refused, "declaring that she had rather die, not only the most Ignominious, but the most cruel Death that could be invented at home, rather than be sent Abroad to slave for her Living." The author of Standford's biography in the *Lives of the Most Remarkable Criminals* was baffled by Standford's position, and he interrupts the telling of her story to present a lengthy defense of the institution of convict transportation. He describes life as an indentured servant in the American colonies in rosy terms by claiming that convicts are "removed into another Climate, no way inferiour to that in which they were born," where they "perform no harder tasks, than those who work honestly for their Bread in *England* do."[25] The author makes transportation sound like a compelling alternative to execution, but the reality of a transported convict's life overseas did not easily match his depiction of it, and some criminals valued their liberty over enforced servitude, even if it meant their own death.

After counseling Standford as she awaited her execution, James Guthrie, the minister at Newgate Prison, described her as "grosly Ignorant of any thing that is good," and went on to say that "she was neither ingenious nor full in her Confessions, but appeared obstinate and self-conceited." Standford continued to maintain her innocence in the affair with Smith. She also appeared to be indifferent about the fate of the child she was leaving behind and expressed to Guthrie the hope that the parish would take care of it. Guthrie notes, however, that "she acknowledg'd herself among the chief of Sinners."[26]

Mary Standford was executed along with three other criminals on Wednesday, August 3, 1726 at Tyburn at the age of 36. One of other criminals was John Claxton, alias Johnson, who was put to death for returning twice from transportation before his seven-year sentence had run out.[27]

The Procession to the Convict Ship

When the convict merchant was finally ready to make the trip across the Atlantic, the convicts were released from prison and loaded on the ship, along with dry goods and perhaps a few indentured servants. Convict voyages were generally timed to leave just after the spring and autumn sessions of the assize courts. After the eight-to-ten-week voyage, the ships would usually arrive in Maryland or Virginia either in June and July or in October and November.[28]

Jonathan Forward and other transportation contractors used part of the payments they received from the government to cover the jailer's fees for releasing the prisoners they were supposed to transport. For every convict who was discharged for transportation in London, the Keeper of Newgate Prison charged 14s.10d. Since jailers and justices of the peace maintained tight control over the delivery of convicts in and out of prison, convict merchants who did not have guaranteed contracts with the government had to maintain good relationships with these officials in order to secure future transportation contracts and receive reasonable cooperation in transferring convicts to the ship.[29]

Transportation contracts were struck between merchants and justices soon after sentences were handed out in court. A transportation bond was then drawn up, which included a fine of 50 pounds if an authentic certificate of the convicts' arrival from the governor or chief customhouse officer at the American destination could not be produced by the contracted firm. The firm also agreed to transport the prisoners within a specified amount of time after the contract was signed and not to lend aid to any transported convicts who might attempt to return to England before the end of their terms.[30]

The release of the convict from prison was an important moment, because the term of transportation, be it seven or 14 years, began as soon as the keeper of the prison delivered the criminal to the captain of the convict ship. Upon leaving the prison, the convicts were chained together two by two and then marched through the street and down to the docks. This parade of convicts, which occurred three or four times a year, would generate considerable attention. People in London would follow the chained group as they emerged from Newgate and then made their way through the streets down to Blackfriars at the edge of the River Thames to board the convict ship.[31] The curious among the crowd could sometimes buy from a vendor a list of the criminals who were being transported. The novelty of convict transportation as a punishment caught the attention of the press as well. Accounts of trials that ended with transportation as a verdict were circulated in the coffee houses, and newspapers reported on the loading of convicts aboard ships and their departure for the American colonies, a practice that continued right up until convict transportation to America ended.

"A Gang of Men and Women Transports Being Marched from Newgate to Blackfriars" from *The Newgate Calendar*, 1735

(Source: Project Gutenberg, http://www.gutenberg.org)

On August 20, 1752, 11 convicts were scheduled to be led down to the ship that was to take them from Bristol to America.[32] A large crowd had gathered to witness the procession, but most of them wanted to see one convict in particular: Daniel Bishop. Bishop had been found guilty of murdering his girlfriend, Winnifred Jones, and he was sentenced to death. But Bishop received a reprieve from execution—perhaps through the help of family or political connections—and his sentence was instead changed to transportation for life, a reversal that did not sit well with the gathering crowd.

Ten of the prisoners exiting the prison were chained together two by two, and each pair was placed on a horse. Not seeing Bishop, the crowd grew restless and started crying out, "Where's Bishop?" Finally, he emerged from the prison and was put on a single horse without chains. As soon as he appeared, the crowd started shouting at him. One woman cried, "Hang the Dog!" and told him that she was "glad to see him come to this."

Unmoved by the crowd, Bishop boldly waved his hat and shouted along with them. As more people gathered along the street to see the parade, Bishop's displays of self-assurance began to ignite the mob. Shouts of "Hang the Dog---Hang the Dog.---A Halter,---A Halter" filled the air, as did dirt that the people were now picking up to throw at him. The noise became so intense that six of the other convicts were thrown from their frightened horses. One woman approached Bishop with a halter in her hand and cried out that "She would be glad to see him hang'd up to her Sign Post, for that he had killed her good honest Servant Maid, Winnifred Jones," to which he insolently responded, "What should I be hang'd for? I have been hang'd a great many times to such as you."

Eventually, Bishop began to show his frustration with the taunting crowd when he several times struck a young man who had thrown dirt at him. This action incensed the mass of people, and they now eagerly threw stones as well as dirt at him. Were it not for the guards protecting the prisoners, Bishop would have been torn to pieces by the mob, which at this point had reached several thousand. The transfer of Daniel Bishop to the convict ship was more extreme than what usually took place, but similar scenes occurred throughout the age of convict transportation.

When dealing with bureaucratic institutions in the 18th century, money artfully placed in the proper hands could often buy special privileges, and convict transportation was no exception. But one blatant case of purchased privilege that occurred in 1736 was so egregious, it was reported in newspapers on both sides of the Atlantic. Henry Justice, "a Gentleman of Fortune, and a Barrister at Law"—what other profession could he have had with such a last name?—was accused of stealing a quantity of books from the Trinity College Library in Cambridge and from other university libraries in London and Middlesex. He then sold the pilfered books both in England and overseas before he was arrested and put on trial at the Old Bailey.[33]

Justice began his trial by complaining that he could not hear the Judge due to his deafness and a "wretched Cold, which has stuck by me all the Winter," so he was relocated to the inner bar and closer to the judge. Justice then brazenly claimed that more books were seized from his apartment than were named in the exceedingly long list of books that appeared in his indictment and asked that the court return to him the ones that were not listed. His request was ignored, and the proceedings continued. Justice pleaded not guilty to the charges against him and argued that he was entitled to use the books that were found in his apartment, because he was a student at the university. But this claim proved to be false. The Librarian of the Trinity College Library confirmed that the books found in Justice's possession belonged to the university and demonstrated to the court that small tracts found in Justice's apartment were cut out of larger volumes that remained back in the library. On the strength of the librarian's testimony, Justice was found guilty. The Deputy Recorder sentenced him to transportation and said that his offense "was greatly aggravated by his Education, his Fortune, and the Profession he was of, and his Guilt much greater than it would have been, if he had been an ignorant or an indigent Person."[34]

Several days after Justice received his sentence, 100 convicts were paraded through the London streets early in the morning from Newgate Prison to Blackfriars in order to board the *Patapsco Merchant*, but Henry Justice and several other convicts who were sentenced to transportation for robbery were not among them. William Wreathock, an attorney; James Ruffet, alias Ruf-head, a butcher; George Bird, a bailiff; and George Vaughan, otherwise known as Lord Vaughan, instead rode in two hackney coaches down to the shore to board the ship. Justice traveled separately in one of the coaches and enjoyed the company of none other than Jonathan Forward.[35]

While most of the felons were confined in the hold of the *Patapsco Merchant* throughout the voyage and were sold as soon as they reached shore, these five men paid for the privilege of enjoying the captain's cabin and were presumably given their freedom as soon as they landed. *The Virginia Gazette* commented at the time, "Thus, by the wholesome Laws of this Country, a Criminal who has Money (which Circumstance, in all other Countries, would aggravate his Guilt, and enhance the Severity of his Punishment,) may blunt the Edge of Justice, and make That his Happiness which the Law designs as his Punishment."[36]

The fact that these five men most likely purchased their freedom in America was not entirely unusual, although it was not typical. The sale of convicts upon arrival in America helped convict merchants and captains both recover the costs of transporting their cargo and realize a profit. But convicts who paid up front what they would normally command at auction in the colonies were free to pursue their own interests once they landed. What did the merchants or captains care whether they received compensation for transporting convicts across the ocean from a plantation owner or from the criminals themselves? If convicts with money did not have enough to pay for their freedom outright, they could pay to have their terms of servitude reduced. Ironically, convicts with desirable skills, such as carpentry, generally commanded higher prices in America and consequently faced a greater challenge in purchasing their own freedom.[37]

In Daniel Defoe's 1722 novel *Moll Flanders*, Moll uses her connections and wealth to obtain special privileges for her trip to Virginia after she is sentenced to transportation for theft. Not only is she able to secure travel with her husband in the captain's lodgings, as opposed to being thrown into the hold of the ship with the rest of the convicts, but she is also able to take a number of goods with her on board, so that she can sell them for a profit after they land in America.[38] Moll's experience, though, was not the norm. The great majority of transported convicts were in no position to pay for the cost of their voyage, let alone carry a quantity of goods with them, since financial destitution was usually what put them in such a position in the first place.

Sometimes, though, fiction mirrors reality. Mary Young, a.k.a. "Jenny Diver," who quickly rose up the ranks to lead a gang of thieves on the strength of her innovative schemes for emptying pockets,* was finally caught shoplifting in 1728 and sentenced to transportation under the name of Mary Webb. During her four-month stay in Newgate Prison while she waited to be transported, she became a fence—i.e., a receiver of stolen goods. Her insistence that the gang put aside a percentage of the profits it received from its thefts, so that members who were caught could buy privileges while in prison, also paid off. So by the time Young was put on board the convict ship, she had acquired a wagonload of goods, and she enjoyed freedom and ease throughout her voyage to America after paying off the captain.[39]

Young was dropped off at the first port they came to in Virginia along with her goods, which she sold for a great profit. She lived for a short time in America in high style, but soon realized that the opportunities for plying her trade as a thief were fewer here than in England. She ingratiated herself to a young gentleman, who secured passage for both of them back to

---

* For the background of Mary Young, see pages 24-26.

London, but when the ship arrived at Gravesend, Young robbed the young man of everything she could get her hands on and executed a swift getaway.[40]

Young was transported once more in June 1738, this time under the name of Jane Webb.[41] On December 30, 1738, the *Newcastle Courant* reported that "Jane Webb, alias Jenny Diver," had returned from transportation, well before her sentence had run out. This same article also reported that three of the men who were transported along with Henry Justice—George Vaughan, George Bird and William Wreathock—had also returned from transportation early.[42]

Both Vaughan and Bird were caught soon after their return. Vaughan was picked up in Chester, England after taking part in a coining scheme involving the filing and engraving of half crowns. He was returned to London, where both he and Bird were found guilty of returning early from transportation. Bird was sentenced to transportation for life, and Vaughan was sentenced to transportation for 14 years. Wreathock never appeared again at the Old Bailey, so he may have remained at large for the duration of his life. Henry Justice managed to leave America as well, although he remained outside England and settled in Dunkirk, France.[43]

Young went undetected for more than two years after she returned from her second transportation stint until she was caught once again and convicted of robbery. This time, she was sentenced to death and was executed on Wednesday, March 18, 1741.[44]

Passengers on the *Jonathan*

Most convicts transported to America did not have the resources to buy the preferential treatment that Henry Justice and Mary Young received. A look at the convicts who in 1723 boarded the *Jonathan*—a former slave ship and at the time the newest addition to Jonathan Forward's fleet of convict ships[45]—provides a more accurate picture of the types of people who were generally transported in the 18th century.

James Bell, who was transported after he stole a book and then hid out in a dog kennel, was one of the *Jonathan*'s passengers. He was joined by 35 other convicts, and Margaret Hayes was one of them. On December 1, 1722, Hayes walked into a shop and began to bargain with Elizabeth Reynolds, the shop's owner, over the price of some stockings. Hayes was a 30-year-old widow with a dark complexion, and she lived in the parish of St. Giles-in-the-Fields, a section of London notorious for heavy gin drinking.[46] In the middle of the negotiations, Hayes grabbed a pair of stockings on display that were selling for two shillings and ran out of the shop.

Reynolds called out that she was being robbed, and several people who heard her cries attempted to stop Hayes. Realizing that she was going to be caught, Hayes dropped the stockings on the ground, but they were quickly picked up along with the offender. Hayes was swiftly brought to trial on December 5, and even though she denied ever having gone into the shop, she was found guilty of theft. The jury showed some sympathy for her by devaluing the goods she took to 10 pence, thereby ensuring a sentence of transportation to the American colonies for seven years, as opposed to death by hanging.[47]

Sarah Nutt was another passenger on the *Jonathan*. On November 25, 1722, Nutt entered Joseph Manning's chandler shop and sat down by the fire to enjoy a drink, most likely gin. Chandlers often sold more than just candles. They also specialized in selling basic items in small quantities to the poor, like coal and soap, and they offered food staples at prices below what they would normally cost in an alehouse. The poor tended to rely on chandlers for their daily allowance of bread, cheese, and small beer, but as the gin craze increasingly took hold over London, they increasingly bought just bread and gin. In general, chandlers were considered the lowest type of shopkeeper.[48]

Nutt was 22 years old at the time, had brown hair, and was unmarried. She lived in the parish of St. James's Clerkenwell not far from New Prison. At one point Manning leaned over to stir the fire, and Nutt quickly pulled a handkerchief out of his coat pocket and took it with her when she left the store. Nutt later discovered that a gold ring was wrapped in the handkerchief. She decided to give the ring to Mary Herrick, a cook, as repayment for a debt she owed her for some food. Herrick in turn sold the ring to Nutt's cousin, Mary Mark.

After missing his handkerchief and gold ring, Manning was eventually able to trace the ring back to Mary Mark, and he had Nutt arrested. At her trial on December 5, Nutt admitted that she took the handkerchief and the gold ring, which was valued at five shillings. She was found guilty of pickpocketing, which carried an automatic death sentence if the goods stolen were valued over one shilling. The jury showed her little sympathy, because they refused to devalue the ring, as they had done for the stockings that Margaret Hayes stole, so Nutt was sentenced to death. Two months later, Nutt received a conditional pardon and her sentence was changed to transportation to the American colonies for 14 years.[49]

John Watkins, a 21-year-old carpenter with brown hair, also joined John Bell on the trip to America. On December 6, 1722, Watkins was walking along a wharf on the Thames not far from his home. He came upon a pile of raisins sitting out in the open and made an impulsive, yet fateful decision. He grabbed a basket full of raisins, which was later valued at eight shillings, and continued on his way. Watkins was easily caught, and the owners of the raisins, Benjamin Longuet and Mark Weyland, brought him to trial on January 16, 1724 at the Old Bailey. Theft along the docks of the Thames was rampant at the time, and the two owners must have been eager to prosecute him. Watkins was found guilty of simple grand larceny, and he was sentenced to transportation for seven years.[50]

The set of trials held in January when John Watkins was convicted of stealing the basket of raisins was not without its theater. John Dyer, a hat-maker, was accused of stealing three hats from a workshop, even though he claimed that they were given to him on the street by a man who was drunk. In a classic case of early hotel theft, John Harris, a 25-year-old baker, was indicted for taking a pair of flaxen sheets after spending the night in the Windmill-Inn on St. John's Street. Both men were found guilty and sentenced along with Watkins to transportation for seven years.[51]

Sarah Wells, otherwise known as "Callico Sarah," also faced trial in January for returning early from transportation. Two years earlier, Wells was found guilty of stealing a silver watch and received a death sentence. Afterward, she and five other women who also faced death by hanging all "pleaded their bellies"—i.e., they claimed to be pregnant in the hope that they could delay their execution. Only one woman out of the six was actually found to be pregnant by a jury of matrons, and Wells was not the one. But even though she was not found to be pregnant, Wells was able to avoid execution when she received a conditional pardon to be transported to America for 14 years.[52]

At her subsequent trial for returning early from transportation, Wells was once again found guilty and sentenced to death for her crime, and once again she tried the same tactic of pleading her belly. This time it worked—Wells was indeed found to be pregnant. This change of events helped her secure yet another conditional pardon, and she was transported a second time to America under a 14-year sentence. Wells did not travel with the others on the *Jonathan*, perhaps so that she could have her baby before making the trip. Instead, she headed out in July on the next ship, the *Alexander*, along with Mary Godson, a.k.a. "Moll King." Both Wells and King at the time were associated with Jonathan Wild, and it turned out that he was behind both of their convictions.[53]

On February 18, 1723, James Bell, Margaret Hayes, Sarah Nutt, John Watkins, John Dyer, and John Harris—along with 30 other convicted felons, including a brickmaker, a wheelwright, three weavers, a painter, and a glass grinder—were paraded through the London streets from Newgate Prison to the docks along the Thames to board the *Jonathan*.[54] Jonathan Forward placed his trusted captain, Darby Lux, in charge of his new ship. Lux had previously carried out two convict voyages to America for Forward as captain of the *Gilbert*. On board Lux's first voyage in October 1720 was "Callico" Sarah Wells, who was on her first trip to America for theft. Wells, along with several other convicts, did not appear on the landing certificate for the *Gilbert*, so she may have escaped and returned to London before or soon after the ship arrived in Maryland.[55] Since Wild often "recruited" convicts who returned early from transportation into his criminal organization, it was at this time that Wells most likely fell under his grip.

The passengers on board the *Jonathan* and the trip itself were representative of most convict voyages. At least two of the convicts died during the crossing of the Atlantic: Elizabeth Knight, who was found guilty of stealing two riding hoods valued at two shillings; and Charles Lynch, who, along with his brother, ran away with a bag of clothes belonging to a traveler who had stopped to ask the two directions.[56] But what happened to the *Jonathan* after it arrived in America was unusual. Some time after the ship landed in Annapolis, Maryland, it caught fire and sank, and the authorities suspected that the convicts were ultimately responsible for setting the fire. In the end, Jonathan Forward's newest member of his fleet made only one convict voyage. Darby Lux, on the other hand, made many more trips with convicts before settling in Maryland in 1738 to become Forward's principal agent in America.[57]

Final Goodbyes

Ships transporting convicts tended to be separated on the docks from those transporting commodities, so there was plenty of space between the convict ship and any other vessel.[58] First-hand accounts of convicts being loaded on the ship include descriptions full of tears, embraces, and goodbyes as the prisoners were finally separated from their families and friends, possibly for the rest of their lives.[59] This sad moment is depicted in a doggerel poem called *The Poor Unhappy Transported Felon's Sorrowful Account of His Fourteen Years Transportation at Virginia in America* (1780) by James Revel, which, despite its bad poetry, is fairly accurate in its details about convict transportation in general:

> My father vex'd[,] my mother she took on,
> And said alas! alas! my only son,
> My father said, it cuts me to the heart,
> To think on such a cause as this we part.
>
> To see him grieve pierced my very soul,
> My wicked cause I sadly did condole,
> With grief and shame my eyes did overflow,
> And had much rather chuse to die than go.
>
> In vain I griev'd and in vain my parents wept,
> For I was quickly sent on board the ship,
> With melting kisses and a heavy heart,
> I from my dearest parents then did part.[60]

The moment of boarding the ship could be particularly harsh for couples who were convicted of committing a crime together and who were both sentenced to transportation. Government officials would generally go out of their way to separate the two by sending each of them to different colonies on different ships. If they could afford to do so, husbands and wives could book passage on the same ship together instead, just like Moll Flanders and her husband were able to do, or try to arrange to become indentured servants in the same colony, but such arrangements rarely happened.[61]

Not all departures were somber. On January 5, 1769, *The Virginia Gazette* ran a report from England that "Saturday morning between four and five o'clock the transports, to the number of eighty, were conveyed from Newgate and put on board a close lighter at Black-friars, in order to be forwarded to the British plantations. They went off very merry, huzzaing; and declared they were going to a place where they might soon regain their lost liberty."[62] In 1767, *The New York Journal* published another account of a group of Newgate felons boarding the *Trial*: "While the securing Chain was putting upon them, the Hand of one of them was caught in the Captain's pocket."[63]

Once the transports boarded the ship, they were sent below deck to a prison hold where they spent most of the eight- to 10-week voyage until they reached port in America. The captain, the jailer, and other witnesses then signed the transportation bond that ensured the convicts being transported were secured safely on board. These documents were delivered to the Treasury to prove that the criminals had been transferred and that payment was due. After a month or so, payment was made to the convict contractor, and the documents were copied word for word into the Treasury Money Books.[64] With the signing of the transportation bond, the convicts were now set to embark on their voyage across the Atlantic to America.

Once the ship left port, family members who may have depended on the convict for their subsistence now had to fend for themselves. Most likely, they ended up in workhouses or fell into a life of crime themselves.

Chapter Five: Convict Voyages

In the early summer of 1774, Captain John Ogilvie was carrying 94 convicts from London to Virginia on the *Tayloe* when one morning he spotted an extraordinarily beautiful bird sitting on the bowsprit. As soon as Ogilvie saw the bird, he knew he had to have it, so he called for his gun and shot it. His aim was less than perfect. The bird fluttered out over the water for a while until it fell dead into the ocean.

Undeterred from his desire to possess it, Ogilvie called out to the convicts that "which ever of them would procure for him the bird, should immediately receive his freedom." Several of the convicts stripped off their clothes and plunged into the water to retrieve the prize. Just as the first convict arrived at the floating bird and reached out to grab it with one arm, a shark rose up out of the water and bit off his other arm. Desperate for the promise of freedom and with the bird in tow, the convict struggled to return to the ship with his remaining arm. The crew hauled the prisoner up out of the water, and he delivered the trophy to the captain before dying on the spot.[1]

In an event reminiscent of Samuel Taylor Coleridge's *Rime of the Ancient Mariner*, lightning later struck Ogilvie's ship as it headed to shore in the Chesapeake Bay. The bolt destroyed the mast and stunned the people on board, but fortunately nobody was injured.[2]

Bad treatment by captains like Ogilvie was only one of the hazards convicts faced on transport ships. Severe weather and pirates could threaten voyages. Convicts were also vulnerable to outbreaks of disease due to the cramped, suffocating conditions in which they were transported. And the prisoners themselves posed risks, with their constant vigilance in seeking opportunities to overthrow the ship and escape. Crossing the Atlantic was risky enough in the 18th century, but especially so on a ship full of disgruntled criminals.

The Convict Ship

Convict ships in general were not large. Even though slave ships were sometimes used to transport felons, most convict ships were better suited to carry tobacco and other commodities for the trip back across the Atlantic than to transport human cargo to the colonies. The ships were generally made in America—mainly in Maryland or New England—where abundant forests offered plenty of wood. About a third of the ships were constructed in Britain, and an even smaller percentage of them were seized from the French as booty during wartime.[3] The ships tended to be old and worn down from frequent trips back and forth across the ocean, and their rotting hulks often required costly repairs that cut deeply into the profits of the convict contractors.[4]

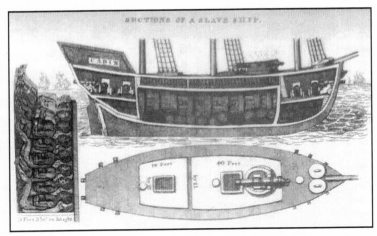

Sections of a slave ship. Note the narrow space for human cargo that sits above the hold for regular cargo.
(Source: Wikipedia Commons, http://commons.wikimedia.org)

Convict ships heading directly to America after leaving London traveled down the Thames on the ebb current and then anchored at Dover, Cowes, or the Downs to wait for favorable winds to take them out to sea. Some London ships traveled to additional British ports to pick up even more prisoners before heading out, although major seaports like Bristol relied on their own convict transportation firms.[5]

Ships going from Great Britain to the Chesapeake along the northern route of the Atlantic traveled in a direct west-southwest direction. In good weather, the trip could take as little as seven to eight weeks, although encounters with bad weather could extend the time of the voyage considerably. During the winter when cold and bad weather were more common, the trip could take 12 to 14 weeks. Return trips back east to Great Britain took much less time—sometimes only six or seven weeks—with the winds and the Gulf Stream helping to move the ship along at a faster pace.[6]

Sailing from England to America was a serious affair due to the real possibility that those embarking would never return. Sailors feared most the frequent storms on the Atlantic, since ships that ran into them were at the mercy of the high winds and roiling waters. Storms could not only severely damage ships and cargo, but they also made travel extremely uncomfortable for passengers as the vessel was battered around. After a particularly stormy trip to the American colonies in 1708, Ebenezer Cook wrote a poem describing his experience:

> Freighted with Fools, from *Plymouth* sound,
> To *Mary-Land* our Ship was bound,
> Where we arrived in dreadful Pain,
> Shock'd by the Terrours of the Main;
> For full Three Months, our wavering Boat,
> Did thro' the surley Ocean float,
> And furious Storms and threat'ning Blasts,
> Both tore our Sails and sprung our Masts.

Food was nearly impossible to cook during rough weather, but seasickness usually eliminated passengers' hunger anyway.[7]

In 1767, bad weather hit a convict ship so hard and so often that once the harrowing voyage was over, newspapers from London to Virginia to Boston carried a detailed account of the journey that was drawn from the captain's log.[8] The trip began inauspiciously in early October when Captain Nicholas Purdy discovered before leaving English waters that the convicts had hatched a plan to take over his ship. Purdy took steps to prevent such an uprising, and on October 10 the *Rodney* set sail into the Atlantic with "clear weather and steady breeze."

One month later, Purdy noted in his log that the convicts were wet, which indicates that the ship was suffering from structural damage or decay. Subsequent days were cloudy, but on December 15 a heavy gale struck. The ship labored through the storm, and water poured into the convict hold. Four days later, the first convict died. A series of gales continued to hit the ship, and another prisoner died. On the 26th, the crew discovered that the great storm they suffered on Christmas day had broken the bolts holding down the deck boards, so that water now freely poured from the top deck down into the holds of the ship. On December 29, the ship met with still more heavy winds and high seas and lost the ability to steer when an enormous wave broke the tiller off of the rudder. The crew was now forced to pump water out every half-hour, and they nailed canvas over the bow and into the seams of the deck in an attempt to slow the leaking. By the next day, the crew was so overwhelmed by the effort to keep the ship afloat that Purdy put the convicts to work pumping out water in shifts.

At this point, the ship had been out to sea so long that food became an issue. It had only 30 pieces of pork and 700 pounds of bread for 105 people without any prospect of reaching Virginia anytime soon. The convicts were practically starving and nearly drowned from the water pouring into the decks below. Food was rationed to only two biscuits per day. Yet the sea continued to pound the ship. On the morning of December 31, the sea beat the ship so hard that they now had to keep one pump going constantly. In a desperate move, Purdy redirected the ship southward in the hope of reaching South Carolina. Still, the weather would not cooperate, and high winds prevented the ship from heading westward. With yet another convict dying and only 24 pieces of beef, 22 pieces of pork, and 600 pounds of bread left to feed 104 people, the ship continued south towards Antigua.

By January 5, the ship's provisions were practically gone. Convicts were limited to three ounces of bread a day, which left them so desperate and hungry that they ate the vermin they picked off of themselves. The condition of the crew members, upon whose lives everyone depended, was not much better. On January 7, Purdy examined the convicts, and what he discovered horrified him. They were covered in ulcers and sores and had been sitting in water for three weeks straight. Convicts now began dying off at a rapidly increasing pace. On the morning of January 20, the ship's provisions completely ran out. The prisoners had long ago eaten their leather breeches and every shoe that could be found on the ship. With no options left, the captain finally opened a 100-pound cask of cheese consigned to Charles Carroll of Annapolis. At noon that same day, the ship finally spied Antigua seven leagues in the distance.

On March 31, more than six months after beginning their journey in England, Captain Purdy and about 70 convicts finally arrived in Annapolis.[9]

Pirates, privateers, and hostile navies also threatened voyages. The Atlantic was full of vessels either acting alone or sanctioned by enemy states looking for other boats to seize and plunder, and convict ships were not immune to such threats.[10] In 1746, the *Virginia Gazette* reported that the *Zephyre*, a French Man of War armed with 30 guns and 350 men, attacked the

Plain-Dealer, a convict ship bound for Maryland and commanded by Captain James Dobbins. Forty of the 106 convicts on board took part in the two-and-a-half-hour fight against the French, but the enemy's numbers eventually overwhelmed the English ship. The *Zephyre* took most of Dobbins's men and some of the convicts, but it sank during its return to France, which resulted in the death of all but seven Frenchmen who managed to make it back to shore.[11]

Diet and Health

Even though external threats of bad weather and pirates could seriously jeopardize convict voyages, the internal elements of diet and disease were more immediate sources of agony for the convicts. Transported felons received meager provisions throughout their voyage, and the extent to which disease spread through the ship often determined how many of them would make it safely to American shores.

The amount of provisions supplied to each convict was generally spelled out in the transportation contract signed by the merchant and the government, although nothing was ever stated about the quality of the food the prisoners were to receive. In order to increase their profit margin, some captains cut corners by buying old provisions at a discounted rate or by ignoring the stipulations in the contract altogether and underfeeding the convicts.[12]

Ships generally carried food that tended to keep well—bread, biscuits, salted meat, peas, and cheese—but which made for a monotonous diet. Even though such food resisted spoilage, it was sometimes carried by ships for years, until the meat went putrid and the biscuits became full of worms. Any fresh provisions brought on board—such as beef, water, and beer—went bad after the first month. With voyages lasting anywhere between six and 12 weeks, passengers were practically guaranteed to be eating spoiled, rotten food by the end of the trip.[13]

Convicts were fed in messes of six with set amounts of food allotted for each group. Francis Place, who in the 19th century collected records relating to convict transportation to America, itemized the weekly provisions given to a group of six convicts on one particular voyage: "34 lbs. of bread, 19 lbs. of beef, 11 lbs. of pork, 7 lbs. of flour, 2 lbs. of suet, 5 gills* of brandy, 134 quarts of water, and 4 quarts of pease."[14] By Place's reckoning, each convict received one pound and four ounces of food per day. This store of food was supposedly shelled out to each six-man group over the course of the week in roughly the following manner:

- Sunday: 4 lbs. of bread, 3 lbs of pork, 1 1/2 qts. of pease, and 18 quarts of water.
- Monday: 4 lbs. of bread, 2 qts. of oatmeal, 1 1/2 ozs. molasses, 1 lb. cheese, 18 quarts of water.
- Tuesday: 4 lbs. of bread, 4 lbs. of beef.
- Wednesday: 1 1/2 qts. of pease.
- Thursday: 18 quarts of water.
- Friday: 4 lbs. of bread, 2 qts. of oatmeal, 1 1/2 ozs. of molasses, 1 lb. of cheese, 18 quarts of water.

---

* One gill = four ounces or one-fourth of a pint.

- Saturday: 4 lbs. of bread, 2 qts. of oatmeal, 3 gills of Geneva [i.e., gin] at night.

This diet was quite possibly more balanced and more plentiful than what some of the convicts were used to eating back in England, although the amount of alcoholic spirits given to them on board the ship was probably much less than what they were used to enjoying.

Disease was by far the greatest killer of convicts at sea. Prisoners cooped up in crowded, filthy jails brought gaol fever, smallpox, and other diseases with them before being piled on a ship. Needless to say, these diseases spread rapidly through the confined quarters. In 1721, 19 of the 50 convicts on board the *Owners Goodwill* died during the voyage. Even crew members and regular passengers could contract disease from felons and die before reaching their destination. The mortality rate for transported convicts ranged between 11 percent and 16 percent, so about one out of every eight convicts did not survive the journey.[15]

Death, no matter how low the percentage, would have been traumatic for the convict passengers given the tight conditions in which they traveled. The sick suffered through their disease while connected by irons to five other passengers on a ceaselessly rocking ship with no bedding on which to lie down. Convicts undoubtedly would have woken up in the morning to find themselves chained to a corpse and wondered if they were next in line for such a fate. The dead were removed, wrapped in a sack weighted down with stones, and thrown overboard with little ceremony.[16]

Worried that convicts were bringing infectious diseases on shore with them, the Maryland Assembly in 1766 passed an act requiring any ship that arrived with sick passengers be quarantined to help prevent the spread of diseases among the colony. Convict merchants fought the act, arguing that it seriously affected the convict trade. The act stood, however, which prompted merchants to furnish their ships with ventilators and to open portholes in order to air out the decks holding the prisoners. These measures greatly reduced the spread of disease, and the mortality rate fell to just 2.5 percent by the time of the American Revolution.[17]

Traveling to America in Chains

In 1770, Matthew Kennedy and his brother were found guilty of murdering John Bigby, a watchman, during a riot on Westminster Bridge. Matthew played a larger part in the crime and was sentenced to death, but his politically connected family managed to have his sentence changed to transportation. In order to arrange a comfortable passage for Kennedy, the Earl of Fife paid John Stewart, the Contractor for Transports to the Government at the time, 15 guineas. But just before Kennedy's ship left port, the widow of the murdered man lodged an appeal of the revised sentence, so Fife hurried to retrieve Kennedy. In a letter to George Selwyn, Fife describes the condition in which he found Kennedy when he arrived at the ship:

> I went on board, and, to be sure, all the states of
> horror I ever had an idea of are much short of what
> I saw this poor man in; chained to a board, in a hole
> not above sixteen feet long; more than fifty with

> him; a collar and padlock about his neck, and
> chained to five of the most dreadful creatures I ever
> looked on.[18]

This snapshot of the dreadful circumstances under which convicts were transported under John Stewart—who had a reputation for actually improving the conditions in which they were shipped—also reveals Stewart's unscrupulous nature, when he threw Kennedy in with the other criminals even after Fife had specifically paid for special treatment for Kennedy.

Convict ships were akin to floating dungeons. The prisoners were chained together in groups of six in small, cramped quarters that were either too hot or too cold, depending on the time of year. The number of convicts being transported could range anywhere from one to 150 or more. More than half of the ships that arrived in Maryland between 1746 and 1775 carried more than 90 passengers.[19] Convicts in general enjoyed more room on ships than slaves, but less room than indentured servants. The lower decks of slave ships, which were sometimes used to carry convicts, usually had ceilings only four-and-a-half feet high, so most convicts traveling on these ships would not be able to stand up straight. In essence, convicts went from one miserable prison on land to an even worse one floating on water.[20]

Voyages across the Atlantic could be pure misery, even for regular passengers. A common traveler from Germany to Philadelphia in 1750 describes his trip in horrifying terms:

> [D]uring the voyage there is on board these ships
> terrible misery, stench, fumes, horror, vomiting,
> many kinds of sea-sickness, fever, dysentery,

headache, heat, constipation, boils, scurvy, cancer, mouth-rot, and the like, all of which come from old and sharply salted food and meat, also from very bad and foul water, so that many die miserably.

Add to this want of provisions, hunger, thirst, frost, heat, dampness, anxiety, want, afflictions and lamentations, together with other trouble, as *c. v.* the lice abound so frightfully, especially on sick people, that they can be scraped off the body. The misery reaches the climax when a gale rages for 2 or 3 nights and days, so that every one believes that the ship will go to the bottom with all human beings on board. In such a visitation the people cry and pray most piteously.[21]

The hardships experienced by this normal ship passenger would have been multiplied for convicts, who made the journey in less amenable conditions.

The incessant tossing of the ship by the ocean waves was a major cause of misery for the convicts. Seasickness was of course an omnipresent source of discomfort for many of them. But the constant rocking of the ship also caused the chains attached to them to rub their skin raw. Minimal movement of iron against skin is painful; being thrown around from side to side by rough waters while sitting on a wooden plank is excruciating. The extreme heat and poor ventilation in the hold also caused convicts to sweat profusely, and the resulting body odor only added to the stench emanating from the tubs full of excrement and from the vomit brought about by seasickness. The groans of the sick and the shrieks of those terrified by the tossing and turning of the ship were a constant soundtrack.[22]

Both jailers and convicts often referred to those sentenced to transportation as having been sent or sold into slavery.[23] The comparison is apt, especially when one considers the circumstances under which convicts and slaves alike were carried across the Atlantic. The similarity between the two trades is not surprising, since both dealt in the transportation of human cargo, and many of the contractors, captains, and ships in the convict trade also worked in the slave trade.

Even though merchants in both the convict and slave trades had a financial incentive to keep their passengers healthy, to some degree convicts were treated worse than slaves. Slave traders only profited from the sale of slaves at the end of their voyage, and since slaves commanded higher prices than convicts, ship captains had a big incentive to deliver the slaves in as healthy a state as possible. In contrast, the British government paid the Contractor for Transports a subsidy for each convict transported before he even left port, so the temptation to increase profits by cutting corners on the amount and quality of provisions allotted to the prisoners was great. Convicts who were old and infirm were especially vulnerable to harsh treatment, since they were unlikely to be sold for a profit at the end of the voyage and consequently were considered expendable.[24]

Harsh Captains

Captains of convict ships were hired for their experience in transporting human cargo, and many of them came from the slave trade. They were tough men who wielded strict discipline.

They would not hesitate to whip and beat those who disregarded their orders or to place unruly convicts in double irons. Crew members were often treated miserably by captains as well. Not only were they subjected to low wages, poor provisions, and a high mortality rate, but they also could be beaten and whipped by the captain for insubordination.[25]

Some captains were completely incompetent. In one case, Edward Brockett, captain of the *Rappahannock Merchant*, spent almost the entire 1725 voyage drunk. He turned the boat into a party ship and squandered the ship's provisions by giving those on board open access to the food and by encouraging passengers to drink to excess. Brockett and another merchant who was along for the ride each kept a mistress in his cabin. When the ship arrived in Virginia, George Tilly, one of Jonathan Forward's agents, reported that the ship had no provisions left and that it was in terrible condition due to the neglect of the captain, the mate, and the ship carpenter to employ the pump.[26]

In 1739, Andrew Reid succeeded Jonathan Forward as Contractor for Transports to the Government, and four years later Reid saw two of his captains, John Sargent and Barnet Bond, grossly abuse their positions of power in separate incidents. In 1742, Sargent was preparing to leave for Maryland on the *Forward* with 190 convicts when he was approached by the husband of Catherine Davis, who was sentenced to transportation in October 1741 for stealing a pair of leather pumps and a shirt.[27] Davis's husband handed Sargent three guineas and asked him to give his wife preferential treatment during the voyage. Sargent promised to allow Davis to travel in the steerage rather than be confined with the rest of the convicts, so she boarded the ship with two trunks full of clothes and valuables. Davis's husband was keen to make sure his wife traveled in comfort because she was pregnant.

Sargent left London in September. After a voyage of eight weeks and four days, he arrived in Maryland having lost almost half of the convicts he was carrying—40 men and 43 women. Sargent complained to Reid, "I did expect either to be killed by the felons every day, or the ship to sink; but they never offered nothing, and all the damage they did was in [the] hould in drinking out all the bear and wine they could get at." The death of so many convicts and the poor condition of those who survived meant that Reid lost out on a considerable sum of money in the sale of his cargo. Reid blamed the owner of the contracted ship for not maintaining it properly: "both sea and rain were unavoidably lett in upon the felons thro' the ship's upper works, and that soon after their arrival several more of them died which was owing likewise to their having catched colds and other distempers." Sargent tried to console Reid over his losses by maintaining that 25 of the dead convicts were "old men not worth 25 [pounds]."

Determined to receive retribution for his losses, Reid brought criminal charges against Sargent. During the trial, a different picture of the voyage emerged than the one Sargent drew up in his initial report to Reid. During the voyage, convicts were routinely brought up on deck under Sargent's orders to be stripped and searched, and Sargent then confiscated any money or valuables that were found on them. After discovering a guinea on one prisoner, Sargent pocketed it and forced the man to take gin as compensation. Crew members testified that Sargent sold gin to any convict who could afford it, and they claimed that 40 of the felons died from excessive drinking. Sargent then seized the clothes of the deceased and sold them on deck for his own profit.

Catherine Davis was also subjected to Sargent's system of abuse and extortion. As soon as the ship left port, Sargent sent Davis below deck to travel with the rest of the convicts with the excuse that Reid had prohibited felons from traveling in the steerage for fear that they would spread disease throughout the ship's crew. Three weeks into the voyage, Davis went into labor during a violent storm. All the while, water gushed into the convict hold and soaked Davis, which caused her to shiver and go into disorders. Most of the people who witnessed the childbirth thought she would not survive. Davis remained sick after her delivery, and two weeks later her child died.

Fearing that she was going to die as well, Davis tried to entrust her trunks to one of the crew, who refused on account of his fear of Sargent. Catching wind that the trunks contained objects of value and knowing that Davis could offer only feeble resistance in her condition, Sargent ordered Davis's two trunks to be brought up on deck. Davis pleaded with Sargent that he could take anything he wanted from the trunks as long as he left her some clothes. Sargent ended up taking four watches, some handkerchiefs, and three or four guineas on the pretext that he suspected them to be stolen goods. In an attempt to cover his tracks, he spread a tale around the ship that Davis had given him watches and other valuables as presents.

At the end of the trial, all of the charges against Sargent were dismissed, because the evidence against him was considered too weak. After Davis returned to England for the trial, she was arrested again for shoplifting, this time under the name of Mary Shirley. Before evidence was even heard at her trial, the prisoner "begged the Court to give her what punishment they pleased, and not transport her; for she would rather be hanged than transported again." Davis, alias Shirley, was again found guilty and again sentenced to transportation.[28]

At the same time that John Sargent was charged with "robbery on the high seas," another captain of Reid's, Barnet Bond, was accused of committing "murder and felonies on the high seas."[29] In the spring of 1743, Bond took command of the *Justitia* and 163 convicts. As the felons came on board his ship, he searched them and confiscated all of their money, knives, and razors. But despite his precautions, several convicts found a way to pry their irons off before the ship left London, so Bond called everyone back up on deck and searched them again. During the second search, Bond discovered at least two guineas hidden away by one of the convicts and pocketed them.

The *Justitia* left port with enough water for every person on board to receive three quarts a day, plus more to boil food and make medicine. Inexplicably, Bond immediately ordered that each convict receive only one pint of water in the morning and one pint in the evening. Bond maintained the rationing throughout the voyage, even though the doctors and other officers argued that such an allowance could not support life for very long. When sick convicts were given barley water or water-gruel, Bond made sure that the equivalent amount of water used to make the meal was subtracted from their regular ration. Felons who were allowed on deck showed Bond their dry, furry tongues and pleaded with him to give them something to drink. Bond denied their requests and then beat them. Some convicts became so desperate for any kind of liquid that they drank their own urine.

At one point during the voyage, Bond learned that after all of his searching some of the convicts still had money in their possession, so he hatched a plan to get it. He granted one prisoner freedom to walk on deck—all the convict had to do in exchange was seize any money he could discover among the passengers and turn it over to Bond. As the end of the voyage neared, the felons demanded that Bond return all of the money he had taken from them. Not only did Bond refuse to return the money he took, but he demanded from each convict half a crown. Those who could not come up with the sum were tied to a rope, pulled up to the yardarm that went across the mast, and then dropped into the ocean two or three times. Bond even threatened Hannah White, who had just had a baby during the trip, with this punishment, but in terror she was able to scrape together enough money to avoid it.

Forty-five convicts died during the voyage. Bond reasoned that since those who died were originally under his care, he was entitled to all of their possessions. At one point, he wore a pair of breeches around the ship that had belonged to one of the now-dead felons. When the *Justitia* finally arrived in Maryland, it was still carrying a full third of its drinking water.

Bond was charged with four separate counts of murder on the high seas. Despite the testimony of the ship's crew and doctors against Bond, he was honorably acquitted by the jury. Bond never worked in the transportation trade again and died a few years later after settling in Maryland with his wife and children.

Rebellion at Sea

In 1767, a group of friends on a pleasure cruise were blown off course, and they stumbled across a ship with its sails furled and in distress. They reported that:

> perceiving no body on board, we made up to her, and hailed her; but receiving no answer, we ventured to go on board, where we found a parcel of poor women lying in a fever, quite delirious, and not able to give any account of themselves, whom we relieved as well as we could, with what necessaries our little vessel afforded.
>
> Upon searching further, we found the cocket of the vessel, which discovered her to be the transport ship, Capt. Ford, Commander, bound for East-Florida from Dublin, with 150 convicts on board. By all appearance, we supposed the hands have been murdered and thrown overboard, as we found on board their compass, quadrants, cloaths, &c.

The group notified the officers in the custom house of the distressed ship once they returned to shore. The authorities later confirmed that Captain Ford and the entire ship's crew had been murdered by the convicts they were carrying. The malefactors discovered a way to knock off their chains in the night, surprised the crew, threw them overboard, and then headed for shore without being detected. Some of the convicts were subsequently apprehended and recommitted to the Dublin jail.[30]

Captains feared the criminal backgrounds of their passengers and the threat they posed in taking over the ship, so they confined convicts in the lower decks throughout most of the voyage. Only occasionally were convicts let up on deck in short shifts of several prisoners each to enjoy the fresh air. Slaves, on the other hand, were regularly brought up on deck during their transport in the interest of keeping them healthy, although these visits into the open were hardly pleasurable for them. The slaves were usually forced to "dance" as exercise, and the rubbing of their chains against their skin was excruciating.[31] So perhaps the convicts were better off staying below deck.

Despite the precautions taken by captains to minimize the possibility of rebellion by the convicts, insurrection did occur. In the fall of 1724, Jonathan Forward sent Captain William Taylor of the *William and Mary* to Lincolnshire to pick up 18 convicts, who would be transferred in London to the *Forward*, which would then take them to America. Shortly after the felons were loaded on the *William and Mary*, they seized the captain and his crew, threw them in a cabin, and escaped on the ship's longboat. Apparently, Captain Taylor had only two or three other sailors with him on board during a moment when the convicts were unfettered and unsecured on deck, so they were easily overtaken. The county authorities later managed to recapture 11 of the 18 felons who escaped, and in November 1725 the captured convicts were successfully put on board the *Rappahannock Merchant*, which was bound for Virginia from London. This group of convicts would have been better off had they not initially escaped. When the ship arrived in Virginia, 48 of the 108 prisoners on board died during the trip, with only one of the group that originally escaped from the *William and Mary* having survived.[32]

In 1736, northern newspapers in America carried a bizarre account about a woman by the name of Mrs. Andrew Buckler of Dublin, who was traveling with her husband to Annapolis, Maryland. The ship they were traveling on had a tough, long voyage, and they were forced to land in Nova Scotia for water. The only water they could find, however, was snow, so the crew put as much as they could in barrels and brought it back to the ship to melt.[33]

The passengers decided to take advantage of the proximity to land and sent a maid and a "Negro Boy" on shore to wash clothes, but the two never returned. In the belief that the two servants were taken by Indians, the passengers and crew remained on board the ship in fear, which was so great that they all started to die slowly of thirst. When Mrs. Buckler was the only one left standing, a group of Indians boarded the ship, stole any gold, silver, watches, and jewelry on board, and "carried her ashore to their Wigwams." Mrs. Buckler was eventually found by Mr. Mitchel, a deputy surveyor of the woods, at a "French House." He took her to Colonel Armstrong, the Lieutenant Governor of Nova Scotia, who wined and dined her before sending her off to Boston, where she boarded a ship heading back to London.

Even though Mrs. Buckler had left for England, the government continued to investigate the affair. In talking with the Native Americans, the authorities discovered that the "whole of her Story now proves to be false, and she to be an abominable Impostor, if not one of the vilest piratical Murderers." Before traveling to America, Andrew Buckler had earlier traveled to Dublin, Ireland—where he and his wife lived—with a ship full of rum from Barbados. After unloading the rum, Buckler agreed to transport 40 felons and several indentured servants to Annapolis, Maryland. Since Buckler's wife did not accompany him on the trip, authorities believed that the woman who claimed to be Mrs. Andrew Buckler was one of the convicts, a Miss Matthews, "who had received Sentence of Death for Theft, and was reputed to be a common Strumpet in *Dublin*, and always of ill Repute." They speculated that she impersonated Buckler's wife in order to take possession of the abandoned ship and its possessions.

As the ship neared American land, the convicts murdered the captain and the rest of the crew, and then landed the ship in a remote area in order to plunder it. During the investigation into the affair, the maid and servant boy who were supposedly sent out to wash clothes were found dead on shore, with the boy's throat cut from ear to ear. Even though the pretend Mrs. Buckler claimed to have buried her "husband," his body was never found, but a lot of dried blood was discovered between the decks of the ship. The rest of the convicts were thought to have dispersed among the French and Indians, and Miss Matthews presumably made it back to London unscathed, the new information coming too late to do anything about her return to England.

James Dalton and the Escape to Vigo

Crime ran strong in the Dalton family. The father was originally a tailor from Dublin, Ireland, but after he fought in the wars in Flanders and rose to become a sergeant, he moved to

London and became a notorious card cheat. After robbing one of his marks, he was sentenced to execution, and so his son, James, vividly experienced the strong-arm of the law at a young age when he sat between the knees of his father as he rode in the cart that took him to gallows to be hanged. After the father's death, the mother married a butcher, but she was soon caught committing a felony and was transported. Her daughter was also said to be transported to the American colonies for a separate crime. Yet, all of the examples that were set by watching each member of his family punished for their crimes failed to deter James Dalton from following in their footsteps.[34]

Starting at a young age, Dalton committed robberies, burglaries, and other crimes in and around London, and he soon started working for Jonathan Wild's criminal organization. On March 3, 1720, Dalton found himself in court charged with stealing some aprons. He was convicted on the evidence of William Field, one of the leaders in Wild's gang, and he was sentenced to transportation. In May, he was loaded on to the *Honour*, a convict ship commanded by Captain Richard Langley.[35]

Wild must have been doing some housecleaning in his organization around this time, because several other members of his gang appeared on board the convict ship along with Dalton, including William Bond, Charles Hinchman, Martin Grey, and James Holliday. Another notable passenger on the ship was William Smith. Long ago, Smith helped throw Wild into the Wood Street Compter debtor's prison, where he languished for several years after his second arrival in London. Now, sitting at the head of a criminal empire, Wild was in a position to exact revenge. Wild had Smith arrested as an accessory to burglary—Smith had helped send a small boy through the window of a house in order to rob it—and Wild even testified against him in court, as did William Field. Smith was found guilty and sentenced to transportation for seven years.[36]

The *Honour* set sail for Virginia, but it quickly hit a storm off the coast of Spain and began to take on water. Short on sailors, Captain Langley was forced to let some of the convicts on board out of their irons so that they could help keep the ship afloat. Dalton took the opportunity to form a conspiracy, and when he gave the signal, the convicts grabbed some firearms, bound the captain, and took possession of the ship. Langley pleaded for his life and in exchange promised to drop the conspirators anywhere they wished. Dalton requested that they be dropped in Vigo, Spain, but a storm forced Langley to drop them off at Cape Finisterre. The convicts robbed the ship of gold and jewelry worth a total of 100 pounds before 16 of them boarded a longboat and headed for shore. James Holliday later claimed that he paid five shillings to go to shore with the rebellious group.[37]

After landing in Spain, Dalton and the other members of Wild's gang made their way across the mountains to Vigo. Soon after they arrived in town, they ran into their old captain, who cordially greeted them. During the course of their conversation, Langley gave a signal to his crewmates, and Dalton's group was captured and brought before the mayor to face charges.

The gang was forced to return the gold and jewelry they stole from the ship, but to the frustration of Langley, the mayor refused to prosecute them. He even issued the malefactors passes to travel through the country. After the group left Vigo they realized that the passes said "English thieves" on them, so they decided to burn the documents and take their chances by avoiding towns as they traveled through the countryside.

The gang eventually reached the north coast, boarded a Dutch ship, and made their way back to England via Amsterdam. Despite the rebellion, the *Honour* eventually made it to Virginia, although under the command of a different captain. Some reports indicated that the group killed Captain Langley during the affair, but William Bond, one of the convicts, later repudiated the report and claimed that Langley traveled safely to the West Indies and eventually died in Virginia.[38]

Slowly but surely, the convicts who escaped to Vigo and returned to England were captured. In September 1720, James Holliday and Anthony Goddard were both charged at the Old Bailey with returning early from transportation. During the same court session, James Wilson, another Vigo escapee, was charged with committing highway robbery, and both Jonathan Wild and William Field testified against him at his trial. Holliday, Goddard, and Wilson were all found guilty and were executed. In February 1721, William Bond was also caught and hanged for returning early.[39]

Even though William Smith, the man who threw Wild into debtor's prison, was not involved in the Vigo affair, he also returned to England early. Wild caught him again in 1721, and this time Smith was sentenced to transportation for 14 years, although he died during this second journey back to America.[40]

Dalton was discovered in Bristol after he was arrested for burglary, and Wild arranged to have Dalton transferred back to

London to face charges of returning early from transportation. On March 1, 1721, Dalton and seven other convicts involved in the Vigo escape—including Charles Hinchman, Martin Grey, Mary North, and Jasper Andrews—were put on trial.[41]

Even though everyone in the group was found guilty, Hinchman and Grey were the only ones who were hanged. Somehow both Dalton and Andrews escaped the gallows, despite being found guilty and disturbing the prisoners while awaiting execution. In fact, their behavior on death row was so egregious that the Ordinary of Newgate described how several other convicts who went on to be executed:

> were loud in their Exclamations to God, declared they died in Charity towards all Men; but said they should have been more prepared for Death, had they not been disturbed by two Boys, Jasper Andrews and James Dalton, who interrupted their Devotions; and even as they slept play'd vile Tricks, burning their Feet, and pouring Water, &c

The Ordinary reported that Mary North, another Vigo fugitive, also disturbed the prisoners while they awaited their execution, but for an altogether different reason:

> Mary North had the unhappiness, she said, to be at certain Times Lunatick, she was some Times troublesome to the Prisoners, and to all who heard her, using most wicked Expressions; That she should go to Hell, that she cared not if she was damned, that she could not say the Lord's Prayer she had so much Enmity in her Heart, and that she would hang herself that Night, or if she could not,

> she would dash out her Brains against the Stones.
> But at other Times, when she was right in her Mind,
> she appear'd to be very Devout, and earnest in her
> Addresses to Heaven for the Pardon of her Sins.

North avoided execution by receiving a conditional pardon for undergoing an inoculation experiment for smallpox.[42]

How exactly Dalton and Andrews escaped execution is not clear. Wild possibly saved them by arranging some kind of conditional pardon in exchange for transportation instead, because Dalton boarded the *Prince Royal* in August 1721 under the name "John Dalton." But before the ship embarked, he was caught trying to commit yet more mischief.[43] *Saturday's Post* for August 19, 1721 reported:

> When the Convicts were lately carried on board a
> Ship at Limehouse-hole, in order to be transported
> to Virginia, a Ginger-bread Cake belonging to one
> Dalton (who was before transported and whose
> Father was hanged) was accidentally broke up, with
> which there was a File so conveniently bak'd up,
> that we may easily believe the Handcuffs could not
> long have withstood it. Upon which the said Dalton
> was tyed to the beers and dealt with according to his
> Deserts.[44]

After landing in America, Dalton threatened his owner into setting him free. He then teamed up with a notorious robber named Whalebone, and over the next two years the two made a business of kidnapping African slaves, stealing boats, and then traveling between the Caribbean islands and the American colonies to find the best means of selling them off. Any slaves that they could not unload were tied up and thrown into the ocean.[45]

Dalton returned to England, but he was immediately pressed into naval service and sent to fight in the siege of Gibraltar in 1727. Back in London, he continued his life of crime, and he regularly appeared in court to give evidence that over time led to the conviction 14 of his colleagues. Dalton was eventually arrested for robbery and was sentenced to death based on testimony given by a professional false witness named John Waller.[46] But before Dalton was executed, William Field, who helped secure Dalton's first transportation conviction, was himself convicted of theft and transported to Annapolis on the *Forward* in November 1729. Field experienced a terrible voyage: Thirty-two out of the 199 convicts on board died before reaching their destination.[47]

While waiting for his execution, Dalton confessed to the Ordinary of Newgate that when he was in America he "debauch'd and ruin'd some Widows and Girls." Several of Dalton's wives in London also visited him together, and Dalton claimed that he had many others besides these, some of whom were transported or were left by him in America.[48] Dalton's reputation of being a ladies' man played into the appearance of his name in Plate 3 of Hogarth's *The Harlot's Progress*, where over the bed of Moll Hackabout, who at this point is working as a common prostitute, is a box labeled, "James Dalton his Wigg Box." Dalton was a well-known criminal by the time he was executed on May 12, 1730, and his name was used in headlines to advertise many collected accounts of notorious criminals for a long time afterward.

Plate 3 of William Hogarth's *A Harlot's Progress*
(Source: Wikipedia Commons, http://commons.wikimedia.org)

* * *

The sight of land was an occasion for great rejoicing among all parties on the convict ship, since it meant that those on board had survived the perilous journey. They survived rough weather, disease, pirates, and possible rebellion by the prisoners. But it was also a time of trepidation. What kind of life awaited the convicts? How would they adjust to the new world that greeted them? What kind of work would they be expected to perform? And who would serve as their master?

Chapter Six: Landing in America

When Nicholas Purdy of *The Rodney* desperately cracked open the cask of cheese he was transporting to give its contents to his starving convict passengers and crew, little did the convicts know that they could end up working for the man who owned the cheese they were about to enjoy, Charles Carroll of Annapolis.* Carroll commanded several plantations in Maryland on thousands of acres of land and was part owner of an ironworks company. He was one of the richest men in the colony, and he attained this position by building on the estate he inherited from his father, Charles Carroll the Settler.

Carroll the Settler emigrated from Ireland to Maryland in 1688 to find an environment where his Roman Catholicism would not impede his political and economic ambitions. That same year, the Glorious Revolution back in England put his plan in jeopardy, since the new Protestant government placed limits on office-holding by Catholics in colonial America as well as in Britain. Yet despite this setback, the Settler managed to accrue a fortune in America through land, slaves, money lending, and mercantilism.[1]

---

* For an account of the voyage of the *Rodney*, see Chapter 5, pages 120-122.

Roots

When Charles Carroll the Settler arrived in Maryland in the latter part of the 17th century, he found a heavily wooded land, only a smattering of human settlements, and a capital that was basically a hodgepodge of rustic buildings. This wilderness and lack of infrastructure might have posed significant challenges for someone arriving in America with few resources, but the Settler enjoyed several advantages over most immigrants from Great Britain.

Carroll's main advantage was that he arrived as a free man. The majority of people who came to America from the British Isles during this period were indentured servants, so it would be years before they could gain independence in the new land. But like most indentured servants, Carroll did not arrive jobless. Waiting for him when he landed was the middle-level post of Attorney General in the proprietary government with an annual salary of 50 pounds sterling. To put his income in perspective, an ordinary Maryland planter could expect to earn only 10 to 15 pounds a year.[2]

Despite his comfortable salary, Carroll harbored ambitions to join the ranks of the Maryland elite, and he climbed up the social ladder with a time-tested strategy: He married well. A year after arriving in America, he became engaged to Martha Ridgly Underwood, an older wealthy widow with four children. Martha originally came to America as an indentured servant, but she married Robert Ridgly, the master who purchased her. When Robert Ridgly died, she inherited a sizeable estate, which included two plantations. She then married Anthony Underwood, who was a bound servant and law clerk for her former husband. Underwood had gained admission to the provincial court one year before the two married, and he eventually rose up through the government to become a member of the lower house of the Maryland assembly. At his death, Underwood left Martha an estate worth 550 pounds sterling and 2,000 acres of land.3

Charles Carroll served as executor to Underwood's estate, and he married Martha six months after her second husband's death. The marriage did not last long. Martha died in childbirth one year later, followed three days later by the death of the baby. Carroll did not inherit much of his wife's estate—the bulk of it went to her surviving children—but he continued to live in her house in St. Mary's County. The marriage helped to improve Carroll's social and political standing, though, and despite growing restrictions on the ability of Catholics to practice law, he gained the patronage of Colonel Henry Darnell, who oversaw Lord Baltimore's interests in Maryland. Even more importantly, he met Darnell's 15-year-old daughter—a girl less than half his age—and married her.

Carroll's new father-in-law gave him 1,381 acres of land in Prince George's County after the wedding and appointed him clerk of Maryland's land office, which placed him in the middle of all land transactions throughout the colony. Carroll used this new position to increase his wealth substantially, which he accomplished through diversification as a planter, banker, lawyer, merchant, and officeholder. By the time Carroll died in 1720, he owned 47,777 acres of land.4

Charles Carroll of Annapolis (1702-1782) inherited his father's vast wealth and built it into one of the great fortunes in colonial America. His son, Charles Carroll of Carrollton (1737-1832), later became the only Catholic signer of the Declaration of Independence. Both of these Carrolls employed convicts to work on their plantations and in their ironworks company.

The New World

One word can sum up the first impression that English immigrants would have had upon seeing American land for the first time: green. New arrivals—especially those from London— would have been immediately struck by the open spaces and the lushness of the American countryside. The clear, bright blue skies and the warm sun provided a sharp contrast to the dingy haze that generally hung above London. Shady trees and fields stood in place of the twisty city streets lined with tall buildings that blocked out the sun. The singing of birds, the wafting of gentle winds through trees, and the murmuring of brooks substituted for the constant din of shouting vendors and horseshoes hitting cobblestones. And the sweet, fragrant aroma of the countryside replaced the putrid odors of urine, feces, and burning coal that hung about London.[5]

New arrivals would have marveled at the bounty of the New World. The Chesapeake Bay and the numerous rivers that fed into it were full of herring, sturgeon, shad, chub, flounder, whiting, and trout, as well as whales, porpoises, sharks, dog-fish, and stingrays. The coasts were home to small turtles, crabs, oysters, mussels, cockles, and shrimp. The rich soil of the land produced cherries, plums, and persimmons; mulberries, raspberries, strawberries, and grapes; chestnuts, hazelnuts, hickories, and walnuts; and Indian corn, peas, beans, potatoes, and tobacco. The woods, marshes, swamps, and savannahs sported swans, geese, ducks, cranes, and herons; beavers, otters, muskrats, and minxes; wild turkeys, pheasants, partridges, and pigeons; deer, hares, foxes, raccoons, squirrels, and possums; and bears, panthers, elk, buffaloes, and wild hogs.[6]

The standout feature of the Chesapeake area was its rivers. William Eddis, who traveled from England to America in 1769, commented, "A few weeks since, the Thames was the most considerable river I had ever beheld; it is now, comparatively, reduced to a diminutive stream." The rivers and creeks were so numerous and winding that they often impeded travel, although bridges and ferries helped to mitigate the inconvenience they posed. At the same time, these rivers allowed goods to be delivered back and forth from the inland to the coast and prompted Eddis to note, "It is almost impossible, on viewing the natural advantages of this country, to avoid anticipating the future political and commercial importance of America."[7]

Travelers who floated down the rivers would have seen thick woods with occasional clearances for plantations and abandoned fields that could no longer support the growth of nutrient-sucking tobacco plants.[8] An Englishman traveling through Maryland in 1746 describes the setting:

> On every Side [of the rivers] you might discern the
> Settlements of the Planters, with their industrious
> Clearings, surrounded by the native Woods of the
> Country; whilst the distant Curlings of the aspiring
> Smoak, wantoning in the Breeze, direct your Eyes to
> the happy Places of their Residence, where they,
> generally bless'd with Innocence and Cheerfulness,

> a compliant comfort, and a numerous Race at their
> Boards, enjoy Life much to be envy'd by Courts and
> Cities.[9]

But the idyllic settings of the plantations also raised criticism from this Englishman for their effect on their owners:

> this Property is attended with this ill Consequence,
> that being so well seated at home, they have no
> Ambition to fill a Metropolis, and associate together
> ... [T]he Capitals and other Towns in these two
> Colonies, are very slightly peopled, and very badly
> situated, and remarkable for little else than the
> Residence of Governors, and the Meeting of the
> three Estates, Governor, Council and Assembly.[10]

Both Baltimore and Annapolis were sparsely populated throughout the colonial period and functioned more as towns or villages than as cities. In 1722, Robert Beverley could only single out three notable public buildings in all of Virginia: the college, the capitol building, and the governor's house. He also noted a structure adjacent to the capitol in Williamsburg that would have struck a chord with a transported convict: the public prison. Beverley described it as "a large and convenient structure, with partitions for the different sexes, and distinct rooms for petty offenders. To this is also annexed a convenient yard to air the criminals in, for the preservation of their life and health, till the time of their trial; and at the end of that, another prison for debtors." The people in these American cities looked different from their London counterparts as well. The traveling Englishman remarked, "'Tis an odd Sight, that except some of the very elevated Sort, few Persons wear Perukes, so that you would imagine they were all sick, or going to bed: Common People wear Woollen and Yarn Caps; but the better ones wear white Holland or Cotton."[11]

Baltimore, 1752

(Source: U.S. History Images, http://ushistoryimages.com)

The challenge facing newcomers to America was not a lack of available resources; it was in knowing how to exploit those resources to make life sustainable. Many of the people coming over from England did not arrive with ready-skills to take advantage of the abundant resources and had to learn on the fly. Likewise, most of the convicts transported to America were ill-equipped to handle the work that they would be expected to carry out. One of the ideas behind the creation of convict transportation was that while serving out their terms of punishment, convicted felons could gain valuable experience and skills that they could then use to make something of themselves. The reality is that criminals who served out their terms had a difficult time settling in America. Buyers of transported convicts were better positioned to take advantage of the opportunities that the land afforded them, but even they faced considerable challenges.[12]

The Buyers of Convicts

Most of the planters in Maryland and Virginia who purchased convict labor were like the Carrolls in that they had roots in America going back to the mid-17th century, well before convict transportation was institutionalized. They generally were the sons of middling English merchants who could afford to travel to America as free passengers and who came in search of economic opportunity. Immigrants from the elite classes back in England were mainly merchants, gentry, and government officials, and those from the middle ranks included small merchants, petty retailers, and craftsmen. These early settlers were rough, tough, and eager to get rich, but establishing life in America was not easy. Disease claimed the lives of many of them. Tobacco, their chief crop, offered only moderate returns, and cultivating it required a lot of work. These early settlers lived in modest houses, because they did not have the time or money to spend developing their estates beyond supporting basic agriculture.[13]

By the 17th century, the rich were getting richer and the poor were getting poorer. Because tobacco is such a labor-intensive crop, the income of planters was proportional to the number and efficiency of their laborers, not to the amount of land that they owned. Land was cheap in colonial America; labor was not. Only about 25 percent of the planters in the Chesapeake area could afford to buy slaves, but those who could were able to produce more tobacco. And with the greater profits that came with growing more tobacco came the ability to buy more slaves.[14]

By the 1720s, some planters were rich enough to begin building the stately mansions that are associated with southern plantations today. Through the use of slaves, indentured servants, and convicts, great planters like the Carrolls were able to grow their businesses quickly and came to dominate the area both economically and politically. Below these slave-owning tobacco planters were family farmers, who owned a house, some land, and perhaps a servant. Most of the tobacco planters in Maryland and Virginia ran small estates with a total worth of less than 100 pounds. They had few possessions; many did not even own candlesticks. If these lesser tobacco farmers were ever in a position to purchase more labor, they would often turn to convicts or indentured servants to help work their fields.[15]

In general, plantation owners were perceived as arrogant, domineering, and greatly concerned with their social standing.[16] John Adams, in his diary entry for February 23, 1777, brought a Boston bias to his harsh assessment of the people of Maryland:

> The Manners of Maryland are somewhat peculiar.
> They have but few Merchants. They are chiefly
> Planters and Farmers. The Planters are those who
> raise Tobacco and the Farmers such as raise Wheat
> &c. The Lands are cultivated, and all Sorts of Trades
> are exercised by Negroes, or by transported
> Convicts, which has occasioned the Planters and
> Farmers to assume the Title of Gentlemen, and they
> hold their Negroes and Convicts, that is all

labouring People and Tradesmen, in such
Contempt, that they think themselves a distinct
order of Beings. Hence they never will suffer their
Sons to labour or learn any Trade, but they bring
them up in Idleness or what is worse in Horse
Racing, Cock fighting, and Card Playing.[17]

Other contemporaries described planters in more
benevolent terms. William Eddis said of the people of Maryland,
"The inhabitants are enterprising and industrious; commerce
and agriculture are encouraged; and every circumstance clearly
evinces, that this colony is making a rapid progress to wealth,
power, and population." But he also noted their "litigious spirit"
and was astounded by how many cases were brought before the
courts at each session.[18]

Planters' houses were generally situated at the top of hills,
both to command authority and to survey the rest of their
property and buildings. The great plantations essentially
functioned as miniature communities run by a patriarch who had
a strong sense of independence. John Mason, the son of George
Mason, described 18th-century plantations as self-contained
worlds:

It was very much the practice with gentlemen of
landed and slave estates in the interior of Virginia,
so to organize them as to have considerable
resources within themselves ... Thus my father had
among his slaves carpenters, coopers, sawyers,
blacksmiths, tanners, curriers, shoemakers,
spinners, weavers and knitters, and even a distiller.
His woods furnished timber and planks for the

carpenters and coopers, and charcoal for the blacksmith; his cattle killed for his own consumption and for sale supplied skins for the tanners, curriers, and shoemakers, and his sheep gave wool and his fields produced cotton and flax for the weavers and spinners, and his orchards fruit for the distiller.[19]

The most prominent buildings on the plantations were private homes made of brick. The houses were large, but relatively low to the ground, since there was no need to build up with large expanses of land available. As colonists became wealthier, they began building houses that had more stories, larger windows made of crystal glass, and richer furniture. The rooms were built large in order to keep them cool in the summer, and all of the cooking and washing took place in separate buildings for the same reason. Servants and slaves lived in separate quarters, although their living spaces were sometimes attached to buildings used for other purposes, such as smokehouses, kitchens, or laundries. Their quarters ranged anywhere from 12 by eight feet to 40 by 20 feet, with an average size of 345 square feet. Other structures on the plantation included tobacco houses, dairies, henhouses, and storage facilities for grains and meat.[20]

An Old Maryland Manor House

(Source: U.S. History Images, http://ushistoryimages.com)

Charles Carroll of Annapolis was like most planters in that he was distrustful of outsiders. He vigorously defended his interests, refused to be subordinated to any man or group, and rarely parted with his own money, a trait that grew out of his strong sense of self-determination. Doohoragen, Carroll's main plantation, functioned almost as its own town. It had a tobacco barn, flour and grist mills, a house for weaving, a cobbler shop, a blacksmith shop, a fulling mill, a tanyard, a ciderhouse, a brickyard, a repair yard, and a quarry. Carroll supplied most of the food needed for his large labor force from his own plantations. Each plantation had large gardens, which grew cabbage, broccoli, endive, lettuce, onion, and beans. Orchards supplied apples, pears, peaches, and cherries. Each year, his plantations produced between 22,000 and 23,000 gallons of cider. Carroll continually cleared land to grow corn that was increasingly in demand and helped to feed his workers. In the fall, he slaughtered hogs.[21]

An Old Virginia Mansion
(Source: U.S. History Images, http://ushistoryimages.com)

The self-sufficient nature of plantations meant that planters were always on the lookout for anyone who could perform skilled labor and not just work in the fields or in the house. The problem was that anyone who freely came over with such skills probably wanted to start his own business and did not want to work for anyone else. He might even be looking for specialized labor to support his own enterprise. The labor shortage in the colonies was severe, and convicts were a potential solution to this problem.[22]

The Sale of Convicts

The circumstances of William Green's arrival in America were quite different from Charles Carroll the Settler's. At the age of seven, Green moved to London with his parents, where he attended free school for seven years and then was bound as an apprentice to a weaver in Old Cock-Lane, near Shoreditch.[23] He probably did not learn much in the trade, because most weavers simply took on apprentices as easy sources of cheap labor.[24] While serving as an apprentice, Green fell in with "idle company," who convinced him to run away from his master and join them in committing crimes in Sherwood Forest, most likely highway robbery. One of the gang members was eventually caught, and to save himself he impeached all of the other members, including Green. Green was sentenced to transportation for seven years on March 19, 1762, shipped from Nottinghamshire to London, and then loaded on the *Sally* at Iron-Gate, near the Tower of London. "There were twenty-six of us unhappy felons," he said of the ship's passengers, "and a most wicked crew as ever went over, most of us did smoak, but all did swear."

Green and his company set sail for Maryland on May 1. After losing sight of land, Green and his fellow convicts were put below deck to prevent them from rebelling. From that point on, they were let up on the top deck only six at a time, which, Green said, "amazed us." Convicts who were not used to the sea got sick. On the fifth day of sailing, Green's turn to go up on deck finally arrived, but his respite from the convict hold was far from comforting. When he walked out into the light, "I looked round and saw that I had brought myself to a scene of misery." The long passage wore on his nerves: "I often thought, but all in vain, for my spirits were very low and faint, God knows, and this being the sixth week of our passage, I never should see land any more." But his fears were put aside when the ship finally entered the Chesapeake Bay and headed towards its destination in Maryland. Once the *Sally* landed, the captain and crew began preparations to turn Green and his fellow convicts into saleable commodities.

After a convict ship pulled into port, the captain would send for the factor, an American representative for the British government who reviewed the list of convicts, noted any deaths, and evaluated the condition of those remaining. The factor then issued an arrival certificate for the captain to take back to Great Britain to prove that the convicts had indeed been delivered to their destination. Back in London, these arrival certificates were presented by the contracted merchant to the Treasury, which entered the names of each convict into the Treasury Money Books. While serving as Lord of the Treasury, Robert Walpole, the future Prime Minister of Great Britain, authorized and signed many such petitions for payment.[25]

Once the convicts were inspected, the American representative of the convict merchant posted notices and placed advertisements in newspapers, such as the *Maryland Gazette*, announcing the impending auction of the prisoners. Advertisements gave the date of the sale, the number of convicts to be sold, and a general idea of the skills they possessed. Oftentimes, though, the market for convicts was so good that advertisements were not needed, and the ship sold its entire cargo of prisoners soon after landing. In fact, at one point convict labor was in such high demand that the Bristol-based firm of

Stevenson, Randolph & Cheston had standing orders to supply plantation owners with convicts months before they arrived by ship.[26]

The sale of criminals into indentured servitude was not a requirement of the Transportation Act of 1718. Convict merchants essentially gained a property interest in the labor of the convicts they transported, so they sold them in America both to cover the cost of transporting them and to capitalize on this interest. In the early years of convict transportation, felons generally sold for terms that matched the time that they were banished from Britain—seven or 14 years—but as time went on, convicts were sold for seven-year terms no matter what their sentence was. As long as the sale both covered the cost of transporting the convict across the Atlantic and resulted in a profit, captains did not care how long the servant's term would be.[27]

William Green described his condition and that of his companions after their rough passage across the Atlantic as, "A wretched crew as are was seen, / Our cloths ragged, our bodies lean." While the captain of the *Sally* took care of paperwork, Green and the other passengers were ordered to wash themselves, comb their hair, and the men to shave off their beards. Sometimes shipmasters supplied headdresses for the women and caps for the men.[28] Despite the best efforts of captains to clean them up for sale, convicts still made a poor presentation at the end of their journey. One colonist described with dismay the condition of about 100 convicts who were up for sale in Williamsburg:

> I never see such pasels of pore Raches in my Life,
> some all most naked and what had Cloths was as
> Black [as] Chimney Swipers, and all most Starved
> by the Ill [usage] in their Pasedge By the Capn, for
> they are used no Bater than so many negro Slaves.[29]

After being cooped up in the ship for weeks on end, no amount of freshening up could rid the convicts of the pungent odor they acquired. One runaway ad in the *Virginia Gazette* for July 26, 1770 described the runaway convicts as having "been but a few days from on board the ship, and all have a peculiar smell incident to all servants just coming from ships." Another advertisement for two runaway convicts in the *Virginia Gazette* for April 22, 1775 claimed that "To those used to the Smell of Servants just from a Ship they will easily be discovered, unless they have procured new Clothes."[30]

In addition to cleaning up the convicts, captains prepared for their sale by procuring a hogshead of rum in order to make a large bowl of punch to serve to prospective buyers. On the day of the sale the prisoners were ordered up on deck and, as one contemporary described it, "placed in a Row together, like so many Oxen or Cows." Planters flocked on board the ship, first to hear the news the captain relayed from England and then to look over the convicts. They were especially on the lookout for any joiners, carpenters, blacksmiths, weavers, tailors, and other specialty skills among the criminals.[31] Buyers had to be careful, however, because sometimes prisoners claimed they had skills in handicrafts for which they had little or no experience in the hope of procuring a more desirable position. Sellers of convicts might also try to hide the true origins of their cargo and pass them off as regular indentured servants, who commanded higher prices. In one case, a ship arriving from Dublin with 66 convicts was discovered with 22 wigs, which were intended to make some of its passengers appear to be more respectable, and consequently more expensive, than they really were. In order to prevent such deception, Maryland passed an act requiring that copies of the felons' convictions had to be presented upon the arrival of a convict ship, with a fine of 10 pounds for failure to do so.[32]

Potential buyers examined the convicts by feeling their muscles, looking into their mouths to evaluate the condition of their teeth, and asking them questions to determine their morals and potential obedience. They also looked over the prisoner's conviction papers, which contained the convict's crime, length of sentence, and where and when the convict had been jailed in England. But even the closest examination might not reveal if the felon was carrying certain diseases like venereal disease. To help mitigate this possibility, the firm of Stevenson, Randolph & Cheston offered partial refunds to buyers who returned with evidence that the convict they bought was defective in some way that was not detectable at the point of sale. After the planters had sufficient time to examine the human cargo and make their decisions, the convicts were sold to the highest bidder.[33]

In 1771, James Revel was sentenced to transportation for 14 years in Surrey and was placed on board the *Thornton* for Virginia.[34] In his *Poor Unhappy Transported Felon's Sorrowful Account of His Fourteen Years Transportation at Virginia in America*, Revel provided a complete description of his sale in America:

The women from us separated stood,
As well as we by them to be thus view'd,
And in short time some men up to us came,
Some ask'd our trade, others ask'd our name.

Some view'd our limbs turning us around,
Examining like horses, if we were sound,
What trade my lad, said one to me,
A tin man, sir. That will not do for me.

Some felt our hands, others our legs and feet,
And made us walk to see if we were compleat,
Some view'd our teeth to see if they were good,
And fit to chew our hard and homely food,

If any like our limbs, our looks and trade,
Our captain then a good advantage made,
For they a difference make it doth appear,
'Twixt those of seven and those of fourteen years.

Another difference too there is allow'd,
Those who have money will have favour shew'd,
But if no cloaths nor money they have got,
Hard is their fate, and hard will be their lot.

At length a grim old man unto me came,
He ask'd my trade, likewise my name
I told him I a tin-man was by trade,
And not eighteen years of age I said.

Likewise the cause I told which brought me here,
And for fourteen years transported were;
And when from me he this did understand,
He bought me of the captain out of hand. 35

After the passage of the Transportation Act, sales of convicts began competing with those for indentured servants, European immigrant servants, and African slaves. Despite grumblings in the American press about the dumping of convicts on the colonies, planters were eager to buy them up. By 1745, half of all indentured servants arriving in Annapolis were convicts, and by 1755, 22.4 percent of all white employees in Maryland were transported felons. Such large numbers prompted a French traveler to the American colonies to remark in 1765, "the number of Convicts and Indented servants imported to virginia [is] amazing."[36]

Convict labor was able to compete so well with other forms of labor because it offered some distinct advantages. When compared with slaves and other European servants, convicts had the benefit of speaking English and so could adjust more easily to the colonial lifestyle. Some planters simply found convicts to be better laborers than slaves. Felons also served almost twice the time as indentured servants—seven years as opposed to four—and they were generally not subject to freedom dues, which were contractually awarded to indentured servants who served out their terms. These dues could be quite costly, as they usually consisted of a small parcel of land, seed, some tools, and sometimes even money. The criminal backgrounds of convicts were not as much of a problem as one might think, either. Planters could be just as skeptical about hiring indentured servants, because they suspected that anyone who willingly subjected themselves to four years of servitude must have been fleeing something at home. At least with a convict, they presumably knew what they were getting.[37]

But the biggest reason convict labor was so popular among planters was price. Even though convicts were bound to serve for only a set number of years, they were much cheaper to acquire than slaves or indentured servants. Slaves generally cost about 30-35 pounds sterling, and a healthy male could cost as much as 50 pounds; most male convicts, on the other hand, sold for 10-14 pounds, and females sold for only 5-9 pounds. When compared to indentured servants, the per-year value of convicts was 35 percent lower, so planters who could look beyond a convict's past could find a bargain. Lesser planters who could not afford to buy slaves often turned to convicts, and wealthier planters would use convicts to augment their slave labor or to perform specialized tasks as overseers, schoolmasters, carpenters, coopers, weavers, and blacksmiths.[38]

A variety of factors dictated the final price of convicts. The typical transported felon was an unskilled adult male of average height who received a seven-year sentence for larceny and cost 12.84 pounds sterling at auction. Convicts who could provide skilled labor not only sold for more—a skilled craftsman could go for as much as 25 pounds—but the seller could demand cash from the buyer. Others could be sold for credit or exchanged for tobacco. Manual laborers were in greater demand than those who were literate and well-educated, although convicts often claimed to be schoolteachers in an attempt to avoid manual labor. Adult servants were more valuable than teenagers, and taller convicts sold for 20 percent more than those of average height, because in both cases the former were considered more productive than the latter. The specific crime that convicts committed also affected their price. Those who committed arson, received stolen goods, or stole horses went for lower prices than those who committed simple theft.[39]

Convicts who were sick, old, lame, or judged useless were lumped and sold together or were simply given away. In some cases, the convict contractors actually had to pay to have such convicts taken off their hands. Later in the 18th century, as more people settled inland away from the tidewaters, groups of convicts were purchased by "soul drivers," who would buy up large groups, parade them through the countryside, and sell them to planters along the way.[40] Such was the fate of William Green:

> ... we were put all on shore in couples, chained
> together and drove in lots like oxen or sheep, till we
> came to a town called *Fike*, where was a great
> number of men and women, young and old, came to
> see us; they search us there as the dealers in horses
> do those animals in this country, by looking at our
> teeth, viewing our limbs to see if they are sound and
> fit for their labour, and if they approve of us after
> asking our trades and names, and what crimes we
> have been guilty of to bring us to that shame, the
> bargain is made.

As eager as planters were to buy up convicts, captains were just as eager to sell them off, both to relieve them of the responsibility for their welfare and feeding and to make sure that the sale did not interfere with their plans for the trip back to England. As soon as convict ships emptied their holds of human cargo, they filled up the space with tobacco to take back to London, Bristol, or another British port. Once the convicts left the ship, they also ceased to be of any concern to the British government. Unlike in Australia, convicts sent to America were not officially watched over or disciplined by any governmental authority, which is why it cannot be said that convicts transported to America were sentenced to serve in a penal colony.[41]

Convict transportation raised important issues of identity and freedom for the convict, the plantation owner, and the other servants. Once on the plantation, criminals had to renegotiate their social position. They suddenly found themselves bound to a fellow Englishman who claimed ownership over them and everything they did. During the sale of William Green, a man came up and asked him his name, his trade, and the crime he committed back in England. Green's answers must have satisfied the gentleman, because he immediately purchased him. Whereas Green knew nothing about his new owner or where he was headed, the man may have been motivated to buy Green on the strength of knowing that the two grew up within 20 miles of each other back in England.

Chapter Seven: On the Plantation

> My master was a man but of ill fame,
> Who first of all a transport thither came,
> In Raphannock country he did dwell,
> In Raphannock river known full well.
> —James Revel, *The Poor Unhappy*
> *Transported Felon's Sorrowful Account of*
> *His Fourteen Years Transportation at*
> *Virginia in America*

Most of the convicts who ended up in Virginia lived north of the York River, mainly in the Northern Neck between the Rappahannock and Potomac rivers. In Maryland, about three-quarters of the convict population lived in four of the colony's 14 counties: Baltimore, Charles, Queen Anne's, and Anne Arundel. Maryland by far had the highest concentration of transported convicts, since it received more felons from Great Britain and its total population was half that of Virginia.[1]

Whereas convicts transported to Botany Bay in Australia were forced to work in a state-run penal colony, convicts sent to America were sold to private individuals who were on the lookout for specific skill sets that could prove useful on their plantations. The most common occupations among convicts were shoemaker, weaver, blacksmith, carpenter, sailor, tailor, barber, joiner, gardener, butcher, and bricklayer. Convicts were also engaged as soldiers, silversmiths, coopers, chimney sweeps, perukers, and fishermen.[2] Those who possessed some form of education could try to land a position as a schoolteacher. A young George Washington was educated in reading, writing, and accounts by a convict servant who was purchased by Washington's father for just this purpose.[3]

Convicts and other servants who could perform one of the aforementioned occupations generally received better treatment from their masters than those who could not. But most convicts came from the lower orders and arrived as laborers with no identifiable skills. These felons generally worked on plantations as common field hands along with African slaves.

A Rude Awakening

When transported convict and doggerel poet James Revel arrived at his new master's house in America, his European clothes were taken away from him and replaced with a canvas shirt, trousers, and a "hop sack frock."[4] His master did not provide him with a pair of shoes or a hat, so he had to go out into the tobacco fields in bare feet and with nothing to shade his eyes from the blazing sun.

Revel worked alongside five other convict servants and 18 African slaves, and all of them were expected to perform the same amount of work. Four other female transports worked as servants in the main house and attended to the master's daughter and wife. Revel and his fellow servants began work at daybreak and continued out in the fields until sunset. But their day did not end here. They then headed to the mill to ground corn until midnight or one o'clock before returning to bed and rising again with the sun the next day. This schedule went on for six days until the seventh day of the week, when the servants tended a separate piece of land where they were expected to grow their own food. Servants on plantations generally lived away from the main house in huts or cabins of their own fashioning, but even if convicts worked alongside slaves out in the fields, as in Revel's case, the two groups generally occupied separate living quarters.[5]

From Hugh Jones, *The Present State of Virginia* (1724)

(Source: Google Books, http://books.google.com/)

At one point Revel fell seriously ill, but his affliction did not secure him a reprieve from work. As long as he could stand up and "hold the hoe within my feeble hand," he was forced to go out into the fields. Through this experience, he realized that his master treated him and his lot in a worse manner than he did his slaves:

> Much hardship then I did endure,
>
> No dog was ever nursed so before,
>
> More pity then the negroe slaves bestow'd
>
> Than my inhuman brutal master show'd.

Transported convicts such as Revel had dual status in the colonies: They were both British felons and American indentured servants at the same time. They worked on the plantation alongside regular indentured servants—who had some agency in their decision to travel to America to start a new life—and African slaves, who, like the convicts, were forced to emigrate. Convicts fell somewhere in between these two servant groups in terms of status, so they could either be treated like other indentured servants or be subjected to forms of degradation that were usually reserved for African slaves.[6]

Plantation owners who purchased the labor of a convict servant acquired complete legal control over him or her: They could rent the service of the convict out to another plantation owner; they could transfer complete ownership of him or her over to someone else; they could even use the convict as a wager in a card game. Owners could freely use corporal punishment to control the criminals, as long as they were not deemed overly cruel in handing out punishment. They could prohibit convicts from engaging in any trade outside of their normal duties on the plantation and generally did so for fear that the servants would pilfer goods from the plantation in order to sell them. Any money that convict servants happened to earn through exercising a craft could be confiscated, since the labor used for that craft was considered the property of their owner.[7]

If an owner died, convicts were passed along as property. A 1767 inventory of the deceased John Brice of Anne Arundel County in Maryland listed under "Sundries" one mill saw, two blank books, and John Matthews, a convict servant and carpenter with three and a quarter years left to serve on his term. Owners also had the power to grant convict servants their freedom and simply let them go. Despite all of these limitations, convicts generally had more legal rights than slaves, mainly because their bonded condition was temporary and because they could petition courts to prevent excessive abuse. But as the 18th century wore on, convicts steadily lost legal rights to the point where there was not much difference between them and slaves in the eyes of the law.[8]

Around the time that convict servants began arriving in America in large numbers, slavery was rapidly becoming a critical part of the Chesapeake economy. Back in the 17th century, menial plantation work was generally carried out by white servants, but in the 18th century it was increasingly assigned to African slaves. This transformation in the composition of laborers on plantations brought about an attendant change in the perception of the very category of unskilled labor, which began to assume a demeaning stigma that was not associated with it during the previous century. So as the 18th century progressed, convicts—who generally arrived in

America with low reputations and few specialized skills—were treated more and more like slaves by their masters than as indentured servants. Convicts with valuable skills, on the other hand, tended to be grouped with indentured servants, who at the time were increasingly purchased to perform specialized rather than menial forms of labor.[9]

Still, neither criminal nor indentured servant generated much respect from later colonists. William Eddis, an English observer of Maryland society in the early 1770s, wrote that the perceived difference between the indentured servant and the convicted felon was nominal, since colonists thought that anyone who abandoned family and friends to become an indentured servant in a distant land must somehow be lacking in character. Both indentured servants and convicts were considered social outcasts with no real ties to the community, and as plantation owners became more and more dependent on slave labor, the working conditions of white servants deteriorated as well. Eddis went on to write:

> Negroes being a property for life, the death of
> slaves, in the prime of youth or strength, is a
> material loss to the proprietor; they are, therefore,
> almost in every instance, under more comfortable
> circumstances than the miserable European, over
> whom the rigid planter exercises an inflexible
> severity. They are strained to the utmost to perform
> their allotted labour; and, from a prepossession in
> many cases too justly founded, they are supposed to
> be receiving only the just reward which is due to
> repeated offences. There are doubtless many

exceptions to this observation, yet, generally
speaking, they groan beneath a worse than Egyptian
bondage.[10]

Sometimes convicts were put in charge of overseeing slaves. William Barton was transported once by Francis March in 1716 and then again in 1719. The second time around he was sold as a servant for 18 pounds, "but was not used as a Slave, but set to overloook the Negroes in their Work, and to lash them when they neglected it." Barton went on to say that his experience on the plantation "was the happiest Part of his Life; that he endured no Wretchedness, had no Care, but found whatever was requisite for the sustaining Life provided for him." But most convicts did not enjoy the lifestyle that Barton apparently did, nor did they react to being in America in such glowing terms. They had to eat food that was foreign to them, wear clothes made of cotton or linen rather than wool, and drink water rather than beer. Some convicts reported that they were fed only corn and were given nothing to wear on their feet but skins. They often endured whippings, especially if they were unruly, and they were forced to wear iron collars and chains if their master thought they needed to be restrained. Even Barton himself stole away from the plantation in the summer of 1720 to return to his wife back in England. Ten months later he was executed for committing highway robbery.[11]

James Revel worked on the Rappahannock plantation for 12 years, but with two years left to go on his 14-year term his master died, and the widow decided to sell the plantation and all of its contents. A lawyer from Jamestown purchased all of the slaves, but he refused to buy the convicts, so Revel and the other white servants were put up for sale to the highest bidder. Revel was lucky. He was purchased by a cooper from Jamestown and was surprised when his new owner "used me so tenderly and kind" and "said he would not use me as a slave, / But as a servant if I'd well behave." His new owner even offered to send Revel back home after his time expired. Two years later the cooper followed through on his promise, and Revel enjoyed a tearful reunion with his parents back in England.

Adjustment

Convicts who led idle lives through pickpocketing or theft back in England and were not used to manual labor probably had the most difficulty adapting to the new circumstances of colonial America. Some of them engaged in the grueling and most dreaded task of clearing trees and brush so that the soil could be turned over to create arable land. Falling timber was a skill that was rarely brought over from Europe, so servants had to learn it on the fly. Once acquired, though, it was considered a highly valuable skill.[12]

The climate of the Chesapeake, with its greater temperature extremes than in England, was itself a source of misery for the convicts. William Green noted, "It is exceeding cold in the fall of the year, and in the summer it is prodigious hot and sultry." Servants in Maryland received some respite in the summer, when they were generally allowed three hours of rest during the high heat of the day. But if adjusting to the extremes of the climate was not enough, convicts also had to contend with exposure to new diseases—that is, if they did not already arrive with an illness that they had picked up before or after stepping on the ship in Great Britain.[13]

Spring was an especially busy time for plantations in Maryland and Virginia, because tobacco plants required special attention early on in their development. Tobacco seeds were first planted in beds, where they were carefully cultivated and weeded for a month. Once the plants reached the size of a hand, they were transferred in wet weather one-by-one to the hills. Spring was also the time when ships arrived from England loaded with china, silver, wine, dresses, and other English items the planters had ordered over a year ago using the tobacco they grew as exchange. But the most difficult month for field hands was August, when both the heat and the backbreaking work intensified as the plants neared harvest time. Come September, temperatures began to cool, but the pace of tending to the tobacco plants increased with harvesting, curing, storing, and shipping the leaves. These tasks were no small matters, since tobacco needed to be dried carefully before it was gently packed inside barrels for shipment to England.[14]

From Hugh Jones, *The Present State of Virginia* (1724)
(Source: Google Books, http://books.google.com/)

Convict servants led fairly isolated lives. They had few opportunities for building community relationships, either on or between plantations. The simple presence of other convict servants on a plantation did not guarantee companionship, especially if the others came from different parts of England or Ireland and the customs that they practiced were different from their own. Building connections with slaves, who faced even greater cultural alienation in America, was even less likely to occur.[15]

Servants could not marry without the consent of their owner. Without such permission, some convicts developed illicit relations with one another that sometimes resulted in bastard children. Since fathers were generally responsible for the cost of raising their own children, which a convict servant could rarely do given his circumstances, these children were turned over to the county. The owner of the convict then paid the county the amount needed to care for the child, and the court tacked on extra years to the convict's service in order to compensate his owner. Another payment option was for the court to seize the convict father after his original term of service was over and then sell him back into servitude, with the profit from the sale going towards offsetting the costs of raising his child. The mother of the bastard child was often required to provide an extra year of service to her owner to compensate him for the time lost during her pregnancy and childbirth, even though the time she needed to carry the baby to term was much shorter than the tacked-on service.[16]

Abuse

On the whole, servants were treated much worse in America than they were in England. Many plantation owners ruled over their personal empire with an iron fist. One Englishman traveling through the Chesapeake once reported to the *London Magazine*, "Prodigious Numbers of Planters are immensely rich, and I think one of them, at this Time, numbers upon his Lands near 1,000 Wretches, that tremble with submissive Awe at his Nod, besides white Servants."[17]

Masters who abused their servants often did so through beatings or by limiting their food to bread and water. One published account about the experience of an indentured servant tells the story of how Chevalier James, an "Unfortunate Young Nobleman," is tricked into indentured servitude and ends up on a ship bound for Pennsylvania. There, he is purchased by a cruel master named Drumon, who puts him to work cutting timber for pipe staves, which were used for making wooden barrels. Drumon repeatedly whips James and withholds meat from him as punishment for his initial incompetence in carrying out this unfamiliar labor. James soon realizes that Drumon will never be satisfied with the quality of his work, because his master seems to relish handing out punishments to all of his laborers.[18]

Another published account from the time, *The Fortunate Transport*, documents the story of a transported convict who is also treated cruelly by her master.[19] After being transported for theft to Virginia, Polly Haycock is purchased by a planter, and the narrator's description of him does not cast a positive light on planters in general:

> He was a meer Planter, consequently cruel,
> haughty, and mercenary, without any soft
> Sentiment of Humanity in his Breast; and his Years
> had laid the Fever in his Blood so much that he had
> no Thoughts but how to work the Value of his
> Money out of the Slaves, and make the most of
> them without regard to their Happiness or Misery.
> In a Word, like most of the Tribe of Planters, he had
> no Appetite but for Money; nor Pleasure in any
> Pastime but torturing the unhappy Wretches in his
> Power.

After acquiring Polly, the planter makes her a cook's maid despite her inexperience in this line of work. One day, as punishment for not roasting a turkey properly, the planter has Polly stripped naked, tied to a post, and whipped by an African slave. While this cruelty is being carried out, the planter sits down to eat, with the background "Musick" of Polly's cries heightening the enjoyment of his meal. Luckily for Polly, a justice of the peace happens to be passing by and witnesses the scene of the slave unmercifully applying a cat-o'-nine-tails to her back. The justice quickly puts an end to Polly's beating and threatens to bring the planter to justice. Even though the planter knows that the Assembly would probably side with him if the case were brought before them, he offers to give Polly to the justice in exchange for not pursuing the matter, which the justice readily accepts.

Not all planters treated their servants with such cruelty. The Carrolls of Maryland understood the value of treating their servants and slaves well, and to help keep their servants in line they instituted a series of graduated privileges and rewards to encourage proper behavior among their workers. But they were also quick to punish behavior that was detrimental to the running of their plantations and would just as readily use severe discipline on their white servants, especially their convict servants, as they would on their black slaves. When the young Charles Carroll of Carrollton was unable to control the gardener Harry White, the older Charles Carroll of Annapolis had the convict servant flogged and then collared. Afterward, the father lectured his son, "it is imprudent to threatten to whip Servants or to keep them in dread of it, when they really deserve it, give it to them as soon as possible." According to the younger Carroll, White had been whipped six or seven times previously, and he attributed his ill behavior to the distractions of Annapolis. After the last incident they moved White to Doohoragen, a more isolated plantation, in an attempt to improve the convict's disposition. When White turned out to be just as "exceedingly idle" there as in the city, with the result that "never was a garden in a worse condition than mine," the young Carroll had the servant whipped yet again.[20]

White's fellow convict servant in the garden, John Turnbull, was just as troublesome. The older Carroll described Turnbull as "a perfect Blackguard & Brute when He is drunk," which apparently was often the case. After Turnbull came home one night intoxicated and abused Carroll's wife—and then later in the week returned home drunk once again with another laborer—Carroll had him whipped. Turnbull's service at the time had almost run out, but he must have had extra time tacked on his term for his bad behavior, since he arrived in Maryland in 1763 and this incident occurred in 1774. Carroll offered Turnbull a good wage to stay on with him at the end of his term, but only on condition that the servant would agree to be whipped when he deserved it. Carroll confidently predicted that Turnbull would accept his offer, but apparently the convict had had enough and left the plantation. Yet another convict servant belonging to the Carrolls, Daniel Squiers, was ordered by the older Carroll to be whipped with 15 lashes and collared after he attempted to run away. But in the end Carroll did not administer the whipping and explained his decision to his son: "Squiers was not whipt, He Wears a Collar in terrorem to others & as a Punishment wh He justly deserves."[21]

Few convicts or indentured servants left behind first-hand accounts of their experiences on plantations. But in one of the few extant letters written by an indentured servant, Elizabeth Spriggs poignantly illustrates the cruelty that could be wielded by plantation owners when she wrote to her father in 1756:

What we unfortunate English people suffer here is beyond the probability of you in England to conceive. Let it suffice that I, one of the unhappy number, am toiling almost day and night, and very often in the horses' drudgery, with only this comfort that: "You bitch, you do not half enough:" and then tied up and whipped to that degree that you'd not serve an animal; scarce anything but Indian corn and salt to eat, and that even begrudged. Nay, many negroes are better used: almost naked, no shoes or stockings to wear, and the comfort after slaving during Master's pleasure what rest we can get is to wrap ourselves in a blanket and lie upon the ground.

This is the deplorable condition your poor Betty endures, and now I beg, if you have any bowels of compassion left, show it by sending me some relief. Clothing is the principal thing wanting.[22]

Elizabeth's letter is heart-wrenching, but it never made it to her father.

The Ironworks

The intense labor required for the cultivation of tobacco may have served as the initial justification for shipping convicts to America, but just as convict transportation began in earnest, iron production in the Chesapeake started to develop as well. Unskilled prisoners who did not end up working as common laborers on plantations most likely ended up in an ironworks.

Bound with an Iron Chain

After great profits were made on tobacco in the 17th century, prices began to lag in the 18th century. Plantation owners were eager to find alternative sources of income, and expanding their operations into growing grains and corn was one way to supplement their tobacco income. But as Chesapeake planters shifted away from labor-intensive tobacco and towards growing more grains, their workforce had more time on its hands, so in order to keep their workers busy, large planters sought to diversify their economic activities even more by creating an ironworks.[23]

A group of English capitalists, iron-masters, and merchants founded the first iron company in Maryland by first establishing an iron forge in 1715 and then creating the Principio Ironworks Company in 1720. At its peak, the Principio Company produced half the iron exported by Maryland. In Virginia, the Accokeek Furnace was founded in 1725 in the Northern Neck and was soon followed by many others. Even though Charles Carroll of Annapolis concentrated his efforts on agriculture and banking—and abandoned his father's methods of acquiring wealth by combining the two activities with mercantilism, office holding, law, and land speculation—he pooled his money with a group of wealthy gentlemen in 1731 to create the Baltimore Iron Works. The Carrolls owned a fifth interest in the company, which grew to be the second-largest iron enterprise in Maryland after the Principio Company and ended up generating 400 pounds sterling a year for the family.[24]

Another important family in the Chesapeake iron industry was the Tayloes.[25] William Tayloe was born in London in 1645 and moved to Virginia sometime before 1680. In 1685, he married Anne Corbin, the daughter of a wealthy Middlesex County planter, and together they founded a plantation in Rappahannock County using funds that William inherited from a deceased uncle. William became an important planter and political leader, and when he died in 1710 he passed along 3,000 acres and 21 slaves to his son, John Tayloe I.

Tayloe I was born in 1687, and he added to the fortune he inherited from his father by marrying Elizabeth Gwynn Lyde, a widow who brought with her 1,000 acres, 10 slaves, 200 pounds sterling, and 264 pounds of tobacco. The Tayloes were mainly planters, but they also engaged in agricultural processing, mercantile activity, money lending, craft services, shipbuilding, and investing in towns and industry. After his marriage, Tayloe I became involved in county politics in order to increase his new wealth and social connections, and by the 1730s he obtained a seat on the Colonial Council of Virginia. The Council controlled the land-grant process, and his seat basically guaranteed that all of his land speculation ventures would be approved. In 1737, Tayloe I founded the Neabsco Ironworks, and his position on the Council secured him a break from paying port duties on the iron ore he imported from Maryland to process in his factory. Tayloe I died 10 years later and left 20,000 acres and 320 slaves to his only son, John Tayloe II. Like his father, the younger Tayloe was active in politics and used his positions to continue the expansion of the Tayloe fortune. In 1756 he added yet another ironworks company to the family portfolio, the Occoquan Ironworks. The new company was on the Occoquan River in Prince William County, but eventually the Tayloes ran it and the Neabsco Ironworks as one company.

Bound with an Iron Chain

The Neabsco Ironworks sat on 5,000 wooded acres around the Neabsco Creek. The processing complex took up 18 acres and included two blast furnaces, a water-powered gristmill and a sawmill, workers' quarters, pit mines, trench mines, a water-collection pond, an ore-roasting area, a small forge, and storage facilities for iron ore, coal, and equipment. Forging, smithing, and processing took place on one side of the creek, while the iron-making and living quarters for the workers were on the other side. The rest of the acreage provided the massive fuel needed to run the works. Most of the iron ore had to be shipped in from the western shore of Maryland, so the company also owned a full line of boats and vessels.

Combining tobacco and iron interests made a lot of sense for large plantation owners, because geography was definitely on their side. The extensive ore and timber resources on their lands could easily support a thriving iron industry, and in the same way that the Chesapeake water system offered advantages in moving and transporting tobacco, those same advantages held true for the shipping of raw iron. Another advantage that large plantation owners gained by growing tobacco and making iron was the savings they could realize on shipping costs. Tobacco took up a lot of space on ships but it was very light, so ironworks owners could negotiate free shipping for iron, which acted as stabilizing ballast for ships carrying tobacco.

Iron-making was the most technologically advanced industry in colonial America, and one of the most lucrative. Around 50 ironworks operated throughout the Chesapeake during the middle of the 18th century, and by 1775 the American colonies produced a third of the world's raw iron.[26] But as with plantations, the greatest challenge in operating an ironworks was acquiring adequate labor.

In 1767, Charles Carroll of Annapolis transferred his one-fifth interest in the Baltimore ironworks company to his son, Charles Carroll of Carrollton. The son immediately became active in the operations of the company, and one of his first steps was to propose replacing hired workers with cheaper and more reliable sources of labor—i.e., indentured servants and slaves. Even though the Baltimore company had employed convict servants from at least 1746, Carroll's proposal met resistance from the company's board. And when he finally convinced the group to follow his plan, he had trouble obtaining slaves and servants who could meet the rigorous demands of working iron. But by 1775 the company had acquired 10 convicts—the maximum number the manager wanted to employ—and had instituted a policy of regularly buying slaves.[27]

Given the difficulty of finding an adequate labor supply for ironworks, companies used a combination of indentured servants, slaves, slaves hired from other owners, and convicts. Some companies bought up whole groups of convicts to labor in their ironworks. Tayloe II bought convict servants to work in his iron company throughout his lifetime, and in the 1770s he even ventured into importing and selling prisoners himself using a convict ship that he appropriately called the *Tayloe*.[28]

Jobs at the ironworks included timbering, coaling, mining, carting, milling, iron making, and shipping. The work was difficult, constant, and exhausting, and workers often expressed discontent. William Eddis called working in the iron mines "the most laborious employment allotted to worthless servants."[29]

Widespread unhappiness among the workforce led many of the laborers at ironworks to cause trouble. In 1732, Charles Carroll of Annapolis received a letter from one of his partners about their workers, warning that "none here are to be trusted without a watchful Eye & Strict hand." In 1734, a slave named Caesar, hired to work in the Baltimore Iron Works, returned after an unexcused absence holding a note from his true master stating that he should not be beaten for his disappearance. Stephen Onion, the manager of the company at the time, honored the request of Caesar's master, but he placed an iron collar around Caesar's neck as a corrective measure. Otherwise, Onion reasoned, "youl have by Turns most of the negroos running to Annapolis to Know Where they must work and Overseers will be of little use." But more positive approaches to discipline were also used at the Baltimore company, which used an incentive or "overwork" system to encourage laborers to meet or exceed their quotas or tasks. Workers who surpassed expectations, even slaves, were rewarded with cash or goods.[30]

Despite such incentives, indentured servants, convicts, and black slaves all ran away from the Baltimore Iron Works with some frequency. In fact, convicts employed in the harsh iron industry ran away at a higher rate than in any other profession by far, and advertisements for convicts who ran away from ironworks belonging to John Tayloe and Charles Carroll regularly appeared in *The Maryland Gazette* and *The Virginia Gazette*.[31] But the trouble convict servants caused was not limited simply to running away. Many continued their criminal ways after they landed in America, much to the consternation of colonists.

Chapter Eight: Committing Crime and Running Away

On June 12, 1751, the *Maryland Gazette* reported in the same article that in Annapolis, Maryland, Onesiphorus Lucas received an execution sentence for committing burglary, Thomas Poney was sentenced to be burned in the hand for committing a felony, and in Queen Anne's County, Jacob Windsor was executed.[1] Windsor had apparently caused quite a bit of trouble before he was finally executed, because he "had been four Times since whipp'd and pillor'd, once for stealing a Bible." The crimes that these three committed were not out of the ordinary, but what was particularly noteworthy was the fact that they were all transported convicts. Newspaper reports like this one helped confirm in the minds of American colonists what they initially feared: that the Transportation Act of 1718 would drastically increase the number of crimes committed in the colonies.[2]

Soon after Great Britain started sending convicts to America, colonists began complaining about the number of crimes they committed. In 1724, Hugh Jones, the Rector of Jamestown, Virginia, claimed that "the abundance of [convicts] do great Mischiefs, commit Robbery and Murder, and spoil Servants that were before very good."[3] Likewise, the Baltimore County Court complained in 1723 that "the great number of convicts of late imported into this Province have not only committed divers murders, burglaries and other felonies, but debauched several of its formerly innocent and honest inhabitants" and that the "very great numbers of said convicts in this County ... encourages them to be more frequent in the perpetration of their villainies."4 The belief that convict servants elevated the crime rate was so widespread that in 1732, John Clayton, the attorney general of Virginia, successfully argued for a higher salary on the grounds that "the increase of Criminals of late Years especially since the importation of Convicts from great Britain" had increased his workload.5

Convicts in the Media

Whether the influx of convicts actually led to a rise in the number of murders, arsons, and robberies in America is debatable, but by the middle of the century the number of newspaper stories about crimes committed by convict servants notably increased.6 A report that appeared in the *Pennsylvania Gazette* in 1752 about two transported convicts who tried to murder their owners in Dorchester County must have struck fear in any plantation owner who employed convict servants. The couple successfully held their assailants at bay until another female convict servant joined the attack. Her appearance prompted the mistress to run upstairs, escape out a window, and hide in a swamp near the house. With his wife no longer in the picture, the master was quickly overtaken and cruelly beaten by the three until they left him for dead. The group then plundered the house and took clothes and 11 pounds in money. The article notes that the master survived the attack and was likely to recover.[7]

One year earlier, the same newspaper reported another attack by a convict on his owner. This time, the convict servant entered the main house with the intention of murdering his mistress with an ax. But when he came face to face with her and saw, as he later said, *"how d----d innocent she look'd,"* he placed his own left hand on a wooden block and chopped it off with the ax. He then threw the detached member at her and shouted, *"Now make me work, if you can."* In a note added to the end of the story, the *Gazette* warns the public that the convict servant had recently been seen begging in Philadelphia and claiming that he had lost his hand in an accident.[8]

Sometimes the reputations of transported convicts followed them to America through the press. *The Boston Post-Boy* reported in 1770 that Captain Blichenden arrived in Annapolis from London with a number of coiners on board his ship, the *Trotman*, and that since their arrival some poorly made counterfeit dollars and a milled shilling had already been discovered. The implication is that the newly arrived convicts were the ones who produced them, even though it is doubtful that they would have had the means or the time between their arrival and the appearance of the report to carry out even poor reproductions of colonial currency.[9]

In 1751, the *New-York Gazette, or Weekly Post-Boy* printed an account of "one of the most audacious Robberies." Two armed men took a ladder to the house of Charles Cole at night, and one of them climbed into the second-story bedroom where Cole was sleeping while the other one served as a lookout.

Once inside the bedroom, the burglar held a pistol to Cole's head and threatened to blow his brains out if he stirred or made a noise. He then tied Cole up and began beating him to get him to disclose the location of his money. Meanwhile, one of Cole's servants, who was sleeping in a nearby house, heard the noise and peeked out his window to investigate. The lookout at the bottom of the ladder spotted the servant and threatened to shoot him dead if he made a sound. Undeterred, the servant grabbed a gun and fired it at the lookout. The lookout fired back. They missed each other, but the shooting was enough to cause the two robbers to run off and leave Cole tied up in his bed. As of the writing of the article, the two armed men were still at large.[10]

A little over a month later, the same newspaper reported that a convict servant named John Connor confessed to the robbery of Charles Cole. He told a magistrate that he was the one who served as the lookout, while another convict servant, Thomas Bevan, went up into Cole's bedroom. After the two escaped, they hid in the pine forests and continued to rob several people. At this point the search for them became so intense that Connor decided to return to his master, who turned him over to the authorities. Bevan also returned to his master, but he did not know that he had already been impeached by his partner. Bevan tried to threaten his owner into helping him escape back to England, but his master, who anticipated his return, managed to stow him away in a cellar, where he was later taken into custody by several people loaded with pistols. The article assures the reader that Bevan is now in Jail, "strongly iron'd, and chain'd to the Floor."[11]

In 1745, James Barrett received a death sentence for the murder of John Cain. Both men were transported convicts, and they committed various thefts with another unnamed convict servant. Cain set out to sell some of the wool that the three had stolen, but he kept the 18 pence he received from the sale for himself. Barrett and the other convict demanded that Cain share the profit, but to no avail, so the two decided to cast lots to determine which of them should kill their partner. The deed fell to Barrett. He confronted Cain one last time, and when the latter once more refused to pay up, Barrett cried, "Then d—n you take that," and stabbed Cain with a long knife. Cain suffered from the six-inch-deep knife wound for nine weeks before finally dying. Even though Barrett was charged with Cain's murder, he "appeared at his Trial, without the least Concern or Remorse."[12]

Newspapers were not the only places where colonists could read about the criminal exploits of transported convicts. An execution broadside sold at the hanging of John Grimes in New Jersey in 1765 gave a detailed account of his criminal life after he was transported to America.[13] Grimes grew up in a small town in Ireland. His parents were poor, did not provide him with any education, and even encouraged the young boy to carry out small thefts. Eventually, he "became so notorious" in the area that he had to leave for Dublin, where he temporarily worked on board ships until he returned to his thieving ways. After being dismissed from his employment "for Dishonesty and Thieving," he joined a gang of street robbers and pickpockets, but when the leaders were all captured, they impeached Grimes, so he fled to England. While in London, Grimes was arrested for robbery and sentenced to transportation at the Old Bailey.

Grimes was shipped on the *Dolphin*, and ended up in Patapsco, Maryland. He was sold as a servant to an ironworks, but he ran away shortly afterward. He decided to pass himself off as a peddler, so he broke into a store and hauled off as many goods as he could carry. He continued as a thief and housebreaker until he was arrested for horse stealing, for which he was burned in the hand and thrown in jail. While in prison, Grimes stole all of the money from a man the sheriff had hired to perform an execution and who was staying in Grimes's jail cell until he could carry out his duty the next day. After a man secured Grimes's release from prison in exchange for his servitude, Grimes robbed the man of his horse and all the money he had with him and headed to New York.

While he was being held in jail, Grimes learned about the details of the house of Joseph Burr, who lived in western New Jersey, so he and two of his criminal colleagues set out to rob it. After carrying out the burglary, the gang stole some horses to get away, hid out in the woods, and got drunk. While in hiding, the group got into a fight over the division of their booty, and the two partners beat Grimes up so badly that he could not move to escape when the authorities discovered him. The other two burglars were eventually picked up as well, and they were all found guilty and executed for their crime.

These are only some of the stories of crimes committed by transported convicts that circulated during the middle of the century. Colonists justifiably worried about transports committing robbery, horse theft, burglary, and murder. Even reports of convicts stealing plate from churches increasingly circulated. Arson was another concern, especially in the

Northern Neck of the Chesapeake. Convicts were blamed for burning down the Thomas Lee mansion. Private residences, tobacco inspection houses, and public buildings were also hit by arsonists. Convicts seeking revenge for their miserable situation were responsible for many of the fires, but in some cases they were hired by rival planters to set them.[14]

Runaways

Convicts tried to run away almost as soon as the practice of transporting them began. When one of the very first ships to transport criminals to America under the Transportation Act landed, seven of the prisoners on board escaped. Samuel Shute, the Governor of Massachusetts at the time, issued a proclamation on November 25, 1718 asserting that the convicts had been committing "many robberies, and other Enormities in the Places whether they are fled" and offered 50 shillings each for their recapture. Convicts often ran away to escape harsh treatment from their owners or to regain their freedom and possibly return to Great Britain. Some of them became pirates, especially if they had been a sailor at one time.[15]

Convicts tended to run away more often than regular indentured servants. Unlike indentured servants, convicts did not choose to come to America, so they were more likely to be resentful of their situation. They were also given little incentive to serve out their terms of service. As in the case of indentured servants, once convicts finished out their terms, owners were required to provide freedom dues. But these legal rights were soon stripped from the convicts, so with no reward waiting for them if they stayed until the end of their service, running away could appear to be an attractive option, even though punishment for it was harsh. Runaway convicts faced corporal punishment and additional service time if caught. Transported convict William Green said that if they ran away, a day was added on to their service for every hour they were gone; for every day absent, a week was added, and for every month, a year. Convicts who were caught stealing or committed murder, he claimed, were put to death. But such punishments seemed trivial compared to the experiences the prisoners had already faced, so they were not much of a deterrent.[16]

Most convicts who chose to run away did so within two years of arriving in America, and if they did not flee soon after they landed, they usually did so six months to a year after their arrival. The incentive to run away decreased as the end of their usual seven-year sentence grew nearer. Most convicts ran away by themselves, but occasionally they would run away in pairs, often with someone who came from the same part of England. Some convicts were even known to run away with an African slave.[17]

Runaway convicts had a difficult time escaping detection due to the many mechanisms in place to bring about their recapture. Servants traveling through the countryside were required to carry papers showing that they either had been discharged or had their owner's permission to be wandering off of his property. Any servant caught traveling without such papers could be questioned and apprehended to see if anyone made any inquiries about his or her whereabouts. Some convicts carried forged papers for just this reason. Property owners were vigilant in keeping an eye out for runaways, mainly because a generous reward was usually offered for their capture and return.[18]

Advertisements in American newspapers helped in the identification of runaway convicts and specified the reward offered. Due to the high cost, though, owners probably did not advertise runaways until they had been missing for a while. Runaway ads usually gave the names of the convicts, a description or their appearance, their age, where they originally came from, and their occupation or skill set. The faces of convicts were often described as being pitted from smallpox, and some convicts were noted as wearing an iron collar or handcuffs. Some ads described behavioral tendencies, such as "addicted to boasting and telling of lies," "loves liquor," "speaks fast," or has "a very remarkable way of staring any body in the face that speaks to him." Many plantation owners kept descriptions of their servants and slaves on file in case any one of them decided to run away.[19] The following runaway ad that appeared in the *Pennsylvania Gazette* illustrates the kind of information that was generally included, even though it provides a more detailed description of the convict than most did.

> *Bohemia, Maryland, April 9. 1752*
> Runaway, last night, from the subscriber, a convict servant fellow, nam'd Jacob Parrott, born in the West of England, and bred in the family of a gentleman in Devonshire. He is about 22 years old, of a fair complection, active and strong, but short for his bulk; he is very handy at any thing, so that he may pretend to be a groom, coachman, gardiner, barber, lawyer, shoemaker, &c. His apparel was a

new felt hat, a new brown and an old grey wig, a new ash colour'd duffel great coat, with a large cape, and white metal buttens, a new darkish grey fine kersey coat, with a small black cape, and black button holes, with carved white metal buttons, double breasted short brown holland jacket, with wash'd yellow buttons, new leather breeches, two or three fine Irish linen shirts, white cotton stockings, and new footed grey yarn ditto, new pumps, and larger pewter buckles. He took with him a brown middle siz'd natural pacing horse, a good bridle, saddle and housing, with plenty of money, which 'tis supposed will soon be spent, he being a very drunken idle fellow, and a lover of dancing, singing, carding, racing, cock-fighting, &c. he will cringe to those he thinks his superiors, but is quarrelsome and abusive to others, in whose company he will brag, chatter, fight, curse, swear, &c. has a scar on his left-thumb, occasioned by a cut with a broad ax: All persons, especially women, are cautioned to beware of him, for he is a great cheat, and a notorious villain. Whoever secures him in any prison, &c so that he may be had again, shall be paid Forty Shillings, Pennsylvania currency, and besides that reward, any person that will bring him home, shall be paid his reasonable charges, &c. by me, his master. Hugh Jones.

N.B. All masters of vessels are forbid to carry him off.[20]

Convict servants who ran away in Virginia or Maryland not only had to contend with vigilant property owners, but also with the terrain. The intersecting rivers that facilitated the transport of crops and iron could make travel on foot extremely difficult. But if the runaway could steal a canoe or small boat, the creeks and rivers could actually aid his or her escape. In an attempt to evade detection, some convicts took extra clothing or even a wig to help them change their appearance. A few smart convicts stole tools of their trade from their owners to help them get started in their profession once they had reached a comfortable distance. Other runaways headed for ports, but even if they made it there, they would have had a difficult time securing passage back to Great Britain without any money or without being detected.[21]

A strange advertisement for a runaway convict placed by David Currie of Lancaster County appeared in the *Virginia Gazette* on July 3, 1752.[22] Currie describes the runaway, Sarah Knox, as being "of middle Size, a swarthy Complexion and has a short Nose, talks broad, and says she was born in *Yorkshire*." He adds, "She may go by the Name of *Sarah Howard, Wilson,* or something else, pretend to be a dancing Mistress, will make a great many Courtesies, and is a very deceitful insinuating Woman, and a great Lyar." Currie apparently had had enough of her, because he also stipulates that if anyone finds her qualified to teach dancing, or wants her as a servant, that person could purchase her five to six years of service that she had left on her term for 15 pounds currency.

By February of the following year, Currie had yet to find Knox, so he placed another advertisement in the *Pennsylvania*

Gazette.[23] But this time he offers more clues to her whereabouts by citing an extract from a letter that appeared in the *Virginia Gazette*.[24] The letter was written by someone living in Chester, Pennsylvania and gives an account of a doctor and surgeon by the name of Charles Hamilton who was going door to door selling various medicines. Even though Hamilton was carrying a pass signed by magistrates from Virginia and Maryland, the doctor was taken up and held anyway when some people suspected that he was actually a woman dressed in men's clothing, which indeed turned out to be the case. She confessed that she had been using the disguise for several years and said that her real name is Charlotte Hamilton. The letter goes on to say, "She is very bold, and can give no good Account of herself; says she is about Twenty-eight Years of Age, though she seems to be about Forty," and it advertises that she will be held in prison for a short time to see if anyone would appear to claim her. After reading this piece, Currie suspected that this doctor in disguise was Sarah Knox, but he was too late in reading it to take advantage of her detainment.

Runaway convicts could be quite dangerous. On September 7, 1738, the *American Weekly Mercury* carried a story about a coach maker named Evans who was found murdered in the woods.[25] Evans was traveling from Rappahannock to Hanover when he stopped at an inn for the night. Before retiring, he handed the innkeeper some money wrapped in a handkerchief for safekeeping. Evans left the inn the next day, but two days later a runaway convict was picked up and in his possession were Evans's handkerchief, his clothes, his horse, and a considerable sum of money. The convict, it turns out, had witnessed Evans handing his money over to the innkeeper and had followed him when he continued his journey the following day. After his capture, the convict was committed to the public jail in Williamsburg, Virginia and charged with "barbarously murdering Mr. *Evans.*"

In July 1773, Archibald Moffman, a soul-driver from Baltimore, got more than he bargained for when he purchased a group of convicts with the intention of reselling them for a profit farther inland.[26] He sold all but four of the convicts by the time he reached the town of Frederick and set out for Hagerstown to sell the rest. About two or three miles outside of Frederick, one of the convict servants complained of fatigue, so the party stopped under a tree along the main road. When Moffman decided that they needed to continue on their journey, the convicts refused to move. But then they all jumped up at once, threw Moffman backwards, dragged him into the woods, and cut his throat from ear to ear. They then stole his pocketbook and proceeded to stop at every tavern they met as they continued to travel over the mountain. At one of the taverns, a man who earlier had happened to spot the group asked them where their master was. The group claimed that he was refreshing himself just a little way behind them, but after the enquiring man rode a couple of miles back without meeting Moffman, he suspected murder. He notified the neighborhood, and the convicts were easily pursued and captured. The group was brought to the jail in Frederick, where they confessed their crime. This story caused quite a sensation at the time, for a number of newspapers from the Chesapeake all the way up to New Hampshire carried the story and followed up on it in later editions. All four convicts received a death sentence for their part in the murder, and they were executed in Frederick on October 22, 1773.

The Reaction of American Colonists

Given all of the accounts of convicts committing crime and running away, it should come as no surprise that the British policy of shipping criminals to America was not well received by colonists. Americans complained that Britain was using their land as a dumping ground for their undesirables in the name of helping the colonies with their labor shortage. A report printed in *The Boston News-Letter* in 1722 with the dateline, "London, Feb. 10" shows the British attitude that prevailed toward convict transportation: "Eighty five Felons have been lately ship'd off for our Colonies in America. Tho' we abound with those Vermin such Numbers of them are order'd for Transportation every Sessions, it is hoped in a little Time the Plantations there will be pretty well stock'd, tho' it were to be wish'd with honester People."[27] But such justifications did not sit well with Americans. Vocal protests by colonists caused some merchants to shy away from carrying convicts. In 1721, the *American Weekly Mercury* of Philadelphia reported that merchants were beginning to refuse to carry convicts to America despite the large sums of money being offered them to do so. The merchants contended that even though the convicts had helped planters who desperately needed their labor, the colonies complained bitterly about how the convicts had generally been corrupting their society.[28]

In *The Present State of Virginia* (1724), Hugh Jones discusses an early design to contain the convicts and prevent them from committing mischief in Virginia. The proposal was to create a penal colony that would function much like the Bridewell workhouse in London where convicts would be put to work producing hemp and flax. The colony would be designated as its own county and be appropriately named "Hempshire." But the project never went anywhere, although Jones says that he still thought it was a good idea and that it could help supply the navy with needed cordage.[29]

In an attempt to curtail if not put an end to the import of British convicts into their colonies, both Virginia and Maryland passed laws to regulate the convict trade. In 1722, Virginia passed an act that levied fees and put in place layers of bureaucracy so as to make it unprofitable for convict merchants to do business in its colony, but Jonathan Forward immediately petitioned to have the colonial act overturned and won. Maryland tried to pass a similar bill that year as well, but Lord Baltimore vetoed it based on the previous decision of the Privy Council.[30] Almost every time Virginia and Maryland tried to pass laws that placed limits on convict transportation, the British government overturned them. In 1725, provincial authorities in Annapolis tried to block Forward's agents from unloading their convict cargo without securing a bond assuring the good behavior of its passengers. The agents, not willing to incur such an expense, were forced to take the prisoners back on board the ship. Once again, Forward complained to the authorities back in London, and once again they ruled that the Annapolis rules violated the terms of the Transportation Act.[31] The only act regulating convict transportation that passed British scrutiny was a Maryland law that quarantined convict ships that arrived with sick felons on board. Virginia tried to pass similar acts in

1767 and 1772, but both failed on grounds that they contained defects in their administration.[32]

Displeasure over convict transportation set the stage for a sarcastic exchange in 1752 between the *Virginia Gazette* and the *Maryland Gazette* about the arrival of convicts into the Chesapeake region. The *Virginia Gazette* reported that a ship carrying 150 convicts bound for Maryland had arrived in the James River and added, "We *congratulate* the Marylanders on the safe arrival of these recruits!" But *The Maryland Gazette* shot back, "Thanks for this Virginia compliment! But the author, it is probable, did not think of the old trite proverb—'The pot should not call the kettle black.' It is said that Captain Gracey, who brought these recruits into the Patowmack, sold the chief part of them on the *south* side of that river."[33]

The increase in newspaper stories at the middle of the century about transported convicts committing crimes in America was accompanied by editorials complaining about Britain's policy. On May 9, 1751, Benjamin Franklin published one of the more biting critiques of convict transportation in his *Pennsylvania Gazette*.[34] Franklin begins on the front page with a series of reports about serious crimes committed in Maryland and Virginia. The accounts include a story about a gang of thieves that broke into a Maryland home and then later that same night robbed a store of goods worth 200 pounds. Other stories involve two separate cases of robbery, a gang of roving bandits in Virginia that boldly robbed its victims in daylight, and a forger who turned to crime after coming under the influence of transported convicts owned by his reputable Maryland family. Franklin also adds a letter from Maryland about how two transported criminals presumably murdered a sea captain and two other seamen.

Benjamin Franklin's *Pennsylvania Gazette*.
(Source: Wikipedia Commons, http://commons.wikimedia.org)

Franklin follows these criminal accounts with an open letter that begins, "By a Passage in one of your late Papers, I understand that the Government at home will not suffer our mistaken Assemblies to make any Law for preventing or discouraging the Importation of Convicts from Great Britain, for this kind Reason, '*That such Laws are against the Publick Utility, as they tend to prevent the* IMPROVEMENT *and* WELL PEOPLING *of the Colonies.*" Franklin continues, "Such a tender *parental* Concern in our *Mother Country* for the *Welfare* of her Children, calls aloud for the highest *Returns* of Gratitude and Duty." He goes on to propose a fair exchange for Britain's convicted felons:

> In some of the uninhabited Parts of these Provinces,
> there are Numbers of these venomous Reptiles we
> call RATTLE-SNAKES; Felons-convict from the
> Beginning of the World: These, whenever we meet
> with them, we put to Death, by Virtue of an old Law,
> *Thou shalt bruise his Head.* But as this is a
> sanguinary Law, and may seem too cruel; and as
> however mischievous those Creatures are with us,
> they may possibly change their Natures, if they were
> to change the Climate; I would humbly propose,
> that this general Sentence of *Death* be changed for
> *Transportation.*

Franklin ends the letter:

> Now all Commerce implies *Returns*; Justice
> requires them: There can be no Trade without
> them. And *Rattle Snakes* seem the most *suitable*
> *Returns* for the *Human Serpents* sent to us by our
> *Mother* Country. In this, however, as in every other
> Branch of Trade, she will have the Advantage of us.
> She will reap *equal* Benefits without equal Risque of

the Inconveniences and Dangers. For the *Rattle-Snake* gives Warning before he attempts his Mischief; which the Convict does not.

But such complaints from American colonists had little effect. The British government and convict merchants resisted any effort by the American colonies to interfere with the convict trade. There was too much social benefit for Britain and too much money to be made by convict merchants to allow the colonies to get in the way of such an expedient means of punishing criminals. And even though Americans could be quite vocal in their opposition to convict transportation, the complaints generally came from those who did not employ convict labor. Editorials about the practice generally appeared in northern newspapers, and the most vocal opposition came from colonies that received few if any convicts from Britain. The fact is that planters who needed cheap labor for their plantations to function continued to buy up felons almost as fast as they landed, and this market force was too strong for arguments based on principle.[35]

Moll Flanders and Moll King

While the American press criticized convict transportation, British writers supported it, and none were perhaps as enthusiastic as Daniel Defoe was in writing his novel *The Fortunes and Misfortunes of the Famous Moll Flanders*. Moll Flanders is the best-known character in literature to have been shipped to America. In many ways, her story offers the most complete account of the life of a transported convict, even if she is only a fictional character and her experience was far from the norm of most transported felons.

Moll Flanders fits into an admittedly short line of both fiction and nonfiction tales involving convict transportation. Most stories about transportation appeared in British and American newspapers. Execution broadsides and collected criminal accounts occasionally included a criminal who had been transported. A few memoirs written by ex-convicts also appeared, but the discussion of their experience as a transported convict usually made up only a small part of the work. Sweeney Todd, the "Demon Barber of Fleet Street," is perhaps the most famous fictional example from the 19th century, when he begins his bloody rampage upon his return to England after being unjustly transported to Australia.

In Defoe's novel, Moll Flanders first learns about convict transportation during a conversation with her mother-in-law after Moll had moved to Virginia with her husband to start a business. To Moll's surprise, her mother-in-law informs her that the colony is filled with productive citizens who first came to America as prisoners: "many a *Newgate* Bird becomes a great Man, and we have, *continued she*, several Justices of the Peace, Officers of the Train Bands, and Magistrates of the Towns they live in, that have been burnt in the Hand."[36] Moll's mother-in-law then goes on to reveal that she herself is a former convict by showing Moll the burn on her hand. This positive account of convict transportation contrasts with the mother-in-law's description of Newgate Prison:

> HERE my Mother-in-Law ran out in a long account
> of the wicked practices in that dreadful Place, and

> how it ruin'd more young People than all the Town
> besides; and Child, *says my Mother*, perhaps you
> may know little of it, or it may be have heard
> nothing about it, but depend upon it, *says she*, we
> all know here, that there are more Thieves and
> Rogues made by that one Prison of *Newgate*, than
> by all the Clubs and Societies of Villains in the
> Nation; 'tis that cursed Place, *says my Mother*, that
> half Peoples this Colony.[37]

Through these conversations Moll, who was born in Newgate Prison, realizes that her mother-in-law is actually her true mother and that her husband is in reality her brother. The shock of this information sends Moll back to England, where she eventually falls into a life of crime.

Defoe himself dabbled as a convict merchant in 1688. He made a tidy profit from the venture, but he never pursued it any further. He published *Moll Flanders* in 1722, four years after the passage of the Transportation Act, but the novel takes place back around the time when Defoe tried his own hand at convict transportation.[38] The mother-in-law's characterization of Virginia being well-populated with convicts, then, is anachronistic to the time period of the novel, since a significant convict population did not develop in the Chesapeake until after Britain institutionalized convict transportation in 1718. In other details, however, Defoe was more accurate.

One of the possible sources of inspiration for the character of Moll Flanders is Moll King, a notorious pickpocket and thief who worked for Jonathan Wild.[39] Just as Moll Flanders protects her identity by telling the reader at the beginning of the book that the name she is using is a pseudonym, Moll King used many aliases throughout her criminal career, among them Mary Godman, Golston, Golstone, Gilstone, Goulston, Gouldstone, Gouldston, Godfrey, Godson, and Bird. All of these aliases make it difficult to trace the history of Moll King accurately, and most likely they confounded the authorities back then as well. The first time we know with certainty that Moll King appeared before the Old Bailey was in 1693.[40] Under the name Mary King, alias Godman, she was found guilty of housebreaking and sentenced to branding. The name "Mary King" appears in the Old Bailey records several times before and after this time, but it is impossible to determine which, if any of them, is actually Moll King.

Moll King was also transported to the American colonies several times under various names. In December 1718, she was indicted under the name of Mary Goulston for stealing a gold watch and chain and was sentenced to death.[41] She turned out to be pregnant, however, and after she had her baby was transported on the *Susannah & Sarah* under the name of Gilstone in 1719. King quickly turned around and returned to London, but soon after she arrived back, Jonathan Wild threatened to expose her as a returned convict if she didn't join his criminal empire and begin stealing for him. After about a year of operating under Wild's thumb, King was caught robbing dress materials from a house on June 14, 1721. During this time, Defoe both wrote and edited newspaper stories about Moll King's return from transportation and about her criminal exploits, and her story very likely gave Defoe the idea of writing a novel about a female criminal. For the robbery of the dress materials, King was transported on the *Gilbert* under the name of Mary Goulstone in 1722. Once again she returned to England, was caught, and was transported on the *Alexander* under the name of Mary Godson in 1723. Accompanying her on this convict voyage was the colorful Sarah Wells, a.k.a. "Callico Sarah."* After Moll King was transported this third time, the certainty of her history becomes muddled once more.

After Moll Flanders returns to England from Virginia, she becomes a successful criminal, but she is caught trying to rob a plate from a goldsmith and finds herself in Newgate Prison with a death sentence hanging over her head. Moll, however, appeals her sentence and receives a conditional pardon of transportation for 14 years. Moll's early experience in Virginia gives her great advantages. Before casting off for America, Moll has her governess buy tools and other items necessary for setting up a plantation, because she knows that these items will cost twice as much to procure once she arrives at her destination. Upon landing in America, she also learns that her deceased mother has left her a considerable sum of money, as well as a yearly stipend from the family plantation in Virginia. With the help of a Quaker, Moll sets up a prosperous plantation and even purchases a female English servant and a black African slave. Few, if any, transported convicts enjoyed such advantages and treatment.

At the book's conclusion, Moll discovers that by turning her energies to forging a productive life in the colonies, she can atone for a previously wicked one. The Preface to the novel maintains:

---

* For the background of Sarah Wells, see Chapter 4, pages 112-114.

> [Moll's] application to a sober Life, and industrious
> management at last in *Virginia*, with her
> Transported spouse, is a Story fruitful of
> Instruction, to all the unfortunate Creatures who
> are oblig'd to seek their Re-establishment abroad;
> whether by the Misery of Transportation, or other
> Disaster; letting them know, that Diligence and
> Application have their due Encouragement, even in
> the remotest Parts of the World, and that no Case
> can be so low, so despicable, or so empty of
> prospect, but that an unwearied Industry will go a
> great way to deliver us from it, will in time raise the
> meanest Creature to appear again in the World, and
> give him a new Cast for his Life. [42]

The entire novel, then, is framed by convict transportation, and the narrative works to argue its benefits. Moll's experiences in America and her improvement at the end makes Defoe's novel one of the most spirited and extended defenses of convict transportation ever written.

Returning to England

That Moll King was able to go back and forth across the Atlantic so many times after being transported was unusual. Most of the convicts sent to America stayed in America. Still, some made it back to their home country, legally or illegally. Those who escaped, ran away, or purchased their freedom soon after landing in America had a greater likelihood of making the trip back across the Atlantic than convicts who ran away after several years had passed or who finished their terms of service.

Convicts who belonged to criminal gangs were also more likely to return to England.[43]

John Poulter, who wrote a best-selling book that gave a full account of his criminal career and exposed the common practices of criminals in the 18th century, describes the method by which convicts returned from transportation:

> After they are in any Part of North *America*, the general Way is this, just before they go on board a Ship, their Friend or Accomplices purchase them their Freedom from the Merchant or Captain that belongs to the said Ship, for about ten Pound Sterling, some gives more and some less; then the Friend of the Convict or Convicts, get a Note from the Merchant, or Captain, that the Person is free to go unmolested when the Ships arrive between the Capes of *Virginia*, where they please.[44]

Once the convicts secured their freedom from the captain of the ship, they then looked for another ship that would take them back to England. Poulter maintains that convicts almost never returned on the same ship that brought them to America. The risk of taking a felon back across the Atlantic would have been too great for convict merchants. The British government prohibited them from helping any convict to return to England, and if they were ever caught doing so, it would have jeopardized their highly profitable business. There were plenty of other captains, though, who were willing to take paying passengers back to England. Convicts who did not have enough money to pay for their passage would look for opportunities to work on board a ship that was heading back overseas.

Bound with an Iron Chain

If prisoners could not secure their freedom upon arrival in America, Poulter says, they would run away from their master, and "lay in the Woods by Day, and travel by Night for *Philadelphia, New York*, or *Boston*, in which Place no Questions are asked them." Poulter goes on to claim that the ease by which convicts could return from transportation "encourages a great many to commit Robberies more than they would, because they say they do not mind Transportation, it being but four or five Months Pleasure, for they can get their Freedom and come home again." This nonchalant attitude toward the punishment showed up in the trial of Bampfylde-Moore Carew, when he was sentenced to transportation. After the judge passed sentence and told Carew that he would now *"proceed to a hotter Country,"* the convict:

> enquired into what Climate, and being told
> *Maryland*, he with great Composure made a critical
> Observation on the Pronunciation of that Word,
> implying, that he apprehended it ought to be
> pronounced *Merryland*, and added, it would save
> him Five Pounds for his Passage, as he was very
> desirous of seeing that Country.[45]

After landing in America, Carew escaped just as he was being sold to some planters. He was eventually caught, and as punishment the captain had him flogged with a cat-o'-nine-tails and secured an iron collar around Carew's neck to prevent him from escaping again.

Any felon returning to England had to remain in hiding, because if he or she were ever caught, the convict could receive an automatic death sentence. The government did not make it easy for returned convicts to go undetected. The reward for identifying and turning in a returned criminal was substantial, and Jonathan Wild took full advantage of this reward system.[46] John Filewood was one such convict who fell under Wild's tight grip. Wild pocketed the 40-pound reward after helping to convict Filewood for returning early from a 14-year transportation sentence. Before his execution, Filewood said to the Ordinary of Newgate that "he died for the Fault of the Planter in America he was sold to; for he invited him, for a Sum of Money, to accept of his Liberty, and when he had his Freedom, the Love of England was natural."[47]

But even with the reward offered by the government, prosecuting returned convicts was apparently quite difficult if one did not have the kind of resources that Wild had at his disposal. *The Virginia Gazette* contended:

> It is certain Numbers do return from
> Transportation; but it being so much Trouble to
> bring them down to the Old Bailey, prove them to
> be the Persons transported, and that did the Fact
> transported for, that People don't care for the
> Trouble of it; especially since the Trying of them for
> the Fact transported for, is too often attended with
> great Trouble and Expence, that poor People are
> scarce able to support it, by which Means Rogues
> often escape.[48]

Notably, convicts who were caught returning to England never showed up in advertisements for runaways in American newspapers.[49] There could be several reasons why this is the case. Most likely, those who ran away from their masters never made it back to England. Convicts needed some combination of money, connections with captains or sailors, and an appearance that did not draw suspicion that they were escaped servants in order to travel back to their homeland. The longer they stayed in America, the less likely these resources were available to them. Convicts who found freedom after their ship encountered problems at sea through shipwreck, piracy, or mutiny were more likely to return to England. But because they escaped before they could be sold in America, advertisements for their capture did not run in colonial newspapers. Another reason convicts caught returning to England did not show up in runaway ads could be that they were either skillful in avoiding detection once they returned, or the methods of detecting them in England were in reality inadequate.

Samuel Ellard was one of the convicts who defied the odds and returned to England. Ellard grew up in Spitalfields and was apprenticed to a butcher.[50] He completed his time as an apprentice and worked in the Spitalfields Market for various people until he was arrested on March 9, 1741 for robbing a cheese shop owned by William Shipman. The night of the robbery, Ellard went behind the counter of Shipman's shop and pulled out 18s. 9d. from the till, but he was spotted by a neighbor who cried out, "Stop Thief! Shipman!" Upon hearing the cries, Shipman seized Ellard, who put up a great struggle, but another neighbor came to Shipman's aid, and the two dragged Ellard to the magistrate.

Shipman and two neighbors, Elizabeth Holmes and John King, testified against Ellard at his trial, and Ellard was found guilty and sentenced to transportation. He later claimed that he was "in Liquor, and did it at the Instigation of a young Fellow a Sailor who was going to Sea."

Ellard had run into trouble before. In May 1736, he and Christopher Freeman were accused of committing theft. Freeman had grabbed a quantity of linen items that Elizabeth Exton had been hired to wash. A neighbor heard Exton's cries after she realized that her laundry had been taken, and he assisted her by grabbing hold of Freeman. While the two scuffled with one another, Ellard appeared and gave encouragement to Freeman by shouting, "Strike him, punch him in the Guts." Just as another neighbor arrived to help, Freeman handed the bundle to Ellard, who turned to run away. Ellard was quickly caught and brought to the constable, and Freeman was captured a couple of days later.

At their trial, Ellard claimed that Freeman simply handed him the bundle during the ruckus and that he never tried to run away. He also arranged to have several people testify that he was at the Butchers-Arms while the robbery was taking place, and he produced a number of other witnesses to speak to his character. Consequently, Ellard was acquitted. Freeman, on the other hand, only managed to call one person to speak to his character, but even this witness could not give a good account of him. Freeman was found guilty and sentenced to death.

After Ellard was found guilty of robbing Shipman's cheese shop five years later, he was transported to Maryland along with 21 other convicts. He was sold to a planter who he later claimed treated him cruelly and was known to have whipped seven men to death. At the first opportunity, Ellard filled his pockets with food and ran away from his owner. He traveled 300 miles through the woods, covering 20 to 30 miles per day. At one point, he caught a squirrel and lived on it for three days. Several times he was caught and held as a runaway, even though he claimed that he had served out his time as a convict servant. But when nobody came forward to claim him, he was let go, and he continued on his journey.

Eventually, Ellard reached Philadelphia and then went to New York, where he found a job working on a ship. After six months he returned to Philadelphia and purchased passage back to London. After returning to England, he worked as a porter, carrying fruit for the vendors at Fleet Market. He worked for two years in this capacity, but he was suddenly taken early one morning and sent to Newgate Prison as a returned convict.

At his trial for returning from transportation, the two people who gave evidence against Ellard for robbing the cheese shop three years earlier, Elizabeth Holmes and John King, showed up in court again to testify against him. Curiously, neither one could positively identify Ellard. King said that Ellard had a fairer complexion than when he last saw him, but when he was asked whether the prisoner had one eye back then, as was the case now, the witness said yes, he believed he did. Contradicting what he would later tell the Ordinary of Newgate about being sold to a cruel planter, Ellard said at his trial that he worked as a butcher in America and that he lived very well, but that he "could not be easy till he returned to his native country."

Ellard was found guilty of returning early from transportation and was executed on November 7, 1744 at the age of about 30. He left behind a pregnant wife, whom he had married eight months before his arrest. She frequently visited him in prison and wept bitterly up until his death.

Chapter Nine: The End of Convict Transportation

If convicts harbored any desire to return to their homeland after escaping or serving out their time, their wishes were probably never realized. Most transported criminals never made it back to Great Britain. Escape was difficult, and the passage back was expensive. Even if convicts were able to return after serving out their seven- or 14-year term, they would have found it a very different place from when they were first transported. With a reputation that would have followed them back, and with few to no connections left in England, they would have had a difficult time finding employment and restarting their lives.

After Servitude

Convict transportation was modeled after indentured servitude, and indentured servants who completed their terms were entitled to "freedom dues." These dues came in the form of goods or money, and they were meant to help servants become planters themselves or establish their own business once they left the plantation. These dues could be negotiated as part of the signed contract between the indentured servant and the plantation owner, although in Virginia, indentured servants who completed their terms of service were entitled by law to a musket, 10 bushels of corn, and 30 shillings (or the equivalent value in goods). Women were entitled to 15 bushels of corn and 40 shillings. In 1748, the Virginia Legislature set freedom dues at a standard rate of £3.10s for both men and women.[1]

Whether convict servants were entitled to the same freedom dues as indentured servants was an open question. Through the early years of convict transportation, convict servants who served out their terms generally enjoyed the same right to collect freedom dues as indentured servants, and in 1749 the Virginia Legislature codified this practice into law. But four years later, the Legislature reversed its decision and specifically excluded convict servants from the legal right to receive freedom dues. The justification for the reversal was that convicts did not deserve the benefit. But this action not only made it much more difficult for felons to start new lives; it also removed one of the few incentives that encouraged them to serve out their terms and not run away.[2]

Few convicts who completed their terms would have been willing to stay on the plantation and hire themselves out to their old master, so planters would have had to replace them either with slaves, who were quite expensive, or with newly arrived transported convicts.[3] Some of the felons who completed their terms during the early years of convict transportation took advantage of cheap land and freedom dues to become planters themselves and even purchased their own indentured servants and convicts.[4] One contemporary observer noted:

> The Convicts that are transported here, sometimes
> prove very worthy Creatures, and entirely forsake

their former Follies; ... Several of the best Planters,
or their Ancestors, have, in the two Colonies [of
Maryland and Virginia], been originally of the
Convict Class, and therefore, are much to be prais'd
and esteem'd for forsaking their old Courses.[5]

But ex-convicts who became planters were the exception. Only
one out of every 10 indentured servants as a whole became an
independent farmer. Another one out of 10 became an artisan.
The remaining eight either died before they could collect their
freedom dues or became propertyless day laborers or vagrants,
or ended up in local almshouses. The odds of achieving success
in America would have been even lower for convict servants, and
only those transported early on in the century would have had
any chance of starting fresh lives in Maryland or Virginia.[6]

As land in the Chesapeake tidewaters became scarcer and
fewer resources were given to convicts after they completed their
service terms, many of them headed for new frontiers, which
were increasingly being settled by poorer people. White laborers
in general left the Chesapeake area as soon as they got the
chance, so laboring jobs increasingly fell to African slaves, who
were imported at a greater rate during this time in order to fill
the labor gap. As heavy labor came to be associated more and
more with black slavery, even the poorest whites would not
consider working such labor-intensive jobs. The overall lack of
opportunity and the degrading status of laboring jobs meant that
a white, agricultural proletariat—where convicts presumably
would have ended up after their terms ran out—never developed
in Maryland or Virginia. Most poor whites moved on to settle in

other areas of the country that offered more opportunity, and convicts were a part of this transient group.[7]

Criminals who finished their terms were eager to leave their wretched past behind them, so many of them changed their names when they moved to other parts of the country. Convicts were for the most part illiterate, and they left few documents that chronicled their lives. Given these circumstances, tracking the fates of individual criminals after they arrived in America is quite difficult, if not impossible. But a few contemporary accounts provide a general indication of what happened to convicts and where they went after they finished their sentence. One letter from Maryland printed in the *Pennsylvania Gazette* in 1751 claims, "I believe we have every Year three or four Hundred Felons imported here from *London*; and if, when their Times are out, or before, they were not many of them to move away to the *Northward*, and elsewhere, we should be over-run with them."[8] Most likely, convicts who served out their terms headed for the Pine Barrens of New Jersey or traveled west to the backcountry. Here, they faced few questions about their past and could set up their lives as they wished, even though the land was not as rich or as useful as in the tidewaters.[9] Others headed south to the Carolinas. A French traveler in 1765 noted that the area around Edenton, North Carolina "is the azilum of the Convicts that have served their time in virginia and maryland. when at liberty they all (or great part) Come to this part where they are not Known and setle here. it is a fine Country for poor people, but not for the rich."[10] Still others believed that once convicts completed their seven-year sentence, they became vagabonds and lived hand to mouth.[11]

In a 1767 letter to the *Maryland Gazette*, one writer defended importing convicts from Great Britain by citing how many of them reformed:

> [A] few Gentlemen seem very angry that Convicts are imported here at all, and would, if they could, ... prevent the People's buying them, and then of course they would not be brought in.
>
> I CONFESS, I am one of those who think a young Country cannot be settled, cultivated, and improved, without People of some Sort, and that it is much better for the Country to receive Convicts than Slaves ... The wicked and bad of them that come into this Province, mostly run away to the Northward, mix with their People, and pass for honest Men; whilst those, more innocent, and who came for very small Offenses, serve their Times out here, behave well, and become useful People.[12]

While this writer fancifully contends that bad convicts were spontaneously siphoned off to the north by running away, thereby leaving the good ones behind in the Chesapeake, he is correct in asserting that at least some convicts became productive members of society. And if the fate of several prisoners who were transported together on the *Pretty Patsy* in 1737 is any indication, transported criminals may have been more successful in establishing lives in America after serving out their terms than previously thought.

Jonathan Ady, Nicholas Baker, and George Gew were all convicted of theft back in England and transported to Maryland on the *Pretty Patsy*. Ady was found guilty of stealing money and a few assorted goods from Isaac Hone. At his trial, Ady pleaded, "I am a poor young Fellow, come out of the Country, and have not any one to stand my Friend. It will go hard with me I know: I beg for Transportation, though it should be for all my Life." Despite Ady's request, he was sentenced to death. While being held in Newgate Prison, the Ordinary reported that "Jonathan Adey was most of the Time sick, weak and infirm, complaining of Pains and Fevers, yet, excepting once or twice, he came constantly to Chapel." Five days before he was scheduled to die, Ady got his wish and was instead shipped to America for a term of 14 years after receiving a royal pardon.[13] Baker was indicted for stealing a pair of women's shoes and some black lace from Benjamin Noble. The jury devalued the goods to 10 shillings, so that he would receive a reduced sentence of transportation.[14] Gew was also found guilty along with James Moulding for stealing from the stable of John Scot a pig and a sack, which presumably was to be used to carry off the pig. Both Gew and Moulding received a sentence of transportation and joined the others on the *Pretty Patsy*.[15]

After finishing out their terms as convict servants, Ady, Baker, and Gew all lived prosperous lives in America. Ady married Rebecca York on March 27, 1743, and settled in Baltimore County, Maryland. Eight months after marrying, he leased 60 acres from *My Lady's Manor*, which he in turn sublet to someone else two years later. At this point, he was identified as a cooper and signed his own name on the mortgage document. He also served as a private during the American Revolution and had 11 children. Ady died in 1801 at the ripe old age of 82. Nicholas Baker married Martha Wood on January 4, 1741 in

Baltimore County, and they had seven children. Martha died by 1764, after which Nicholas married his second wife, Mary Gilbert, and the two of them had two daughters together. In 1768, Baker was listed as a planter and leased 125 acres of the *Hall's Plains* plantation from William Horton for 10 years. Baker died by May 6, 1774 in Harford County, Maryland. George Gew settled in present-day Montgomery County, and by 1747 he was married with children and owned a small farm. He died in 1772 and at that point had eight or nine children.[16] We unfortunately do not know the fate of James Moulding, Gew's partner in crime back in England.

Some convicts had inauspicious beginnings in America, but later put their lives back on track. Mary Slider was transported on the *Loyal Margaret* in 1726 for stealing two shirts from Thomas Shelton. One year after arriving in Maryland, she had a son born out of wedlock and was tried for bastardy. Apparently, this experience wasn't enough to dissuade her from such behavior, because she bore yet another child, a daughter, one year before her marriage in 1730 to Peter Majors. Together, the couple had three or four children, including the daughter born out of wedlock.[17] The experience of Anne Ambrose, who was also shipped on the *Loyal Margaret* in 1726, was similar to Mary Slider's. Ambrose was transported for theft and not long after she arrived had a son out of wedlock named William Ambrose. Years later, she was charged with bastardy in 1731 and then again in 1737. No father was named in any of these cases, but Charles Motherby, who was transported in 1723, was said to be the father of William. In 1749, William Ambrose was called to testify in proceedings against his father, but he failed to appear and was found in contempt of authority. In 1774, William purchased the *Rocky Point* plantation in Baltimore County, but at one point he moved away from Maryland. He died in 1802 in Bracken County, Kentucky.[18]

All of these cases show that it was at least possible for convicts to beat the odds and establish roots in America, so those who defended the punishment could justly claim that criminals who abandoned their past practices and applied themselves could lead productive lives in America. But the ones who fit this category were definitely the exception. In 1739, Governor William Gooch of Virginia complained to the British government that "The great number of Convicts yearly Imported here, and the impossibility of ever reclaiming them from their vicious habits have occasioned a vast Change to the Country."[19] Such objections from the American colonies were perhaps to be expected, but the practice also had its critics back in Great Britain.

Debates Back in England

Almost as soon as the Transportation Act was passed in 1718, convict transportation had its skeptics in England. While the courts saw the punishment as a welcome alternative to executing petty offenders, the public generally regarded the practice as less humanitarian and more severe than corporal punishment, which had commonly been used to punish petty criminals before the Act's passage.[20] But most of the critics in Great Britain were less concerned with severity of the punishment and instead focused on the failure of convict transportation to accomplish its goals.

Critiques in the British press frequently claimed that convict transportation failed to reform criminals and that many of them ended up returning to England before serving out their sentence. In *Lives of the Most Remarkable Criminals* (1735)—a collection of biographies about notorious British criminals—the author contends that the practice did not answer the purpose of preventing crime. He maintains that within a year, many of the convicts returned to England and were "Ten times more dangerous Rogues than they were before; and in the Plantations they generally behave themselves so ill, that many of them have refused to receive them."[21] The author holds up the use of convicts to man the oars of galleys in other nations as a model that Britain should follow, since this punishment subjected prisoners to hard labor yet effectively prevented them from committing any more crimes. He goes on to admit, however, that Great Britain has no need for galleys but believes that similar laborious work could be found that could benefit the country as a whole.

The argument that convict transportation failed to reform criminals was reinforced later in *Lives of the Most Remarkable Criminals* by no less than Ebenezer Ellison, "a notorious Irish thief." His biographical entry includes his last dying speech, where Ellison says, "we generally make a Shift to return after being transported, and are ten times greater Rogues than before, and much more cunning. Besides, I know it by Experience that some Hopes we have of finding Mercy when we are tried, or after we are condemned, is always a great Encouragement to us."[22] It is hard to argue with a criminal who claims that convict transportation does not have any effect on changing the behavior of those within his profession.

Some critics contended that transportation did not go far enough in instilling terror into criminal offenders. George Ollyffe in 1731 was troubled by the fact that even though convict transportation was supposed to rid "the Nation of its offensive Rubbish, without taking away their Lives, greater Numbers still gather."[23] He proposes a more systematic application of hard labor in order to "promote the most sharp and lasting Terror." He envisions prisoners working to defray the costs of their confinement, while "watchful Inspectors ... drive them on in their Work with the utmost Severity" until they determine that the convicts have been sufficiently punished for their crime. He also embraces the idea of either transporting vagrants and beggars to the colonies and then selling them off as slaves, or sending them to work in galleys to help guard the British seas and forts.

In an essay added to the end of *Ways and Means Whereby His Majesty May Man His Navy*, Thomas Robe wonders why convicts needed to be sent overseas to perform work when they could be made to do so in Great Britain.[24] He proposes stripping those who would normally be transported down to their waist and then confining them in workhouses, where they would be made to work in iron forges or in stone quarries. He adds that at night these felons should be manacled and during the day fettered at the ankles. Female felons, on the other hand, should be kept in hospitals and treated similarly—"only not strip to the Waste as the Men"—and be employed to card wool or wind yarn. Those who refuse to work in such a capacity, he goes on to suggest, should be exchanged two for one to liberate fellow countrymen who have been taken as slaves in foreign countries.

But despite all of this criticism, convict transportation also had its supporters. One such advocate was the merchant Joshua Gee, who in *The Trade and Navigation of Great-Britain Considered* proposes expanding convict transportation to include all people who could not find ways to support themselves in Great Britain.[25] He justifies this position by contending that many of the convicts who were shipped to the American colonies have "come to severe Repentance for their past Lives, and become very industrious." Gee suggests that anyone who finishes out their term should receive 100 acres of land or more from the government and then be charged rent for the land in the form of hemp or flax, which could be used to help supply the Royal Navy. He sees his proposal as a win-win situation for both Great Britain and the convicts, since "they would marry young, increase, and multiply and supply themselves with every Thing they want from us, but their Food, by which Means those vast Tracts of Land now waste will be planted, and secured from the Danger we apprehend of the *French* over-running them."

Criminal biographies and newspaper stories that recounted the early return of transported felons to England, along with debates in the British press about the efficacy of convict transportation, gave the public the impression that this experimental form of punishment was a failed policy.[26] In 1752, the British government took the criticism seriously when Parliament began exploring alternatives to sending its convicts across the ocean. Some of the suggestions it came up with included making the prisoners work in the dockyards, toil in the local coal mines, or repair and maintain roads. The government even considered exchanging convicts for English slaves being held in Morocco. But none of these proposals ever took hold, and the prevailing arguments were that some of the measures would end up displacing honest workmen who currently labored in positions that presumably would be handed over to convicts.[27] In the end, convict transportation was too convenient of a punishment for the British government to abandon. But England would eventually find out just how dependent on the practice it had become.

Closing Stages

Beginning in 1770, English courts handed out fewer transportation sentences to its convicted felons, and the growing unease in the American colonies over British rule and its use as a destination for convicts probably had something to do with this trend. Rather than send criminals across the ocean to America, local authorities instead started reviving the use of benefit of clergy, imposing terms of imprisonment on offenders, and instituting hard labor at home. Even so, convict transportation remained an important element of the British criminal justice system.[28]

John Stewart assumed the position of Contractor for Transports to the Government in 1763, but his tenure came to an end with his death in 1772. Naturally, Stewart's business partner, Duncan Campbell, applied for the vacant post. Campbell was descended from the Glasgow family of Scotland. With his marriage in 1753 to the daughter of a wealthy Jamaica planter, he became prominent in the West Indies trade, where he owned both plantations and ships.* During the time that Campbell and Stewart held the government contract, they made a tremendous amount of money. They averaged a profit of six pounds per convict and enjoyed an enormous 70 percent excess profit per freight space. Campbell assumed that he would automatically step in to the position of Contractor for Transports and continue to receive five pounds from the government for every convict he shipped, just as all the others who held this position had in the past.[29]

Campbell was mistaken. The profits that could be realized in selling convicts in America were so great that groups of merchants were already lined up at the Treasury offering to transport felons at their own expense. Since the Treasury no longer needed to pay merchants to take prisoners off the government's hands, Campbell's application was denied. With Campbell's failure to win the government contract, the position of "Contractor for Transports to the Government" was essentially dissolved, and Stewart turned out to be the last person to hold the official post. But even though Campbell did not secure the government subsidy, he continued to make a fortune exporting convicts and remained an influential player in the business.[30]

Market competition may have torn down the original model for how the British government administered convict transportation, but looming on the horizon was an event that would permanently end the entire enterprise: the American Revolution. In the spring of 1775, American ports began refusing entry to ships from England after hostilities had broken out

---

* One of Campbell's ships, the *Bethia*, was later renamed the *Bounty* of Captain Bligh fame.

between the two lands, and on July 4 a convict ship was denied entry to America and was forced to return back to England.[31] This action brought convict transportation to an abrupt halt and marked the beginning of the end for Britain's convenient punishment.

At first, the British government thought that the American rebellion would not last long and that the transportation of convicts to the colonies would soon resume. In May 1776, the Solicitor-General declared before the British Parliament that "when tranquility was restored to America, the usual mode of transportation might be again adopted." His prediction never came to pass. The last known ship to empty its cargo of convicts on American shores successfully was the *Jenny*, which arrived in the James River from Newcastle in April 1776, but at this point well over a year had passed since any other convict ship had landed in America.[32] On December 11, 1776, after America had announced its independence from England in July, a group of convicts who had initially boarded the *Tayloe* for transportation to America were pardoned on condition that they join the British army.[33] Now, rather than work for the colonists in America, convicts would be used to fight against them.

While it cannot be said that convict transportation was a direct cause of the American Revolution, it certainly helped validate in the minds of American colonists their status as second-class citizens under British rule. When Samuel Johnson famously quipped in 1769 that the American colonists "are a race of convicts, and ought to be thankful for any thing we allow them short of hanging," such a sentiment would not have sat well with Americans.[34] After all, the British government was responsible for populating America with its unwanted convicted felons against the wishes of many colonists. And if Great Britain could forcibly dump its criminals and other undesirables in America, what did that say about how it viewed its relationship with the colonies?

After the American Revolution ended the transportation trade, convict firms either closed down or, if they were lucky enough to have been diversified, shifted their operations over to other lines of work. The Bristol-based convict firm of Stevenson, Randolph & Cheston dissolved and closed down its Baltimore office once the American convict trade dried up.[35] British convict firms were not the only ones that had to reorganize their operations. American plantations were also forced to reconsider how they did business after the Revolution. Much of the American economy had relied on the cheap labor provided by British convicts, indentured servants, and African slaves, and the ideal of equality that informed the American Revolution now conflicted with these economic structures. Whereas before the war free immigrants arriving in America were by far the minority, after the war they became the majority. Nearly two-thirds of all immigrants who came to America after the Revolution were free, compared to only about a quarter before this time. Slaves and indentured servants continued to make up the difference until importing African slaves was finally banned in 1808.[36]

The American Revolution may have brought freedom to the colonies, but it did not necessarily mean freedom for convict servants. Even though the Revolution put an end to the British practice of transporting criminals to America, runaway ads for convicts continued to run in American newspapers well after 1776. Despite the divorce between the countries, British convicts were still bound to serve out their terms in America.

Convict Hulks

The sudden end of convict transportation threw Great Britain's criminal justice system into chaos. With no place to send its seemingly never-ending stream of convicted felons, and with no backup plan in place, England saw its prisons and jails quickly fill beyond capacity. The British Parliament needed to act quickly before this crisis of prison overcrowding turned into a catastrophe.[37]

In 1775, Parliament charged William Eden, the Home Office secretary, with finding a solution to the prison crisis. Eden estimated that England would need to find new accommodations for 1,000 convicts a year, and since the country's prisons and jails were already overcrowded, there was literally no place to put them. Both Eden and the British Parliament assumed that the American market for convicts would open up again at the conclusion of the war with America. With this belief in mind, Eden proposed creating a system of prison hulks by docking in English waters ships that had been originally used to transport convicts. These ships would serve as temporary places of confinement for England's prisoners until they could be transferred once again to America. Eden immediately implemented his idea, so starting in 1775, convicts were housed on the *Censor* and *Justitia* prison hulks at Woolwich and were put to work dredging the Thames, building docks, and constructing an arsenal.[38]

Soon after placing the convicts in the newly created hulks, Eden presented two bills before Parliament: one to authorize for two years what was already taking place—namely the housing of convicts on board the ships and the use of their labor on public works projects—and one that called for the erection of a penitentiary. Even though convicts were already residing in prison hulks on the Thames, passage of a bill authorizing the practice was far from certain. George Johnstone, a former governor of West Florida, argued against the hulk bill and contended that criminals should be sent to the West Indies or Canada instead. Johnstone's argument was countered by those who pointed out that colonies that had remained loyal to the British government should not be punished by having convicts forcibly dumped on them. And unlike Maryland and Virginia, his critics continued, these areas had little need for cheap convict labor, especially in the West Indies where there was already an abundance of slave labor. A market for convict servants simply did not exist in these other colonies.[39]

In the end, resistance to the hulk bill was not enough to prevent its approval by Parliament in May 1776, although some doubt about the success of this scheme lingered. During the same session, Parliament passed a provision empowering every county in England to create a house of correction. Convicts under sentence of death could then be granted mercy and be sentenced to hard labor at these institutions for a term not exceeding 10 years, during which time they should "be fed and sustained with bread, and any coarse or inferior food and water or small beer." Women and men judged incapable of carrying out hard labor due to age or health were also to be confined in the houses of correction but would be excused from performing laborious tasks.[40]

Parliament did not pass Eden's proposed penitentiary bill until three years after it approved the hulk bill. This later bill not only authorized building a new penitentiary, but it extended the use of prison hulks for another five years. It also set terms of confinement for prisoners on board the hulks: Offenders liable to seven years transportation could be sentenced to not less than one year or more than five, and offenders sentenced to transportation for 14 years could have their terms commuted to seven years on board the prison hulks.[41]

After passing the first hulk bill, Parliament decided that the prison hulks at Woolwich needed someone to manage them. In the summer of 1776 it awarded the position of Superintendent of the Thames Area to Duncan Campbell, who years earlier had failed to land the position of Contractor for Transports. Despite his failure in securing the Contractor position, Campbell maintained influential friends in the House of Commons, and they handed him this new position as compensation for the loss of his convict transportation business to the war in America. Campbell was now responsible for the welfare of 510 male convicts housed in the prison hulks along the Thames.[42]

**The *Discovery* at Deptford served as a convict hulk
from 1818 to 1834, when it was scrapped.**
(Source: Wikipedia Commons, http://commons.wikimedia.org)

Prisoners called the hulks "floating academies," and they
were lodged in the lower decks of the ship, while officers were
housed in the stern. The above-deck forecastle of the ship was
reserved for the sick, so that breezes could carry away the
malodorous and infected air that emanated from them. During
the day, prisoners were removed from the ship and put to work.
At night, prisoners slept side by side on wooden platforms
measuring six feet long and four feet wide. The two prisoners
shared a single straw pad and one blanket, both of which often
carried vermin. Just as they did on convict ships, gaol fever and
other diseases rapidly ran through the prisoners housed on the
hulks. Of the 632 convicts who were confined on board the hulks

between August 1776 and April 1778, 176 died. During the first 20 years of the hulks' existence, around 8,000 prisoners were housed on them and almost 2,000 of them died. This 25 percent death rate essentially doubled the 12-14 percent death rate of the convict ships. But as bad as conditions were on the hulks, had Eden not come up with the idea of housing convicts in them, prison conditions on land could very well have deteriorated to an even greater degree, if such a state can even be imagined.[43]

Despite the original intention of prison hulks serving as a temporary expedient to prison overcrowding in England, in the end they remained part of the British criminal justice system for the next 80 years.*

One Last Gasp and the Australian Solution

The British criminal justice system had become addicted to convict transportation. The government had come to rely on the low-cost expedient of transporting its unwanted prisoners to America, and now it had trouble finding alternatives. The temporary solution of housing convicts on prison hulks only had a short-term impact on relieving prison overcrowding, because before long the hulks were filled with prisoners as well. And once the British lost the war in America, they also lost any hope of once again using the American colonies as a means of emptying its jails and prisons. Years went by as Parliament resisted expensive solutions, such as building newer and bigger

---

* In fact, the prominence of the hulks in the criminal justice system helped them captured the attention of Charles Dickens. In the opening of *Great Expectations*, Pip encounters Abel Magwitch, who has recently escaped from a prison hulk.

penitentiaries. The government tried sending convicts to West Africa, but this test ultimately failed. It even considered increasing use of the death penalty. The temporary prison hulks and their dreadful living conditions began to look like they were going to become permanent.[44]

In the summer of 1783, the British government decided to push the issue of convict transportation with America, since no treaty or law specifically banned the practice.[45] It hired George Moore, a London merchant, to transport 143 prisoners to America by offering him 500 pounds and whatever profits he could receive from selling the convicts. Moore established contact with a prominent merchant in Maryland, George Salmon, who believed that the two could make a fortune selling convicts once again in America. Salmon was confident that with no law prohibiting the import of criminals and with his significant political connections, he could overcome any potential legal obstacles to the scheme. Even so, George Moore and George Salmon decided to disguise their human cargo as indentured servants and list the ship that was to transport them—which was fittingly called the *George*—as headed to Nova Scotia. That way, once the ship landed in Maryland, they could claim that it did so in distress, even if the true identity of its cargo were discovered. They even changed the name of the ship to the *Swift* to help further obscure its true purpose.

The new name of the ship did not turn out to be nearly as appropriate as its original one. Soon after the *Swift* departed, the convicts rebelled, took over the ship, and ran it aground on the Sussex coast. About one-quarter of the convicts escaped, although some of them were caught and consequently executed.

After spending a month in Portsmouth, the *Swift* started out once again for Maryland, this time with only 104 prisoners. The *Swift* finally arrived in Baltimore on Christmas Eve, and as planned, the captain informed the authorities that the ship had run out of provisions and was forced to cut short its voyage to Nova Scotia. What they had not planned was that news of the hoax had reached Maryland before their arrival. Members of the state assembly in Annapolis were outraged when they first learned of the plan, but when they officially received word on Christmas day that the ship had indeed landed, they were already on recess for the holiday and could not take up legislation to block the ship's entry.

The sale of the convicts went ahead as planned, although demand was low. Only 30 of those on board were sold by mid-January, and several of the convicts who were purchased had already run away from their masters. Moore and Salmon managed to sell most of the convicts by the spring, but they incurred serious losses after having to provide food, clothing, and medicine for those who languished on board the ship until they could be unloaded. Furthermore, the prisoners sold for low prices, and the planters with convicts who ran away refused to honor their debts to the two sellers.

Despite these troubles, Moore attempted another voyage with 179 convicts in April 1784. Once again, the prisoners rebelled. The ship finally made it across the Atlantic after a long trip, but unlike the first time, no American port would allow it to enter. The convicts were finally unloaded in British Honduras, which was none too happy to receive them.

Hugh Williamson, a Congressional representative from North Carolina, said of the attempts to transport convicts to America, "Perhaps a greater insult to any Nation could hardly have been offered."[46] To erase any legal ambiguity about shipping criminals to American soil, Congress passed a law in 1788 that specifically prohibited importing convicts from Europe, and the era of convict transportation to America officially came to an end.

After the botched attempts to re-establish the practice of transporting convicts to America, Great Britain was now on its own in finding an alternative. Back in 1779, Sir Joseph Banks, a naturalist who had accompanied Captain James Cook on an expedition through the South Pacific, had recommended New South Wales as a suitable destination for convicts. But the estimated cost of 30 pounds per head to transport prisoners there—six times what it had cost the government to transport them to America—quickly put the proposal to rest. Now in a desperate spot, the British government was forced to reconsider its decision. In August 1786, Parliament approved sending convicts halfway around the world to New South Wales.[47]

The first fleet of 11 ships carrying 548 male and 188 female convicts set sail from England to Australia in May 1787. The experiences of these convicts were very different from those of their American cousins. After the Australian convicts landed, they were put to work in a penal colony in Botany Bay. Convicts sent to America, of course, were never placed in penal colonies. Australian prisoners were also under tighter control than the American convicts. They fell under the direct supervision of the government and were subject to discipline, including the use of chain gangs, convict barracks, slop clothing, and forced labor. They could not buy their freedom, as convicts shipped to America could. Convict servants in America were essentially treated like indentured servants, so they could basically blend in with the general population. In Australia, convicts and indentured servants were separate entities.[48]

Many believed that transportation to Australia would mean the end of the prison hulks in the Thames, but that did not happen. Convicts sentenced to transportation to Australia were first housed in the hulks to await their passage. If the hulks were too crowded to receive the transports, then the prisoners were sent to Newgate or other surrounding prisons to wait.[49]

More than 160,000 convicts were sent to Australia—more than triple the number sent to colonial America—before the practice was officially abolished in 1850. The first four years of transporting convicts to New South Wales cost the British government a staggering 574,592 pounds. If Parliament had known the cost to establish a penal colony in Australia would be so high, it probably never would have approved the plan. Even more, the distance to Australia not only failed to prevent convicts from escaping and returning to England, but it also eliminated the prospect of the colony ever paying for itself or becoming profitable through commercial means, due to the high cost of shipping convicts and resources to the faraway colony. From now on, Britain would have to pay dearly to punish its criminal offenders.[50]

Conclusion: Winners and Losers

In 1724, Anthony Lamb was nearly at the end of his apprenticeship to Henry Carter, a maker of mathematical instruments in London.[1] Lamb had started working for Carter when he was 14 years old, and by all indications he was a studious apprentice and showed promise for having a successful career. Now at the age of 21, Lamb became star-struck when at the Black Lion alehouse he met and became friends with the notorious burglar and escape artist Jack Sheppard.

Sheppard was born in Spitalfields in 1702. He learned carpentry and lock-making as an apprentice, but he was hardly the model student that Lamb was. He was more inclined to follow his older brother, Thomas, who had fallen in with a gang of criminals. Whenever Jack was sent out to perform a carpentry job at someone's house, he would steal from that person if he got the chance. He spent his nights in the gin houses and brothels on Lewkenor's Lane and used his carpentry and locksmith skills to help Thomas and his gang break into houses. In February 1724, Thomas was caught in an act of burglary, and in order to save himself he impeached Jack. After Thomas's arrest, one of the members of the gang, James Sykes—whose name served as inspiration for the character Bill Sikes in Charles Dickens's *Oliver Twist*—lured Jack to an alehouse on the pretense of participating in a plan to cheat a couple of men at skittles. Unbeknownst to Jack, one of the men at the alehouse was a constable, and having thus set up Sheppard, Sykes collected the reward for Jack's capture. Jack was placed in the St. Giles's Roundhouse, where he immediately escaped through the roof. He was recaptured in May 1724, and this time he was put in New Prison. But using some tools that were smuggled in to him by a member of his gang, Sheppard broke out of his cell, lowered himself into the yard of the Clerkenwell Bridewell next door, and scaled a 22-foot wall to his freedom. Sheppard's escape made him a hero among criminals and apparently earned the respect of Anthony Lamb.[2]

Lamb was eager to impress his new friend, so he suggested that the gang target a master tailor, William Barton, who seemed to have wealthy clients and who rented a room in the house of Lamb's master. Lamb agreed to leave the outside door of the house unlocked on June 16, so that the gang could have easy access to Barton's lodgings. That night, Barton happened to return home drunk from a party at one o'clock in the morning and fell into a deep slumber in his bed. After everyone else in the house had fallen asleep, Lamb snuck downstairs, unlocked the front door, and went back to bed. Sheppard then entered the house, and while his accomplice, Charles Grace, pointed a gun at Barton's head in case he woke up, he ransacked Barton's room, and took a considerable sum of money and expensive clothing.

The burglary went off without a hitch, except for one detail: Sheppard and Grace left the outside door wide open when they left the house. When Henry Carter's wife rose at four o'clock in the morning, she discovered the open door and found Barton still sleeping off the effects of the night, but with his room in total disarray. She woke up her husband and Barton, and the group quickly deduced Lamb's participation in the burglary, given that he had recently been associating with bad company and that there was no sign of forced entry into the house. Carter summoned a constable, who pulled Lamb out of bed and got him to confess the entire plot. Neither the goods nor Sheppard could be found, so with no one else to take the blame, Lamb faced the full brunt of the law. On July 8, 1724, Lamb was found guilty at the Old Bailey for his part in the burglary and was sentenced to transportation to the American colonies for a seven-year term.

Lamb remained in Newgate Prison until October 10, when he was paraded through the London streets in chains and placed cn the *Forward*. Joining Lamb on the ship was Thomas Sheppard, who had been picked up for committing a different burglary with his brother Jack and was sentenced to transportation during the same court session as Lamb.[3] Lamb and Thomas arrived in Annapolis, Maryland, along with 141 other convicts. Thomas must have turned right around and made it back to England, because the following February he showed up again at the Old Bailey—this time for grand larceny—and once again he was sentenced to transportation.[4]

Unfortunately, Lamb's life in Maryland goes dark at this point, because the county court records that would have recorded what happened to Lamb when he walked off the ship have since disappeared. As an apprentice, Lamb would have learned how to engrave metal, ivory, and wood, and anyone with such specialized skills would have been in high demand in the colonies. He could have been sold to a printer, watchmaker, or goldsmith, but we will never know for sure.

Short Stories, Momentous Events

Both Anthony Lamb and James Bell—whose story of stealing a book and hiding out in a dog kennel opened the Introduction to this book—followed similar, and by now familiar, paths to America. Both men were in their early 20s when they exercised bad judgment and committed their crimes, and both of them paid dearly for it. After being transported to America, Bell fell into obscurity, and we will probably never learn his fate. Lamb also fell into the shadows, but unlike Bell, he came to light again when his name later began to appear in colonial newspapers. In 1730, Lamb placed an advertisement in Benjamin Franklin's *Pennsylvania Gazette* for his New York-based mathematical instrument business, which made compasses, quadrants, protractors, and scales. He also advertised his services in the *New York Gazette*, *New-York Mercury*, and *Connecticut Journal*, and he even placed an advertisement for a runaway slave in the *New York Mercury* on April 30, 1753, which is believed to be the first such ad to use an illustration of a slave running away. In the end, Lamb became the first professionally trained maker of scientific instruments in the American colonies and one of the most successful transported convicts to land in America.

There were many winners in the convict transportation trade. Convict merchants made a fortune. Plantation owners also benefited economically from the cheap labor that convicts provided. To be sure, there were risks. Criminals with ill temperaments could disrupt plantation life, and many convicts jeopardized plantation owners' investment in them by escaping and running away. But despite these drawbacks, planters quickly bought up prisoners almost as soon as they arrived in port because they were such a bargain. The British government probably gained the most. Not only was it able to empty its jails of convicts at minimal cost, but it also could quickly dispose and forget about them as soon as they set foot on the American shore.

The convicts, who were uprooted from their family and friends in England and shipped off to a strange land, were certainly the losers. While some of them ended up thriving in their new setting, many died before even arriving in America. Others were mistreated by their new masters once they did arrive. And most of them either ran away or served out their terms before disappearing into anonymity. Advocates for convict transportation wanted people to believe that Anthony Lamb's case was the norm: that given a second chance in America, convicts would rise to become industrious citizens. But most of the thousands of prisoners sent to America ended up like James Bell. Bell may well have become a hard-working if not prosperous citizen after serving out his term, but the odds make it unlikely that he did so.

I have tried to put a human face on convict transportation by telling the stories of Anthony Lamb, James Bell, and all of the other transported criminals, merchants, and politicians who appear in this book. But the story of this unique form of punishment is also about systems. Fundamental economic changes in Great Britain created a burgeoning and wealthy middle class that began to claim more and more valuable resources, which included the use of common lands that for generations had helped support poor agricultural workers. These changes forced many of the rural poor to the cities, where there

Conclusion

were not enough jobs to support them all. Facing destitution, the unemployed and underemployed increasingly turned to petty crime and overloaded an already broken and outdated criminal justice system. Criminal entrepreneurs like Jonathan Wild took advantage of this broken system, and the rise in the crime rate forced Parliament into inventing the new punishment of convict transportation.

The labor system in the American colonies was primed to receive Britain's unwanted criminals. Menial labor came at a premium, which forced plantation owners to seek cheap ways to bridge the labor gap. In the absence of a willing labor force, plantations relied on slavery and indentured servitude, and so the sale of convicts as indentured servants became a welcome addition to the labor pool. Eventually, convict labor became so popular that it essentially replaced indentured servitude, so when convict transportation came to an end at the start of the American Revolution, slavery became the only source of cheap labor available to plantation owners. With white laborers out of the picture, slavery kept the plantation system running, but it also ran counter to the ideals of equality that initially fueled the Revolution. As a result, an ideology of racial inferiority not only began to develop, but became necessary for justifying the continued existence of slavery. Back in Great Britain, as the jails and prisons began to fill up in the absence of a place to send its criminals, Parliament was forced into implementing extreme alternatives by first housing convicts on prison hulks and then shipping them halfway around the world to Australia.

All of these systems affected the individual lives of thousands, and eventually millions, of people. Even though Bell's

249

story of petty theft is short and lacks detail, the episode turned out to be a momentous event for him personally. In being sentenced to transportation, he joined 50,000 other people who could tell a story very similar to his own. Transportation to the American colonies transformed the lives of the people who received this punishment, for good or bad. And this transformation was so profound that those who went through it most likely never could have conceived of what was in store for them before it actually happened to them. For committing what could very well have been an impulsive and desperate act, Bell was swept away on an epic journey across the ocean and into the unknown.

Successes and Failures

In 1785, a parliamentary committee charged with studying the old transportation system concluded the following:

> That the old system of transporting to America answered every good purpose that could be expected from it. That it tended directly to reclaim the objects on which it was inflicted, and to render them good citizens.... That it was not attended with much expense to the public, the convicts being carried out in vessels employ'd in the Jamaica or tobacco trade, that for many years Government paid 5 [pounds] a man and afterwards no premium at all, the contractor being indemnified ... by the price at which he sold their labour....
>
> That the convicts ... were usually removed into the back country and finding none of the

temptations ... which occasioned their offenses at home, it does not appear that the police or peace of the colonies suffered in any considerable degree ...5

We now know that such an assessment does not entirely fit the reality, but how should we assess the successes and failures of the convict transportation system today?

Convict transportation certainly had its successes. From an administrative point of view, the partnership between the British government and private business created a surprisingly efficient system of punishment, and little in the way of bureaucracy was needed to carry out the operation. The Treasury simply required proof that the convicts were loaded on the ships and dropped off in America, and the merchants took care of the rest, which included making arrangements with the jailers for the transfer of the convicts from prison to the ship. Convict transportation was also a successful alternative to the "two strikes and you're out" policy, where petty criminals received benefit of clergy for the first offense and execution for their second. It effectively cleared away space in the prisons at a lower cost than building new ones, and it had its intended effect of lowering the execution rate, which plummeted after passage of the Act. And rather than release criminals back out on the street to commit more crimes, or allow prisoners to languish in prison, or even execute repeat offenders, the new punishment put the convicts to work and gave them a chance to improve their lives. Most likely, if the action of sending convicts to America never took place, executions would have skyrocketed and prison conditions in England would have sunken to unimaginable lows.

But for all of its successes, convict transportation also had its failures. The punishment uprooted thousands of people from their family and friends and put them in a strange land under the power of someone who did not have to answer to anyone about how he treated them. This lack of oversight naturally led to abuses. It also meant that there was no uniformity in how the convicts were ultimately punished for their crime. They could end up with a kind owner or a ruthlessly cruel one, no matter what crime they committed back in their homeland. The new punishment also did nothing to reduce the crime rate back in England, because Parliament never coupled the punishment with actions that addressed the root causes of crime. Not until the 19th century, when England put a professional police force in place to patrol the streets and jobs became more readily available in the cities, did the crime rate begin to fall.

Throughout this book, I have been arguing that convict transportation to America was an entirely new form of punishment. In a way, the answer the government came up with to the question of its crime problem was simple: Ship the convicts crowding the prisons to America to work on plantations that sorely needed the labor. But with this simple solution, the government also created new ways of thinking about the criminal and his or her relationship to society.

Before passage of the Transportation Act, convicts were either branded, held in prison for a short amount of time, subjected to corporal punishment in the town square, or executed in a public display. In each case, the criminal remained a member of British civil society both during and after the punishment took place, and the public spectacle of the punishments reinforced this notion. But in creating convict transportation, Britain pursued a policy that effectively terminated the criminal's relationship to civil society. By physically removing criminals from its borders, Britain figuratively tried to wash its hands of its crime problem. Unfortunately, this simple and cheap disposal of its unwanted citizens diverted attention away from the systemic sources that helped generate its crime problem in the first place. The criminals who were sent oversees were quickly replaced by others, because the conditions that helped produce them remained in place. At the same time, transported convicts were forced to rethink their own relationship to society: They were freeborn Englishmen who found themselves shipped like cattle to the American colonies where they were sold off to another Englishman who put them to work next to African slaves and indentured servants. In committing their crime, they lost the right to be considered full-functioning members of British society and were reduced to their base ability to provide labor.

But perhaps most importantly, convict transportation embodied the idea that criminals could be reformed by redirecting their deviant impulses toward industrious ends. Workhouses at the time were specifically aimed at beggars and vagrants—i.e., the dependent, unemployed poor. They were not created to reform criminal offenders. Convict transportation was the first punishment where reform of the criminal was not accomplished by essentially beating them into submission— which was the aim of the old-style, physical punishments of branding, whipping, and hanging. Instead, reform supposedly came about by exposing the criminal to industrious behavior and hoping that he or she would embrace its values. This new approach to reforming the criminal psychologically rather than physically would become important in the development of long-term incarceration, which began immediately after convict transportation to America came to an end. The result was the invention of the modern-day penitentiary, which uses long-term confinement to force criminals into reflecting on their crimes and behavior with the goal of turning them into self-regulating individuals.[6]

Modern Resonances

The history of convict transportation has modern resonances that are hard to ignore. In recent years, drug crimes in the United States soared, and in response the government implemented strict sentencing laws that followed a "three strikes and you're out" policy. As a result, more than one out of every 100 adults is now locked away behind bars in the United States.[7] Convicts who have committed a wide range of offenses are housed in overcrowded and dangerous conditions, often with nothing to do all day. Prison gangs are rampant, and violent clashes between rival gangs and guards are common. Many prisoners have become institutionalized and see prison as their most comfortable, and perhaps only, way of life. The cost of housing convicts is draining government coffers, and some states have even tried to contract out the management of its criminal offenders to private prisons. Other states are beginning to release their prisoners on parole, not because they have reformed, but because they no longer have the money to keep so many of them locked away. And now the United States and the world face new threats in the forms of cyber crime, financial crime, and terrorism. These new crimes pose new challenges to current criminal justice systems and are changing the idea of what constitutes a criminal. The questions of how we handle our criminals and which crimes merit harsh punishment will continue into the future.

This description of the criminal justice system in the United States today is not unlike that for England in the 18th century. Britain responded to its crime problem by creating a system of punishment that gave in to society's impulse to rid itself of its criminal element through expedient means. "Let's just lock them up and throw away the key" is the modern equivalent and is perhaps a natural reaction when crime seems to be out of control. In transporting criminals to another land where they were out of sight and out of mind, Britain may have been able to remove individual offenders from its society. But criminals are also products of society, and try as Britain might, there always seemed to be more criminals waiting in the wings to replace the ones who were transported. The economic and social conditions that forced people into leading a life of crime remained intact, and so more criminals were essentially generated every day. Likewise, the United States tried to solve its drug problem by locking away its offenders. Yet, the problem remained. Rather than attack the root cause of this activity, namely drug addiction, the government essentially deferred addressing the problem. This misguided approach led to a dramatic increase in the prison population. The overall lesson is that even if we can create an effective, administrative system that removes offenders from the streets, we will not solve our crime problem if we do not at the same time address the circumstances that cause the crime in the first place.

Convict transportation was founded on the idea of personal reinvention: that if convicted criminals were put in a position to work and perhaps learn a trade, that they could eventually improve their lot in life. This idea of giving people second chances is very American. The invention of convict transportation also has an American quality to it with the idea that an effective use of government can create systems where free enterprise can be employed to serve the public good. And the administration of convict transportation to America was all-American as well. Not only was its organization and management completely different from its Australian counterpart, but no citizen was ever banished from a country's borders in quite the same way. Convict transportation in its original manifestation was a uniquely American phenomenon, and like it or not, it played a significant role in the workings of colonial America. But unlike Australia, which has learned to acknowledge and even embrace its criminal legacy, the United States has yet to come to terms with its similar past. In the end, the history of convict transportation requires Americans to re-examine their roots and compels them to recognize the contributions that British convicts like James Bell had in establishing and populating what would eventually become the United States.

Epilogue

While Anthony Lamb and Thomas Sheppard waited in Newgate Prison to be transported to America in July 1724, Jack Sheppard continued to commit burglaries and robberies with another member of his gang, Blueskin Blake. But one of the victims went to Jonathan Wild for help, and Wild used his network to capture Sheppard, who was convicted for robbery and thrown in Newgate Prison.[8] He did not stay there for long. With the help of his cellmate and two other visitors, Sheppard cut away a bar from the door, squeezed through the opening, and then wearing a long cloak walked out of the prison.

Sheppard hid away for a little over a month, but on September 10 the Keepers of Newgate learned that Sheppard and his partner, William Page, a young butcher-boy, were on Finchley Common. A posse of men on horses followed by armed men in coaches spread themselves in a line across the common and advanced together northward to comb the area. They soon spotted Sheppard and Page and captured them. And once again Sheppard found himself in Newgate Prison. He was held there for a little over a month until October 15, when he made the escape that would turn him into a celebrity. He was locked halfway up the Gate Tower in "The Castle," the strongest room in Newgate, and weighed down with heavy chains, fetters, padlocks, and bars. Despite these measures, Sheppard managed to free himself from his irons and made his way up through the rooms of the Gate Tower. Along the way he broke through six iron-barred doors—some of which were secured on the far side with padlocks and bars—using the handcuffs he broke out of and an iron bar that he tore from the Castle chimney as tools. When he finally reached the top of the tower, he retraced his steps back to his cell in order to retrieve some blankets, so that he could lower himself down on the roof of the house next door and then down onto the street. He accomplished all of these feats in total darkness on a moonless night.

Sheppard and the story of his escape became a media sensation, and the details of how he broke out of Newgate ran in newspapers as far as America. He was now the most famous man in England, and people celebrated his escape by pouring into the streets that surrounded Newgate so that they could get a look at where the amazing event took place. Sheppard reportedly mingled among this crowd and enjoyed listening to ballad-singers sing about his exploits. But the party ended on October 31, when the authorities found Sheppard drunk in a gin shop and arrested him. They put him back in Newgate and loaded him down with irons weighing 300 pounds. Hundreds of people paid the Newgate turnkey 3s. 6d. to see Sheppard in his cell. But this time, there was no escape, and Sheppard was hastily executed on Monday, November 16. He was buried in the churchyard of the half-built St. Martin's-in-the-Fields, where he remained until his body was dug up in 1866 to make room for the National Gallery.

Jonathan Wild's role in bringing Sheppard to justice turned out to be the beginning of the end for the Thief-Taker General and was one reason Wild incurred such vitriol at his own execution. Sheppard's popularity drew attention to Wild's methods for capturing criminals, and as details about the true nature of his organization came to light, the public grew more incensed. At his trial for theft and receiving stolen goods, Wild desperately tried to sway the jury in his favor by distributing a list of 75 criminals that he was responsible for bringing to justice and arguing that they never would have been captured were it not for him. Nineteen on the list were convicts who had returned early from transportation, including many of the convicts who were involved in the Vigo escape. Wild's attempt to generate sympathy failed, of course, and he was executed by hanging in front of a large and hostile crowd. But the story of Jonathan Wild does not end there.

As soon as Wild's body was cut down after his execution, a rumor began to circulate that it was being carried off to the Surgeon's Hall for dissection. The bodies of executed criminals were often used in this way, but the practice usually led to a struggle between the surgeons, who tried to take the body of the criminal away, and the disapproving crowd.[9] In this case, Jonathan's wife, Mary Wild, created the rumor as a ruse, so that Wild's body could be properly buried without interference. Her plan did not work. Three or four days after it was buried, Wild's body was dug up from the St. Pancras churchyard by the surgeons.[10] Today, his skeleton can be seen on display at the Hunterian Museum at the Royal College of Surgeons in Lincoln's Inn Fields.

Just before Wild was executed, his son of the same name came to London. He was about 19 years old at the time and was described as "a youth of so violent and ungovernable a disposition that it was judged prudent to confine him while his father was conveyed to Tyburn, lest he should create a tumult and prove the cause of mischief among the populace." After his father's execution, the son settled in Aldgate, London and became a laborer, but five years later, he bound himself as an indentured servant for four years to William Burge of Maryland.[11]

Anthony Lamb—whose friendship with Jack Sheppard resulted in him being transported to America as a convict—died in December 1784, and newspapers throughout the Northeast carried his obituary. One death notice described him as a "respectable inhabitant" of the city and "a steady friend to the liberties of America." It went on to say:

> In him, this country has lost one of the most ingenious *Mathematical Instrument Makers*, that this or any other nation could boast of. Though advanced in life, he retained his faculties to the last; was always remarkable cheerful and facetious.—He was an affectionate husband, tender parent, steady friend, obliging neighbour, and was distinguished for his philanthropy.—He resigned his spirit to God, who gave it, in a good old age, leaving behind him many friends, and we may with confidence say, *no enemies.—*
>
> *But, to say more would be words spent in vain,*
> *His Standing Monument is A GOOD NAME.*[12]

None of the obituaries, however, mentioned the circumstances of how Lamb originally came to America.

Appendix:

Is There a Convict in Your Family's Closet? A Short Primer on Researching Convicts Transported to America

If you suspect that one of your ancestors is a convict who was transported from Great Britain to America, here are some tips to help you get started on researching information about him or her. But remember, genealogical research is often hit or miss, and this principle is especially true when researching transported convicts.

The first place to start looking is in two resources by Peter Wilson Coldham: *The Complete Book of Emigrants, 1607-1776* (CD-ROM) or *The King's Passengers to Maryland and Virginia.* Both sources offer extensive lists of convicts and provide basic information about each one, including the ship in which he or she was transported, the name of the captain, when the ship left England, and when and where the ship was registered in America. The former source is more comprehensive, since the latter only covers convicts who landed in Maryland or Virginia. But *The King's Passengers* helpfully organizes its list of convicts by ship, so you can easily see the names of all the other prisoners who traveled along with your ancestor. You might want to consult both sources, if possible, to compare the information in each. Marion and Jack Kaminkow's *Original Lists of Emigrants in Bondage from London to the American Colonies, 1719-1744* can also be helpful, although it is more limited in both place and time than the other resources. In addition, it is out of print.

If you are able to find your ancestor listed in any of the above resources and the convict was originally from London or Middlesex county, then you are in luck. He or she probably came up for trial at the Old Bailey in London, and you can read a description of the trial where he or she was sentenced to transportation online at the *Proceedings of the Old Bailey* (http://www.oldbaileyonline.org/). This resource is not only fabulous, but it is also free. Do not be surprised if you find yourself searching and reading about other criminal figures that passed through this court. The *Old Bailey* database offers all kinds of search options, so if you do not find your convict right away, or if the name you are looking for is so common that too many results appear, then try a different approach. Limit your search for the years around when your convict was transported, or search for just the first name and add other limiters, such as Punishment: Transportation. Also keep in mind, the spelling of names was not necessarily standardized at the time. Think about how the name sounds, and then try other possible spellings. So for example, if you are looking for a Johnson and you cannot find a match, try Jonson. Likewise Smyth for Smith. This same principle applies to searching the Coldham resources listed above.

If you are unable to find your convict in any of these resources, you might be out of luck, short of traveling to suspected libraries and archives where your convict may have lived, either in Britain or in Maryland or Virginia. But all hope is not lost. You should definitely try searching the Web. Lists of convicts do exist on the Web, but they are spotty. For example, *Ulster Ancestry* provides a list of convicts and vagabonds who were transported from Ulster between 1737 and 1743 (http://www.ulsterancestry.com/ua-free_Convicts-and-Vagabonds.html). Other ancestry websites, either institutional or personal, might offer similar lists.

You might be able to find more detailed biographical information about your convict in databases that reproduce 18th-century newspapers and books. *The Virginia Gazette* (http://research.history.org/DigitalLibrary/BrowseVG.cfm) and *The Maryland Gazette* (http://www.aomol.net/html/mdgazette.html) are both freely available online. *The Virginia Gazette* has an online index where you can look for the name of your convict, but unfortunately, no online index exists for *The Maryland Gazette*. The latter, however, is part of the excellent *Archives of Maryland Online* (http://www.aomol.net/html/index.html), so you can try searching for your convict among all of the other online Maryland records offered on this website if he or she landed in Maryland. If you live near a large university or public research library, then you might have access to two important full-text databases that are subscription-based: *America's Historical Newspapers* and *Eighteenth-Century Collections Online*. Both are mammoth databases, containing American newspapers in the case of the former or British books in the case of the latter. If you are lucky enough to find the name of your convict in one of these resources, then you are likely to find information that will really help fill out the picture of your criminal ancestor.

Notes

Database Key:

AHN = *America's Historical Newspapers, Readex/Newsbank.*

AM = *Archives of Maryland Online*
(http://aomol.net/html/mdgazette.html), Maryland State
Archives.

AMem = *American Memory*: Library of Congress
(http://memory.loc.gov/).

CWDL = *CW Digital Library*
(http://research.history.org/DigitalLibrary.cfm), Colonial
Williamsburg Foundation.

ECCO = *Eighteenth Century Collections Online*, Gale.

IA = *Internet Archive* (http://www.archive.org).

ILEJ = *The Internet Library of Early Journals*
(http://www.bodley.ox.ac.uk/ilej/), eLib.

Preface

[1] A. Roger Ekirch, *Bound for America: The Transportation of British Convicts to the Colonies, 1718-1775* (New York: Oxford University Press, 1987), 113.

Introduction: The Beginning of an Epic Journey

[1] *Old Bailey Proceedings Online* (www.oldbaileyonline.org, 7 April 2008), January 1723, trial of James Bell (t17230116-9).

2 Aaron S. Fogleman, "From Slaves, Convicts, and Servants to Free Passengers: The Transformation of Immigration in the Era of the American Revolution," *The Journal of American History* 85.1 (1998), 44; Franklin Bowdith Dexter, *Estimates of Population in the American Colonies* (Worcester, MA: Press of Charles Hamilton, 1887), 20; J. H. Benton, Jr., *Early Census Making in Massachusetts, 1643-1765* (Boston: Charles E. Goodspeed, 1905); A. Roger Ekirch, "Bound for America: A Profile of British Convicts Transported to the Colonies," *The William and Mary Quarterly* 42.2 (1985), 186-188; A. Roger Ekirch, *Bound for America: The Transportation of British Convicts to the Colonies, 1718-1775* (New York: Oxford University Press, 1987), 1-2.

3 Thomas Jefferson, *The Writings of Thomas Jefferson*, ed. Paul Leicester Ford, vol. IV (New York: G. P. Putnam's Sons, 1894), 158-159.

4 For example, see Charles J. Stillé, "American Colonies as Penal Settlements," *The Pennsylvania Magazine of History and Biography* 12.4 (Jan., 1889), 457-464.

5 James Davie Butler, "British Convicts Shipped to American Colonies," *American Historical Review* 2.1 (1896).

6 See Charles Edgar Gilliam, "Jail Bird Immigrants to Virginia," *The Virginia Magazine of History and Biography* 52.3 (July, 1944), 180-182.

7 Ekirch, "Bound for America," 188.

8 Ekirch, "Bound for America," 186-188; A. Roger Ekirch, "The Transportation of Scottish Criminals to America During the Eighteenth Century," *The Journal of British Studies* 24.3 (1985), 366-74.

9 Aaron S. Fogleman, "From Slaves, Convicts, and Servants to Free Passengers: The Transformation of Immigration in the Era of the American Revolution," *The Journal of American History* 85.1 (1998), 44.

Chapter One: England's Criminal Underworld

[1] Gerald Howson, *Thief-Taker General: Jonathan Wild and the Emergence of Crime and Corruption as a Way of Life in Eighteenth-Century England* (New Brunswick, NJ: Transaction Books, 1970), 274-275.

[2] *The History of the Lives and Actions of Jonathan Wild, Thief-Taker* (London: Printed for Edward Midwinter, 1725; Database: *ECCO*), 77-78; "Particular Account of the Life and Trials of Jonathan Wild," *The Malefactor's Register*, Vol. II. (London: Alexander Hogg, 1779; Database: *ECCO*), 80; "The Life of the Famous Jonathan Wild, Thief-Taker," *Lives of the Most Remarkable Criminals*, Vol. II., (London: John Osborn, 1735; Database: *ECCO*), 63; Howson, 275.

[3] *The Life and Glorious Actions of the Most Heroic and Magnanimous Jonathan Wilde* (London: Printed for H. Whitridge, 1725; Database: *ECCO*), 61; The History of the Lives and Actions, 76-77; "The Life of the Famous Jonathan Wild," 63.

[4] "Jonathan Wild, For Felonies," *Select Trials for Murders, Robberies, Rapes, Sodomy, Coining, Frauds, and Other Offenses: At the Sessions-House in the Old-Bailey*, Vol. II. (London: Printed for J. Wilford, 1735; Database: *ECCO*), 110-111.

[5] Howson, 272.

[6] *History of the Lives and Actions*, 78; "Particular Account of the Life and Trials of Jonathan Wild," 81; Howson, 276.

[7] "The Life of the Famous Jonathan Wild," 68; Howson, 276.

[8] Frank McLynn, *Crime and Punishment in Eighteenth-Century England* (New York: Oxford University Press, 1991), 257-276, especially 264; Tim Hitchcock and Robert Shoemaker, *Tales from the Hanging Court* (London: Hodder Arnold, 2006), 202-204; Richard B. Schwartz, Daily Life in Johnson's London (Madison, WI: The University of Wisconsin Press, 1983), 90, 146-149; M. Dorothy George, *London Life in*

the *Eighteenth Century* (Chicago: Academy Chicago Publishers, 1965), 207; John Bender, *Imagining the Penitentiary: Fiction and the Architecture of Mind in Eighteenth-Century England* (Chicago: The University of Chicago Press, 1987), 238-241; Peter Ackroyd, *London: The Biography* (New York: Anchor Books, 2000), 286-287.

9 Henry Fielding, *An Enquiry into the Causes of the Late Increase of Robbers, &C* (Dublin: Printed for G. Faulkner, P. Wilson, R. James, and M. Williamson, 1751; Database: *ECCO*), 92-94.

10 For full accounts of the economic and social changes in England during the 18th century, see Christopher Hill, *The Pelican Economic History of Britain: Volume 2: 1530-1780, Reformation to Industrial Revolution* (New York: Pelican Books, 1969); Roy Porter, *English Society in the Eighteenth Century*, Revised edition (New York: Penguin Books, 1990); and Paul Mantoux, *The Industrial Revolution in the Eighteenth Century: An Outline of the Beginnings of the Modern Factory System in England* (Chicago: The University of Chicago Press, 1983). For political and philosophical analysis of these changes, see J. G. A. Pocock, *Virtue, Commerce, and History: Essays on Political Thought and History, Chiefly in the Eighteenth Century* (New York: Cambridge University Press, 1985); and Isaac Kramnick, *Bolingbroke and His Circle: The Politics of Nostalgia in the Age of Walpole* (Ithaca, NY: Cornell University Press, 1968).

11 George, 37, 318-320; Liza Picard, *Dr. Johnson's London: Coffee-Houses and Climbing Boys, Medicine, Toothpaste and Gin, Poverty and Press-Gangs, Freakshows and Female Education* (New York: St. Martin's Griffin, 2000), 3; Peter Whitfield, *London: A Life in Maps* (London: The British Library, 2006), 56-65, 87-89, for a map of 18th-century London, see 62-63.

12 Schwartz, 110; George, 105.

13 Schwartz, 8-9, 15-18; Whitfield, 58.

[14] Schwartz, 13-14.

[15] Schwartz, 8-11.

[16] Whitfield, 56-67; George, 109-110; Schwartz, 11-12.

[17] Schwartz, 47-48, 128-130; George, 172.

[18] *Old Bailey Proceedings Online* (www.oldbaileyonline.org, 22 October 2009), December 1722, trial of John Flint t17221205-17).

[19] J. M. Beattie, *Crime and the Courts in England, 1660-1800* (Princeton: Princeton University Press, 1986), 7-8; McLynn, 92-93, 300.

[20] E. P. Thompson, *Whigs and Hunters: The Origin of the Black Act* (New York: Pantheon Books, 1975).

[21] George, 116-120, 146.

[22] J. M. Beattie, *Policing and Punishment in London, 1660-1750: Urban Crime and the Limits of Terror* (New York: Oxford University Press, 2001), 40-48; George, 31-32, 116-157; McLynn, 77-80.

[23] James Guthrie, *The Ordinary of Newgate, His Account of the Behaviour, Confession, and Dying Words, of the Malefactors, Who were Executed at Tyburn, on Wednesday the 18th of March, 1740.* (London: John Applebee, 1740; Database: *ECCO*), 7; "Particular Account of the Extraordinary Exploits of Mary Young, alias Jenny Diver, Who Was Executed for Privately Stealing," *The Malefactor's Register*, Vol. II. (London: Alexander Hogg, 1779; Database: *ECCO*), 382-384; "Mary Young, *alias* Jenny Diver, *and* Elizabeth Davis, *alias* Catherine Huggins, *for a* Robbery, *Jan.* 17, 1741," *Select Trials for Murders, Robberies, Rapes, Sodomy, Coining, Frauds, and Other Offenses*, 2nd ed., Vol. IV. (London: Printed for L. Gilliver and J. Huggonson, 1742; Database: *ECCO*), 343-345.

[24] George, 170-174; Schwartz, 39; "Particular Account of the Extraordinary Exploits of Mary Young," 384-385; "Mary Young," 345.

25 John Gay, *The Beggar's Opera*, ed. Edgar V. Roberts, Regents Restoration Drama Series (Lincoln, NE: University of Nebraska Press, 1969); "Particular Account of the Extraordinary Exploits of Mary Young," 385-387; "Mary Young," 343, 347-348.

26 "Particular Account of the Extraordinary Exploits of Mary Young," 387-389; "Mary Young," 347.

27 Daniel Defoe, *An Effectual Scheme for the Immediate Preventing of Street Robberies* (London, 1731), 9-10.

28 For full accounts of criminal literature in 18th-century England, see Ian A. Bell, *Literature and Crime in Augustan England* (New York: Routledge, 1991); Lincoln B. Faller, *Turned to Account: The Forms and Functions of Criminal Biography in Late Seventeenth- and Early Eighteenth-Century England* (New York: Cambridge UP, 1987); and Anthony Theodore Vaver, *Reading Criminals/Criminal Readings: Early Eighteenth-Century English Constructions of Criminality*, Doctoral dissertation. (Stony Brook, NY: The State University of New York at Stony Brook, 1994).

29 "The Life of the Famous Jonathan Wild," 15-16; Capt. Alexander Smith, *Memoirs of the Life and Times of the Famous Jonathan Wild* (London: Printed for Sam. Briscoe, 1726; Database: *ECCO*), 2; "Jonathan Wild, For Felonies," 54; Defoe, Daniel, *The True and Genuine Account of the Life and Actions of the Late Jonathan Wild* (London, 1725. In Henry Fielding, Jonathan Wild, ed. David Nokes, New York: Penguin, 1982), 230; Howson, 12-13.

30 Defoe, Jonathan Wild, 230-231; "The Life of the Famous Jonathan Wild," 16-17; Howson, 13-20.

31 History of the Lives and Actions, 7; "The Life of the Famous Jonathan Wild," 17; "Jonathan Wild, For Felonies," 54; Defoe, *Jonathan Wild*, 231; Howson, 24, 44-46; George, 92-93.

32 Whitfield, 56-59; George, 54, 74, 90-94, 121.

33 George, 83-86, 94-104, 113; Schwartz, 14.

34 "The Life of the Famous Jonathan Wild," 17; "Jonathan Wild, For Felonies," 54; Defoe, *Jonathan Wild*, 231-232; Eric Partridge, "Buttock and Twang," *A Dictionary of the Underworld, British and American* (New York: Bonanza Books, 1961), 93-94; Howson, 46.

35 "Jonathan Wild, For Felonies," 54; Howson, 47-48.

36 McLynn, 19-20; Beattie, *Crime and the Courts*, 67-73; Beattie, *Policing and Punishment*, 169-225.

37 McLynn, 21; *Crime and the Courts*, 35-55; *Policing and Punishment*, 77-108.

38 "The Life of the Famous Jonathan Wild," 19-23; Defoe, *Jonathan Wild*, 233-237; McLynn, 22-24; Howson, 66-69.

39 For a discussion of salaries and money in 18th-century England, see Schwartz, 44-54.

40 Beattie, *Crime and the Courts*, 50-55; McLynn, 22.

41 Howson, 70-73.

42 "Jonathan Wild, For Felonies," 85-87; Howson, 74-75, 82-84, 106-109; McLynn, 24.

43 "Jonathan Wild, For Felonies," 95; Smith, *Memoirs of the Life*, 5; Howson, 117, 119-120.

44 Howson, 120-121; McLynn 26.

45 McLynn, 24-25; Howson, 82-90, 116-118.

46 "Jonathan Wild, For Felonies," 56; McLynn, 22; Howson, 66-67, 144, 227-228.

47 Howson, 116, 120-121.

48 Howson, 116.

Chapter Two: The Need for a New Punishment

1 J. M. Beattie, *Policing and Punishment in London, 1660-1750: Urban Crime and the Limits of Terror* (New York: Oxford University Press, 2001), 315-338; E. P. Thompson, *Whigs and Hunters: The Origin of the Black Act* (New York: Pantheon, 1975); Frank McLynn, *Crime and Punishment in Eighteenth-Century England* (New York: Oxford University Press, 1991), ix.

2 *Old Bailey Proceedings Online* (www.oldbaileyonline.org, 1 February 2008), February 1718, trial of Richard Wood (t17180227-33); Ben Weinreb and Christopher Hibbert, eds. *London Encyclopaedia* (London: Macmillan, 1983), 544; A. Roger Ekirch, *At Day's Close: Night in Times Past* (New York: W. W. Norton, 2005), 326.

3 *Old Bailey Proceedings Online*, trial of Richard Wood.

4 Tim Hitchcock and Robert Shoemaker, "Crimes Tried at the Old Bailey: Explanations of Types and Categories of Indictable Offences," *Old Bailey Proceedings Online* (www.oldbaileyonline.org, 1 February 2008).

5 *Old Bailey Proceedings Online*, trial of Richard Wood.

6 *Old Bailey Proceedings Online* (www.oldbaileyonline.org, 1 February 2008), February 1718, trial of Edward Higgins (t17180227-19); Weinreb and Hibbert, 686.

7 *Old Bailey Proceedings Online*, trial of Edward Higgins; Hitchcock and Shoemaker, "Crimes Tried at the Old Bailey."

8 Gerald Howson, *Thief-Taker General: Jonathan Wild and the Emergence of Crime and Corruption as a Way of Life in Eighteenth-Century England* (New Brunswick, NJ: Transaction Books, 1970), 125; David Nokes, Introduction, *Jonathan Wild* by Henry Fielding, ed. David Nokes (New York: Penguin, 1982), 10; Beattie, *Policing and Punishment*, 379.

9 J. M. Beattie, *Crime and the Courts in England, 1660-1800* (Princeton: Princeton University Press, 1986), 141-148; Howson, 30-31; Peter Wilson Coldham, *Emigrants in Chains: A Social History of Forced Emigration to the Americas of Felons, Destitute Children, Political and Religious Non-Conformists, Vagabonds, Beggars and Other Undesirables, 1607-1776* (Baltimore, MD: Genealogical Pub. Co., 1992), 36.

10 Henry Fielding, *An Enquiry into the Causes of the Late Increase of Robbers, &C* (Dublin: Printed for G. Faulkner, P. Wilson, R. James, and M. Williamson, 1751), especially 47-52; J. M. Beattie, *Crime and the Courts*, 502; McLynn, 294-298.

11 A. G. L. Shaw, *Convicts and the Colonies: A Study of Penal Transportation from Great Britain and Ireland to Australia and Other Parts of the British Empire* (London: Faber and Faber, 1966), 22; Coldham, *Emigrants in Chains*, 41; Don Jordon and Michael Walsh, *White Cargo: The Forgotten History of Britain's White Slaves in America* (New York: New York University Press, 2007) 27-28; Richard Hakluyt, *A Discourse Concerning Western Planting, Written in the Year 1584*, ed. Charles Deane (Cambridge: John Wilson and Son, 1877) 37.

12 Coldham, *Emigrants in Chains*, 41; Jordan and Walsh, 30-31.

13 Coldham, *Emigrants in Chains, 43; Abbot Emerson Smith, Colonists in Bondage: White Servitude and Convict Labor in America, 1607-1776* (New York: Norton, 1971), 233; Jordan and Walsh, 62-64, 70-73.

14 Alan Atkinson, "The Free-Born Englishman Transported Convict Rights as a Measure of Eighteenth-Century Empire," *Past and Present* 144 (1994): 93; Smith, Colonists in Bondage, 91; Beattie, *Crime and the Courts*, 472-473; Beattie, *Policing and Punishment*, 290.

15 Beattie, *Crime and the Courts*, 475-478.

16 *Hanging, Not Punishment Enough* (London: Longman, Hurst, Rees, Orme, and Brown, 1812 [Originally published: 1701]), 20-21.

17 "Thompson or Thomson, Sir William (1678-1739)," *Dictionary of National Biography*, Vol. XIX, Sidney Lee, ed. (New York: The Macmillan Company, 1909), 706; Beattie, *Policing and Punishment*, 425-426.

18 Howson, 92, 241; Edward Foss, *The Judges of England; with Sketches of Their Lives*, Vol. VIII (London: John Murray, 1864), 174; Beattie, *Policing and Punishment*, 426.

19 Beattie, *Policing and Punishment*, 429, 431.

20 Ibid., 430.

21 Atkinson, 93.

22 Bruce Kercher, "Perish or Prosper: The Law and Convict Transportation in the British Empire, 1700-1850," *Law and History Review* 21.3 (2003): 530.

23 Marion J. Kaminkow and Jack Kaminkow, *Original Lists of Emigrants in Bondage from London to the American Colonies, 1719-1744* (Baltimore, MD: Magna Carta Book Co., 1967), vii.

24 A. Roger Ekirch, "Bound for America: A Profile of British Convicts Transported to the Colonies," *The William and Mary Quarterly* 42.2 (1985): 184.

25 Quoted in Beattie, *Policing and Punishment*, 431.

26 Quoted in Beattie, *Crime and the Courts*, 510.

27 Beattie, *Policing and Punishment*, 443-444.

28 Howson, 92-93.

29 Ibid., 93-94.

30 Ibid., 91-92.

31 Ibid., 238-240.

[32] Ibid., 267.

[33] McLynn, 30.

[34] Coldham, *Emigrants in Chains*, 72, 177; Kaminkow and Kaminkow, 180-181; Smith, *Colonists in Bondage*, 128.

[35] *Old Bailey Proceedings Online* (www.oldbaileyonline.org, 6 October 2008), July 1720, trial of Edward Higgins (t17200712-20).

[36] Peter Wilson Coldham, *The King's Passengers to Maryland and Virginia* (Westminster, MD: Heritage Books, 1997), 8-10.

[37] Gwenda Morgan and Peter Rushton, "Running Away and Returning Home: The Fate of English Convicts in the American Colonies," *Crime, Histoire & Sociétiés / Crime, History & Societies* 7.2 (2003): 62.

Chapter Three: The Business of Convict Transportation

[1] Abbot Emerson Smith, *Colonists in Bondage: White Servitude and Convict Labor in America, 1607-1776*, The Norton Library; N592 (New York: Norton, 1971), 112-113.

[2] A. Roger Ekirch, *Bound for America: The Transportation of British Convicts to the Colonies, 1718-1775* (New York: Oxford University Press, 1987), 70 n.1; Smith, *Colonists in Bondage*, 113; Peter Wilson Coldham, *Emigrants in Chains: A Social History of Forced Emigration to the Americas of Felons, Destitute Children, Political and Religious Non-Conformists, Vagabonds, Beggars and Other Undesirables, 1607-1776* (Baltimore, MD: Genealogical Pub. Co., 1992), 59-60.

[3] Qtd. Coldham, *Emigrants in Chains*, 60.

[4] Qtd. Ibid., 60.

[5] J. M. Beattie, *Policing and Punishment in London, 1660-1750: Urban Crime and the Limits of Terror* (New York: Oxford University Press, 2001), 430; Ekirch, *Bound for America*, 70; Coldham, *Emigrants in Chains*, 71.

6 Introduction, *Proceedings of the Maryland Court of Appeals, 1695-1729*, Vol. 77 (Database: *AM*), xlii-xliv; Coldham, *Emigrants in Chains*, 72.

7 J. M. Beattie, *Policing and Punishment in London*, 430-431; Ekirch, *Bound for America*, 70-71.

8 Farley Grubb, "The Transatlantic Market for British Convict Labor," *The Journal of Economic History* 60.1 (2000), 119.

9 Grubb, "The Transatlantic Market," 95; Coldham, *Emigrants in Chains*, 5.

10 Smith, *Colonists in Bondage*, 19-20, 39; Coldham, *Emigrants in Chains*, 5.

11 M. Dorothy George, *London Life in the Eighteenth Century* (Chicago: Academy Chicago Publishers, 1965), 148-149.

12 Grubb, "The Transatlantic Market," 95.

13 Aaron S Fogleman, "From Slaves, Convicts, and Servants to Free Passengers: The Transformation of Immigration in the Era of the American Revolution," *The Journal of American History* 85.1 (1998), 47; Grubb, "The Transatlantic Market," 107 n.35.

14 James Edward Oglethorpe, *A New and Accurate Account of the Provinces of South-Carolina and Georgia* (London: Printed for J. Worrall, 1732; Database: *ECCO*); Benjamin Marlyn, *An Account Shewing the Progress of the Colony of Georgia in America from Its First Establishment* (London: 1741; Database: *ECCO*); George Hendricks and Louis De Vorsey, "United States of America: Georgia." *The New Encyclopaedia Britannica*, ed. Philip W. Goetz, 15th ed., vol. 29 (Chicago: Encyclopaedia Britannica, Inc., 1991), 322; "Oglethorpe, James Edward," *The New Encyclopaedia Britannica*, ed. Philip W. Goetz, 15th ed., vol. 8 (Chicago: Encyclopaedia Britannica, Inc., 1991), 886.

[15] *An Account Shewing the Progress of the Colony of Georgia*, 20; George, 153-154.

[16] George, 149; A. Roger Ekirch, "Bound for America: A Profile of British Convicts Transported to the Colonies," *The William and Mary Quarterly* 42.2 (1985), 185 n.1; Fogleman, 58.

[17] Kenneth Morgan, "The Organization of the Convict Trade to Maryland: Stevenson, Randolph and Cheston, 1768-1775," *The William and Mary Quarterly* 42.2 (1985), 202; Fogleman, 58-59.

[18] Arthur Pierce Middleton, *Tobacco Coast: A Maritime History of Chesapeake Bay in the Colonial Era* (Baltimore, MD: The Johns Hopkins University Press, 1953), 105.

[19] Ibid., xiii, 42.

[20] Ibid., 114-115.

[21] T. H Breen, *Tobacco Culture: The Mentality of the Great Tidewater Planters on the Eve of the Revolution* (Princeton, NJ: Princeton University Press, 1985), 58.

[22] Breen, 86; Morgan, "The Organization of the Convict Trade," 204.

[23] Morgan, "The Organization of the Convict Trade," 204, 221.

[24] Ibid., 203.

[25] Ekirch, *Bound for America*, 117; Ekirch, "Bound for America," 185 n.1.

[26] *A Complete Guide to All Persons Who Have Any Trade or Concern with the City of London and Parts Adjacent* (London: Printed for J. Osborn, 1740; Database: *ECCO*).

[27] Ekirch, *Bound for America*, 73; Coldham, *Emigrants in Chains*, 61.

[28] Coldham, *Emigrants in Chains*, 61-62; Ekirch, *Bound for America*, 71.

[29] Smith, *Colonists in Bondage*, 121-120; Coldham, *Emigrants in Chains*, 64-65; Grubb, "The Transatlantic Market," 118 n.78; Ekirch, *Bound for America*, 139.

[30] Coldham, *Emigrants in Chains*, 26-27.

[31] Gerald Howson, *Thief-Taker General: Jonathan Wild and the Emergence of Crime and Corruption as a Way of Life in Eighteenth-Century England* (New Brunswick, NJ: Transaction Books, 1970), 91-92.

[32] Peter Wilson Coldham, *The King's Passengers to Maryland and Virginia* (Westminster, MD: Heritage Books, 1997); Coldham, *Emigrants in Chains*, 77.

[33] Ekirch, *Bound for America*, 72-74; Morgan, "The Organization of the Convict Trade," 201; Grubb, "The Transatlantic Market," 104.

[34] Grubb, "The Transatlantic Market," 106-107.

[35] Ekirch, *Bound for America*, 70-76.

[36] Ekirch, *Bound for America*, 73-74.

[37] Coldham, *Emigrants in Chains*, 82.

[38] Morgan, "The Organization of the Convict Trade," 205-206.

[39] Ibid., 209, 207.

[40] Grubb, "The Transatlantic Market," 106. Ekirch estimates an even higher profit margin for the Stevenson, Randolph, & Cheston firm of 26 percent (*Bound for America*, 77).

[41] Morgan, "The Organization of the Convict Trade," 206-207.

[42] Ibid., 206.

[43] Ekirch, *Bound for America*, 73-74.

[44] Coldham, *Emigrants in Chains*, 79, 81.

[45] Grubb, "The Transatlantic Market," 105; Coldham, *Emigrants in Chains*, 86 n.11.

[46] Coldham, *Emigrants in Chains*, 81-82; qtd. in Smith, *Colonists in Bondage*, 115.

[47] Coldham, *Emigrants in Chains*, 66, 79-80; Ekirch, *Bound for America*, 97, 107.

[48] Coldham, *Emigrants in Chains*, 26.

[49] Ekirch, *Bound for America*, 74; Coldham, *Emigrants in Chains*, 27, 82-83.

Chapter Four: From Prison to Convict Ship

[1] *Old Bailey Proceedings Online* (www.oldbaileyonline.org, 22 January 2009), May 1727, trial of John Wilson (t17270517-1).

[2] Alfred Marks, *Tyburn Tree: Its History and Annals* (London: Brown, Langham, 1908; Database: *IA*), 221-222; Peter Linebaugh, "The Tyburn Riot against the Surgeons," *Albion's Fatal Tree: Crime and Society in Eighteenth-Century England*, ed. Douglas Hay, et al. (New York: Pantheon Books, 1975), 103.

[3] Kenneth Morgan, "Petitions against Convict Transportation, 1725-1735," *The English Historical Review* 104, no. 410 (1989), 112-13; Peter Wilson Coldham, *The King's Passengers to Maryland and Virginia* (Westminster, MD: Heritage Books, 1997).

[4] Aaron S. Fogleman, "From Slaves, Convicts, and Servants to Free Passengers: The Transformation of Immigration in the Era of the American Revolution," *The Journal of American History* 85.1 (1998), 43-44.

[5] Seventy-four percent of all transported convicts received a seven-year term, 24 percent received 14 years, and two percent were banished for life. Farley Grubb, "The Market Evaluation of Criminality: Evidence from the Auction of British Convict Labor in America, 1767-1775," *The American Economic Review* 91.1 (2001), 295.

[6] Peter Wilson Coldham, *Emigrants in Chains: A Social History of Forced Emigration to the Americas of Felons, Destitute Children, Political and Religious Non-Conformists, Vagabonds, Beggars and Other Undesirables, 1607-1776* (Baltimore, MD: Genealogical Publishing Company, 1992), 99; Kenneth Morgan, "Convict Transportation to Colonial America (Review of A. Roger Ekirch, *Bound for America: The Transportation of British Convicts to the Colonies, 1718-1775*)." *Reviews in American History* 17.1 (1989), 30.

[7] Coldham, *Emigrants in Chains*, 3.

[8] *Old Bailey Proceedings Online* (www.oldbaileyonline.org, 22 January 2009), December 1728, trial of Elizabeth Howard (t17281204-37).

[9] Peter Whitfield, *London: A Life in Maps* (London: The British Library, 2006), 93. For a discussion of debtors in prison, see M. Dorothy George, *London Life in the Eighteenth Century* (Chicago: Academy Chicago Publishers, 1965), 297-302.

[10] Peter Ackroyd, *London: The Biography* (New York: Anchor Books, 2000), 256.

[11] John Howard, *The State of the Prisons in England and Wales, with Preliminary Observations, and an Account of Some Foreign Prisons* (Warrington: Printed by William Eyres, 1777; Database: *ECCO*), 13.

[12] Batty Langley, *An Accurate Description of Newgate, with the Rights, Privileges, Allowances, Fees, Dues, and Customs Thereof* (London: Printed for T. Warner, 1724; Database: *ECCO*), 35.

[13] George, 291; Frank McLynn, *Crime and Punishment in Eighteenth-Century England* (New York: Oxford University Press, 1991), 294-296; Peter Linebaugh, *The London Hanged: Crime and Civil Society in the Eighteenth Century* (New York: Cambridge University Press, 1992), 28-29; Coldham, *Emigrants in Chains*, 27.

[14] Langley, 3, 8, 42-43, 47, quotation: 43; Ackroyd, 241; Coldham, *Emigrants in Chains*, 19-20.

[15] Langley, 9; McLynn, 294.

[16] Langley, 8-9, 41, 43.

[17] Langley, 42-45.

[18] Langley, 45.

[19] Morgan, "Petitions against Convict Transportation," 111-112.

[20] "The Life of Mary Standford, Pickpocket and Thief," *Lives of the Most Remarkable Criminals*, Vol. II (London: John Osborn, 1735; Database: *ECCO*), 283-284.

[21] "The Life of Mary Standford," 284-286; *Old Bailey Proceedings, Ordinary of Newgate's Account*, 3 August 1726 (OA17260803).

[22] *Old Bailey Proceedings Online* (www.oldbaileyonline.org, 26 January 2009), July 1726, trial of Mary Stanford (t17260711-51).

[23] *Old Bailey Proceedings Online*, trial of Mary Stanford.

[24] *Old Bailey Proceedings Online*, trial of Mary Stanford.

[25] "The Life of Mary Standford," 288.

[26] *Old Bailey Proceedings, Ordinary of Newgate's Account, 3* August 1726.

[27] "The Life of Mary Standford," 290; *Old Bailey Proceedings, Ordinary of Newgate's Account*, 3 August 1726.

[28] Kenneth Morgan, "The Organization of the Convict Trade to Maryland: Stevenson, Randolph and Cheston, 1768-1775," *The William and Mary Quarterly* 42.2 (1985), 207.

[29] Howard, 151, 155; Morgan, "The Organization of the Convict Trade," 209-210.

[30] Morgan, "The Organization of the Convict Trade," 209-210.

[31] Langley, 50; Abbot Emerson Smith, *Colonists in Bondage: White Servitude and Convict Labor in America, 1607-1776*, The Norton Library: N592 (New York: Norton, 1971), 124-125.

[32] The following account is based on "Bristol, May 2," *The Maryland Gazette* (Thursday, August 20, 1752; Database: *AM*), 3.

[33] "Saturday, 8," *The Gentleman's Magazine* (1736; Database: *ILEJ*), 290; "From The 'Political State,' For the Month of June," *The Virginia Gazette* (Parks) (Friday, November 19 to Friday, November 26, 1736; Database: *CWDL*), 1-3.

[34] *Old Bailey Proceedings Online* (www.oldbaileyonline.org, 29 October 2009), May 1736, trial of Henry Justice (t17360505-88); "From The 'Political State,'" 2; "Monday, 10," *The Gentleman's Magazine* (1736; Database: *ILEJ*), 290.

[35] "From The 'Political State,'" 2-3; "Monday, 17," *The Gentleman's Magazine* (1736; Database: *ILEJ*), 290; "*The Trials of* William Wreathock, Peter Chamberlain, James Ruffet, *alias* Ruf-Head, George Bird, *the Younger, and* Gilbert Campbell, *for a Robbery*," *The Tyburn Chronicle*, Vol. III (London: Printed for J. Cooke, 1768; Database: *ECCO*).

[36] "From The 'Political State,'" 3.

[37] Alan Atkinson, "The Free-Born Englishman Transported: Convict Rights as a Measure of Eighteenth-Century Empire," *Past and Present* 144 (Aug., 1994), 95; Bruce Kercher, "Perish or Prosper: The Law and the Convict Transportation in the British Empire, 1700-1850," *Law and the History Review* 21.3 (Autumn, 2003), 533; Gwenda Morgan and Peter Rushton, "Running Away and Returning Home: The Fate of English Convicts in the American Colonies," *Crime, Histoire & Sociétés/Crime, History & Societies* 7.2 (2003), 73-74.

[38] Daniel Defoe, *The Fortunes and Misfortunes of the Famous Moll Flanders, & C*, Ed. G. A. Starr (New York: Oxford University Press, 1971), 293-321.

[39] James Guthrie, *The Ordinary of Newgate, His Account of the Behaviour, Confession, and Dying Words, of the Malefactors, Who*

were Executed at Tyburn, on Wednesday the 18th of March, 1740
(London: John Applebee, 1740; Database: *ECCO*), 7; "Mary Young, *alias*
Jenny Diver, *and* Elizabeth Davis, *alias* Catherine Huggins, *for a*
Robbery, *Jan.* 17, 1741," *Select Trials for Murders, Robberies, Rapes,*
Sodomy, Coining, Frauds, and Other Offenses, 2nd ed., Vol. IV.
(London, 1742; Database: *ECCO*), 358; "Particular Account of the
Extraordinary Exploits of Mary Young, alias Jenny Diver, Who Was
Executed for Privately Stealing," *The Malefactor's Register,* Vol. II.
(London, 1779; Database: *ECCO*), 394; Coldham, *King's Passengers.*

40 "Mary Young, *alias* Jenny Diver," 358; "Particular Account of the
Extraordinary Exploits of Mary Young," 394-395.

41 "Mary Young, *alias* Jenny Diver," 359; Coldham, *The King's*
Passengers.

42 Gwenda Morgan and Peter Rushton, "Print Culture, Crime and
Transportation in the Criminal Atlantic," *Continuity and Change* 22.1
(2007), 52, 67n.11.

43 "London, April 10," *The Virginia Gazette* (Parks) (July 13, 1739;
Database: *CWDL*), 3; *Old Bailey Proceedings* (www.oldbaileyonline.org,
22 July 2009), *Ordinary of Newgate's Account,* August 1739
(OA17390803).

44 Gurthrie, *March, 1740*; "Mary Young, *alias* Jenny Diver," 360;
"Particular Account of the Extraordinary Exploits of Mary Young," 397.

45 Coldham, *Emigrants in Chains,* 73.

46 George, 54.

47 *Old Bailey Proceedings Online* (www.oldbaileyonline.org, 15 April
2009) December 1722, trial of Margaret Hayes (t17221205-19).

48 Richard B. Schwartz, *Daily Life in Johnson's London* (Madison, WI:
The University of Wisconsin Press, 1983), 36-37; George, 49-50, 161.

49 *Old Bailey Proceedings Online* (www.oldbaileyonline.org, 15 April
2009) December 1722, trial of Sarah Nut (t17221205-12).

50 *Old Bailey Proceedings Online* (www.oldbaileyonline.org, 15 April 2009) January 1723, trial of John Watkins (t17230116-19); Schwartz, 113.

51 *Old Bailey Proceedings Online* (www.oldbaileyonline.org, 15 April 2009) January 1723, trial of John Dier (t17230116-1); *Old Bailey Proceedings Online* (www.oldbaileyonline.org, 26 March 2009) January 1723, trial of John Harris (t17230116-25).

52 *Old Bailey Proceedings Online* (www.oldbaileyonline.org, 15 April 2009) January 1720, trial of Sarah Wells (t17200115-47).

53 *Old Bailey Proceedings Online* (www.oldbaileyonline.org, 15 April 2009) January 1723, trial of Sarah Wells (t17230116-22); Coldham, *The King's Passengers*; Gerald Howson, *Thief-Taker General: Jonathan Wild and the Emergence of Crime and Corruption as a Way of Life in Eighteenth-Century England* (New Brunswick, NJ: Transaction Books, 1970), 310.

54 "The Chronological Diary," *The Historical Register*, Vol. 8 (London: C. Meere, 1723), 12 (Internet Archive: http://www.archive.org/stream/historicalregis05greegoog).

55 Coldham, *The King's Passengers*.

56 *Old Bailey Proceedings Online* (www.oldbaileyonline.org, 7 April 2008), December 1722, trial of Elizabeth Knight (t17221205-34); *Old Bailey Proceedings Online* (www.oldbaileyonline.org, 7 April 2008), December 1722, trial of Charles Lynch and Morrice Lynch (t17221205-15).

57 Coldham, *Emigrants in Chains*, 73, 86 n.4.

58 Kenneth Morgan, "The Organization of the Convict Trade to Maryland: Stevenson, Randolph and Cheston, 1768-1775," *The William and Mary Quarterly* 42.2 (1985), 213.

59 Bampfylde-Moore Carew, *An Apology for the Life of Mr Bampfylde-Moore Carew*, 8th ed. (London: Printed for R. Goadby and W. Owen, 1768; Database: *ECCO*), 105.

60 James Revel, *The Poor Unhappy Transported Felon's Sorrowful Account of His Fourteen Years Transportation at Virginia in America* (London, 1780; Database: *ECCO*). A later edition is also available from *Documenting the American South*, http://docsouth.unc.edu/southlit/revel/revel.html.

61 Coldham, *Emigrants in Chains*, 15.

62 *The Virginia Gazette* (Rind) (Thursday, January 5, 1769; Database: *CWDL*), 2.

63 "London, January 23," *The New-York Journal* (April 23, 1767, issue 1268; Database: *AHN*), 1.

64 Marion J. Kaminkow and Jack Kaminkow, *Original Lists of Emigrants in Bondage from London to the American Colonies, 1719-1744* (Baltimore, MD: Magna Carta Book Co., 1967), xi.

Chapter Five: Convict Voyages

1 "Williamsburg, July 28," *The Virginia Gazette* (Rind) (Thursday, July 28, 1774, Database: *CWDL*), 3.

2 Ibid.

3 A. Roger Ekirch, *Bound for America: The Transportation of British Convicts to the Colonies, 1718-1775* (New York: Oxford University Press, 1987), 99.

4 Peter Wilson Coldham, *Emigrants in Chains: A Social History of Forced Emigration to the Americas of Felons, Destitute Children, Political and Religious Non-Conformists, Vagabonds, Beggars and Other Undesirables, 1607-1776* (Baltimore, MD: Genealogical Pub. Co., 1992), 104, 113 n.12.

5 Arthur Pierce Middleton, *Tobacco Coast: A Maritime History of Chesapeake Bay in the Colonial Era* (Baltimore, MD: The Johns Hopkins University Press, 1953), 10.

6 Ibid., 8, 10-11.

7 Ibid., 3, 6.

8 My account of the Rodney is based on "Journal," *The Virginia Gazette* (Rind) (Thursday, April 14, 1768; Database: *CWDL*), 4.

9 "Annapolis, March 17," *The Boston News-Letter* (April 7, 1768, issue 3366; Database: *AHN*), Supplement, 1.

10 Abbot Emerson Smith, *Colonists in Bondage: White Servitude and Convict Labor in America, 1607-1776*, The Norton Library: N592 (New York: Norton, 1971), 207; Ekirch, *Bound for America*, 102.

11 "Extract of a Letter from Capt. James Dobbins," *The Virginia Gazette* (Parks) (May 29, 1746; Database: *CWDL*), 2.

12 Smith, *Colonists in Bondage*, 214

13 Middleton, 15-18.

14 Information about provision amounts all comes from Coldham, *Emigrants in Chains*, 103-104.

15 Coldham, *Emigrants in Chains*, 99; Ekirch, *Bound for America*, 103; A. Roger Ekirch, "Bound for America: A Profile of British Convicts Transported to the Colonies," *The William and Mary Quarterly* 42.2 (1985), 190 n.15; Middleton, 13.

16 Marcus Rediker, *The Slave Ship: A Human History* (New York: Viking, 2007), 274; Middleton, 23.

17 Middleton, 15; Ekirch, "Bound for America," 190 n.15.

18 "The Earl of Fife to George Selwyn," *George Selwyn and His Contemporaries: With Memoirs and Notes*, ed. John Heneage Jesse, Vol. II. (London: Bickers & Son, 1882), 384-392, quotation: 389.

[19] Smith, *Colonists in Bondage*, 117-129; Coldham, *Emigrants in Chains*, 99-112; Ekirch, *Bound for America*, 99, 104.

[20] Rediker, 68; Ekirch, *Bound for America*, 100.

[21] Gottlieb Mittelberger, *Gottlieb Mittelberger's Journey to Pennsylvania in the Year 1750 and Return to Germany in the Year 1754*, trans. Carl Theodor Eben (Philadelphia: John Jos. McVey, 1898), 20.

[22] Smith, *Colonists in Bondage*, 215; Rediker, 120, 267.

[23] Coldham, *Emigrants in Chains*, 115.

[24] Ekirch, *Bound for America*, 97-98; Coldham, *Emigrants in Chains*, 99-100.

[25] Rediker, 6-7.

[26] Ekirch, *Bound for America*, 101; Coldham, *Emigrants in Chains*, 104.

[27] *Old Bailey Proceedings Online* (www.oldbaileyonline.org, 23 June 2010) October 1741, trial of Catharine Davis (t17411014-40); the rest of the information about this voyage is from Coldham, *Emigrants in Chains*, 105, 108-110.

[28] *Old Bailey Proceedings Online* (www.oldbaileyonline.org, 23 June 2010) May 1744, trial of Mary Shirley (t17440510-26).

[29] Information about this voyage is from Coldham, *Emigrants in Chains*, 106-108.

[30] "Extract of a Letter from a Gentleman in Waterford, to His Friend in Dublin, Dated Oct. 18," *The New-York Gazette, or Weekly Post-Boy* (February 12, 1767, issue 1258; Database: *AHN*), 2.

[31] Smith, *Colonists in Bondage*, 125; Rediker, 267.

[32] Coldham, *Emigrants in Chains*, 74; Ekirch, *Bound for America*, 103.

[33] My account of Mrs. Buckler is based on *The Virginia Gazette* (Parks) (Friday, September 24, 1736; Database: *CWDL*), 2-3.

34 Gerald Howson, *Thief-Taker General: Jonathan Wild and the Emergence of Crime and Corruption as a Way of Life in Eighteenth-Century England* (New Brunswick, NJ: Transaction Books, 1970), 139; "James Dalton, for a Robbery," *Select Trials for Murders, Robberies, Rapes, Sodomy, Coining, Frauds, and Other Offenses*, vol. III. (London, 1735; Database: *ECCO*), 320; *The Ordinary of Newgate His Account, of the Behaviour, Confession, and Dying Words of the Malefactors, Who Were Executed at Tyburn, on Tuesday the 12th, of This Instant May, 1730* (London: John Applebee, 1730; Database: *ECCO*).

35 Howson, 247; "James Dalton," *Select Trials*, 321; Coldham, *The King's Passengers*.

36 Howson, 139, 310; *Old Bailey Proceedings Online* (www.oldbaileyonline.org, 31 March 2009) March 1720, trial of William Smith and Mary his Wife (t17200303-19). "The Tryals of James Wilson and John Homer," *A Compleat Collection of Remarkable Tryals of the Most Notorious Malefactors*, vol. IV (London: 1721; Database: *ECCO*), 349. See Chapter One for an account of Wild's stay in debtor's prison.

37 "The Tryals of James Wilson," *Remarkable Tryals*, 351; "James Dalton," *Select Trials*, 322; *Old Bailey Proceedings* (www.oldbaileyonline.org, 31 March 2009), *Ordinary of Newgate's Account*, 19 September 1720 (OA17200919).

38 "James Dalton," *Select Trials*, 322; "The Tryals of James Wilson," *Remarkable Tryals*, 351-352; Coldham, *The King's Passengers*; *The Ordinary of Newgate: His Account of the Behaviours, Confessions, and Last Dying Words of the Malefactors That Were Executed at Tyburn on Wednesday the 8th of February, 1720-21* (London: John Applebee, 1721; Database: *ECCO*), 4.

39 *Old Bailey Proceedings Online* (www.oldbaileyonline.org, 16 August 2010) September 1720 (17200907); "The Tryals of James Wilson," *Remarkable Tryals*; *Ordinary of Newgate ... 8th of February, 1720-21*.

40 Howson, 14, 138-139.

41 *Old Bailey Proceedings Online* (www.oldbaileyonline.org, 31 March 2009) March 1721, trial of John Filewood, Henry Davis, Mary North, Charles Hinchman, Samuel Whittle, Jasper Andrews, Martin Gray, James Dalton (t17210301-61).

42 *Old Bailey Proceedings* (www.oldbaileyonline.org, 31 March 2009), *Ordinary of Newgate's Account*, 3 April 1721 (OA17210403).

43 Howson, 139; Coldham, *The King's Passengers*.

44 Quoted in Howson, 139.

45 Howson, 140; "James Dalton," *Select Trials*, 323.

46 Ibid.

47 Howson, 247.

48 "James Dalton," *Select Trials*, 323.

Chapter Six: Landing in America

1 For a full history of the Carroll family, see Ronald Hoffman, in collaboration with Sally D. Mason, *Princes of Ireland, Planters of Maryland: A Carroll Saga, 1500-1782* (Chapel Hill, NC: The University of North Carolina Press, 2000).

2 Hoffman, 62; Aaron S. Fogleman, "From Slaves, Convicts, and Servants to Free Passengers: The Transformation of Immigration in the Era of the American Revolution," *The Journal of American History* 85.1 (Jun., 1998), 44.

3 Hoffman, 64-67.

4 Ibid., 70.

[5] Robert Beverley, *The History of Virginia in Four Parts* (Richmond, VA: J. W. Randolph, 1855; reprinted from the second revised edition, 1722), 242.

[6] Ibid., 102-123.

[7] William Eddis, *Letters from America, Historical and Descriptive, Comprising Occurrences from 1769 to 1777, Inclusive* (London: William Eddis, 1792), 2-3, 6-7; Hugh Jones, *The Present State of Virginia* (New York: Joseph Sabin, 1865; reprinted from the 1724 edition), 49.

[8] Jones, 35; John Harrower, "Diary of John Harrower, 1773-1776," *The American Historical Review* 6.1 (1900), 76.

[9] "Observations in Several Voyages and Travels in America (From *The London Magazine*, July, 1746)," *William and Mary College Quarterly Historical Magazine* 16:1 (Jan., 1907), 2.

[10] Ibid., 5.

[11] Eddis, 17-19; Beverley, 234; "Observations in Several Voyages," 16.

[12] Allan Kulikoff, *Tobacco and Slaves: The Development of Southern Cultures in the Chesapeake, 1680-1800* (Chapel Hill, NC: The University of North Carolina Press, 1986), 5.

[13] Kulikoff, 86; Fogleman, 47; T. H. Breen, *Tobacco Culture: The Mentality of the Great Tidewater Planters on the Eve of the Revolution* (Princeton, NJ: Princeton University Press, 1985), 34-35.

[14] Breen, 35; Aubrey Land, "The Tobacco Staple and the Planter's Problems: Technology, Labor, and Crops," *Agricultural History* 43:1 (Jan., 1969), 78; Paul G. E. Clemens, "The Operation of an Eighteenth-Century Chesapeake Tobacco Plantation," *Agricultural History* 49:3 (July, 1975), 519; Kulikoff, 23.

[15] Basil Sollers, "Transported Convict Laborers in Maryland during the Colonial Period," *Maryland Historical Magazine* (March 1907), 17; Clemens, 522-523; Land, 71; Arthur Pierce Middleton, *Tobacco Coast: A*

Maritime History of Chesapeake Bay in the Colonial Era (Baltimore, MD: The Johns Hopkins University Press, 1953), 162.

[16] Breen, 32.

[17] Paul H. Smith, et al., eds, "John Adams' Diary: January 1, 1777 - April 30, 1777," *Letters of Delegates to Congress, 1774-1789*, Vol. 6 (Washington, D.C.: Library of Congress, 1976-2000; Database: AMem).

[18] Eddis, 57, 127.

[19] Camille Wells, "The Planter's Prospect: Houses, Outbuildings, and Rural Landscapes in Eighteenth-Century Virginia," *Winterthur Portfolio* 28:1 (Spring, 1993), 28; Breen, 86-88.

[20] Beverley, 235; Clemens 524-525; Wells 16.

[21] Hoffman, 107, 241-242.

[22] Laura Croghan Kamoie, *Irons in the Fire: The Business History of the Tayloe Family and Virginia's Gentry, 1700-1860* (Charlottesville, VA: University of Virginia Press, 2007), 8-9; Abbot Emerson Smith, *Colonists in Bondage: White Servitude and Convict Labor in America, 1607-1776*, The Norton Library; N592 (New York: Norton, 1971), 26-27.

[23] My account of William Green is based on W[illiam] Green, *The Sufferings of William Green, Being a Sorrowful Account, of His Seven Years Transportation* (London: J. Long, [undated, but after 1774] Database: *ECCO*).

[24] M. Dorothy George, *London Life in the Eighteenth Century* (Chicago: Academy Chicago Publishers, 1965), 182.

[25] Batty Langley, *An Accurate Description of Newgate, with the Rights, Privileges, Allowances, Fees, Dues, and Customs Thereof* (London: Printed for T. Warner, 1724; Database: *ECCO*), 50-51; Marion Kaminkow and Jack Kaminkow, Introduction, *Original Lists of Emigrants in Bondage From London to the American Colonies, 1719-1744*, ed. Marion Kaminkow and Jack Kaminkow (Baltimore, MD: Magna Carta Book Company, 1967), xv.

26 Langley, 51; Peter Wilson Coldham, *Emigrants in Chains: A Social History of Forced Emigration to the Americas of Felons, Destitute Children, Political and Religious Non-Conformists, Vagabonds, Beggars and Other Undesirables, 1607-1776* (Baltimore, MD: Genealogical Pub. Co., 1992), 121; Middleton, 171; Alan Atkinson, "The Free-Born Englishman Transported Convict Rights as a Measure of Eighteenth-Century Empire," *Past and Present* 144 (1994), 99.

27 Bruce Kercher, "Perish or Prosper: The Law and Convict Transportation in the British Empire, 1700-1850," *Law and History Review* 21.3 (2003), 533-534, 540.

28 A. Roger Ekirch, *Bound for America: The Transportation of British Convicts to the Colonies, 1718-1775* (New York: Oxford University Press, 1987), 107 n. 3; Smith, *Colonists in Bondage*, 221.

29 Quoted in Ekirch, *Bound for America*, 122.

30 "Eight Pounds Reward," *The Virginia Gazette* (Rind) (July 26, 1770, Database: *CWDL*), 3; "Ten Pounds Reward," *The Virginia Gazette* (Purdie) (April 21, 1775, Database: *CWDL*), 3.

31 Bampfylde-Moore Carew, *An Apology for the Life of Mr. Bampfylde-Moore Carew*, 8th ed. (London: R. Goadby, 1768; Database: *ECCO*), 106-107; *The Ordinary of Newgate, His Account of the Behaviour, Confession, and Dying Words, of the Malefactors Who Were Executed at Tyburn, on Wednesday the 7th of November, 1744* (London: John Applebee, 1744: Database: *ECCO*), 5.

32 Smith, *Colonists in Bondage*, 222; Edward D. Neill, *Terra Mariæ; or, Threads of Maryland Colonial History* (Philadelphia: J. B. Lippincott, 1867; Database: *Making of America*, University of Michigan Library [http://name.umdl.umich.edu/AAV9753.0001.001]), 203; "Proceedings and Acts of the General Assembly, 1769-1770," *Archives of Maryland*, Vol. 62 (Database: *AM*), 165-167.

33 Smith, *Colonists in Bondage*, 222; Middleton, 171-172; Kenneth Morgan, "The Organization of the Convict Trade to Maryland: Stevenson, Randolph and Cheston, 1768-1775," *The William and Mary Quarterly* 42.2 (1985), 21; Farley Grubb, "The Transatlantic Market for British Convict Labor," *The Journal of Economic History* 60.1 (Mar., 2000), 107; Farley Grubb, "The Market Evaluation of Criminality: Evidence from the Auction of British Convict Labor in America, 1767-1775," *The American Economic Review* 91.1 (2001), 300.

34 Coldham, *Emigrants in Chains*, 102.

35 James Revel, *The Poor Unhappy Transported Felon's Sorrowful Account of His Fourteen Years Transportation at Virginia in America* (London, 1780; Database: *ECCO*; a later edition is also available from *Documenting the American South*, http://docsouth.unc.edu/southlit/revel/revel.html), 4.

36 Smith, *Colonists in Bondage*, 132; Morgan, "The Organization of the Convict Trade," 215; "Journal of a French Traveller in the Colonies, 1765, I," *The American Historical Review* 26.4 (1921), 744.

37 Middleton, 162; A. G. L. Shaw, *Convicts and the Colonies: A Study of Penal Transportation from Great Britain and Ireland to Australia and Other Parts of the British Empire* (London: Faber and Faber, 1966), 31; Morgan, "The Organization of the Convict Trade," 215, 220; Kaminkow and Kaminkow, viii-ix.

38 Morgan, "The Organization of the Convict Trade," 220; Coldham, *Emigrants in Chains*, 86, n. 10; Grubb, "Transatlantic Market," 108-109; Middleton, 162.

39 Grubb, "The Market Evaluation," 296-299; Morgan, "The Organization of the Convict Trade," 219; Coldham, *Emigrants in Chains*, 5, 122; Grubb, "Transatlantic Market," 110-111.

40 Smith, *Colonists in Bondage*, 222; Harrower, 77.

[41] Ekirch, *Bound for America*, 123-124; Coldham, *Emigrants in Chains*, 73; Kercher, 540.

Chapter Seven: On the Plantation

[1] A. Roger Ekirch, *Bound for America: The Transportation of British Convicts to the Colonies, 1718-1775* (New York: Oxford University Press, 1987), 141-142; Alan Atkinson, "The Free-Born Englishman Transported Convict Rights as a Measure of Eighteenth-Century Empire." *Past and Present* 144 (1994), 98.

[2] Farley Grubb, "The Transatlantic Market for British Convict Labor," *The Journal of Economic History* 60.1 (Mar., 2000), 111 n. 55 and n. 56; A. Roger Ekirch, "Bound for America: A Profile of British Convicts Transported to the Colonies, 1718-1775," *The William and Mary Quarterly*, 3rd Series, 42.2 (Apr., 1985), 196.

[3] Marion Kaminkow and Jack Kaminkow, Introduction, *Original Lists of Emigrants in Bondage From London to the American Colonies, 1719-1744*, ed. Marion Kaminkow and Jack Kaminkow (Baltimore, MD: Magna Carta Book Company, 1967), ix-x; "Observations in Several Voyages and Travels in America (From *The London Magazine*, July, 1746)," *William and Mary College Quarterly Historical Magazine* 16:1 (Jan., 1907), 15-16; Jonathan Boucher, "On American Education," *A View of the Causes and Consequences of the American Revolution; in Thirteen Discourses, Preached in North America between the Years 1763 and 1775* (London, 1797), 183-184; Worthington Chauncey Ford, *Washington as an Employer and Importer of Labor* (Brooklyn, NY: Privately printed, 1889), 12, 16; Fairfax Harrison, "When the Convicts Came," *Virginia Historical Magazine of History and Biography* 30:3 (July 1922), 252.

[4] My account of James Revel is based on James Revel, *The Poor Unhappy Transported Felon's Sorrowful Account of His Fourteen Years Transportation at Virginia in America* (London, 1780; Database:

ECCO; a later edition is also available from *Documenting the American South*, http://docsouth.unc.edu/southlit/revel/revel.html).

5 The convict William Green worked under similar conditions as Revel, see W[illiam]Green, *The Sufferings of William Green, Being a Sorrowful Account, of His Seven Years Transportation* (London: J. Long, [undated, but after 1774]; Database: *ECCO*), 7; Atkinson, 106; Abbot Emerson Smith, *Colonists in Bondage: White Servitude and Convict Labor in America, 1607-1776*, The Norton Library; N592 (New York: Norton, 1971), 256.

6 William Eddis, *Letters from America, Historical and Descriptive, Comprising Occurrences from 1769 to 1777, Inclusive* (London: William Eddis, 1792), 69; Aaron S. Fogleman, "From Slaves, Convicts, and Servants to Free Passengers: The Transformation of Immigration in the Era of the American Revolution," *The Journal of American History* 85.1 (Jun., 1998), 57; Ford, 12.

7 Smith, *Colonists in Bondage*, 233-234.

8 *Probing the Past: Virginia and Maryland Probate Inventories, 1740-1810* (http://chnm.gmu.edu/probateinventory/index.php) John Brice, 5/1/1767, 184-185; Atkinson, 98.

9 Kenneth Morgan, *Slavery and Servitude in Colonial North America: A Short History* (New York: New York University Press, 2000), 58; Ekirch, *Bound for America*, 152; Smith, *Colonists in Bondage*, 256; Atkinson, 98-100.

10 Eddis, 69-70; Fogleman, 57.

11 *Old Bailey Proceedings* (www.oldbaileyonline.org, 5 November 2010), *Ordinary of Newgate's Account*, 12 May 1721 (OA17210512); Smith, *Colonists in Bondage*, 258; Ekirch, *Bound for America*, 149-150.

12 Smith, *Colonists in Bondage*, 256, 258; Kaminkow and Kaminkow, ix.

13 Smith, *Colonists in Bondage*, 254-255; Robert Beverley, *The History of Virginia in Four Parts* (Richmond, VA: J. W. Randolph, 1855;

reprinted from the second revised edition, 1722), 240; Hugh Jones, *The Present State of Virginia* (New York: Joseph Sabin, 1865; reprinted from the 1724 edition), 49; Ekirch, *Bound for America*, 149-150.

[14] Ronald Hoffman in collaboration with Sally D. Mason, *Princes of Ireland, Planters of Maryland: A Carroll Saga, 1500-1782* (Chapel Hill, NC: The University of North Carolina Press, 2000), 244-245; T. H. Breen, *Tobacco Culture: The Mentality of the Great Tidewater Planters on the Eve of the Revolution* (Princeton, NJ: Princeton University Press, 1985), 106-107; Bampfylde-Moore Carew, *An Apology for the Life of Mr. Bampfylde-Moore Carew*, 8th ed. (London: R. Goadby, 1768; Database: *ECCO*), 110-111.

[15] Ekirch, *Bound for America*, 162.

[16] Smith, *Colonists in Bondage*, 233-234, 270-273.

[17] Morgan, *Slavery and Servitude*, 60; "Observations in Several Voyages," 4.

[18] Morgan, *Slavery and Servitude*, 60-61; *Memoirs of an Unfortunate Young Nobleman, Return'd from a Thirteen Years Slavery in America* (London: J. Freeman, 1743; Database: *ECCO*), 62.

[19] Creole, *The Fortunate Transport; or, the Secret History of the Life and Adventures of the Celebrated Polly Haycock* (London: T. Taylor, [1750?]. Database: *ECCO*), 32.

[20] Hoffman, 257-258.

[21] Ibid, 258-259.

[22] Quoted in Peter Wilson Coldham, *Emigrants in Chains: A Social History of Forced Emigration to the Americas of Felons, Destitute Children, Political and Religious Non-Conformists, Vagabonds, Beggars and Other Undesirables, 1607-1776* (Baltimore, MD: Genealogical Pub. Co., 1992), 130-131.

[23] Laura Croghan Kamoie, *Irons in the Fire: The Business History of the Tayloe Family and Virginia's Gentry, 1700-1860* (Charlottesville, VA: University of Virginia Press, 2007), 8.

[24] Arthur Pierce Middleton, *Tobacco Coast: A Maritime History of Chesapeake Bay in the Colonial Era* (Baltimore, MD: The Johns Hopkins University Press, 1953), 186-187; Kamoie, 24; Ronald L. Lewis, "Slavery on Chesapeake Iron Plantations before the American Revolution," *The Journal of Negro History* 59:3 (July, 1974), 243; Hoffman, 109.

[25] See Kamoie for a full account of the Tayloe family.

[26] Lewis, 242; Kamoie, 62-64.

[27] Hoffman, 229-231.

[28] Lewis, 243; Kamoie, 25-26, 71.

[29] Eddis, 83.

[30] Kamoie, 25-26; Lewis, 244-246.

[31] Kenneth Morgan, "Convict Runaways in Maryland, 1745-1775," *Journal of American Studies* 23.2 (Aug., 1989), 256-257.

Chapter Eight: Committing Crime and Running Away

[1] "Annapolis," *The Maryland Gazette* (June 12, 1751; Database: *AM*), 3.

[2] Alan Atkinson, "The Free-Born Englishman Transported Convict Rights as a Measure of Eighteenth-Century Empire," *Past and Present* 144 (1994), 99.

[3] Hugh Jones, *The Present State of Virginia* (New York: Reprinted for Joseph Sabin, 1865), 53.

[4] Qtd. Basil Sollers, "Transported Convict Laborers in Maryland during the Colonial Period," *Maryland Historical Magazine* (Mar., 1907), 29.

5 Qtd. Arthur Pierce Middleton, *Tobacco Coast: A Maritime History of Chesapeake Bay in the Colonial Era* (Baltimore, MD: The Johns Hopkins University Press, 1953), 169.

6 For different sides of the debate on whether convict transportation increased crime in the colonies, see Abbot Emerson Smith, *Colonists in Bondage: White Servitude and Convict Labor in America, 1607-1776*, The Norton Library; N592 (New York: Norton, 1971), 129 and Atkinson, 100. See also Kenneth Morgan, "Convict Transportation to Colonial America" (Review of A. Roger Ekirch, *Bound for America: Transportation of British Convicts to the Colonies, 1718-1775*), *Reviews in American History* 17.1 (Mar., 1989), 32-33. Gwenda Morgan and Peter Rushton, "Print Culture, Crime and Transportation in the Criminal Atlantic," *Continuity and Change* 22.1 (2007), 55.

7 "Annapolis, April 16," *The Pennsylvania Gazette* (May 7, 1752; Database: *AHN*), 2.

8 "Philadelphia, April 11," *The Pennsylvania Gazette* (April 11, 1751; Database: *AHN*), 2.

9 "Annapolis, December 6," *The Boston Post-Boy* (December 24, 1770; Database: *AHN*), 4.

10 "Annapolis, in Maryland, June 26," *The New-York Gazette, or Weekly Post-Boy* (July 15, 1751; Database: *AHN*), 2.

11 "Annapolis, in Maryland, August 14," *The New-York Gazette, or Weekly Post-Boy* (August 26, 1751; Database: *AHN*), 2.

12 "Annapolis, May 3," *The Pennsylvania Gazette* (May 9, 1745; Database: *AHN*), 2.

13 My account of John Grimes is based on John Grimes, *The Confession of John Grimes* (1765; Database: *Becoming American: The British Atlantic Colonies, 1690-1763*: National Humanities Center, http://nationalhumanitiescenter.org/pds/becomingamer/).

[14] Fairfax Harrison, "When the Convicts Came," *Virginia Historical Magazine of History and Biography* 30:3 (July, 1922), 250-260.

[15] Samuel Shute, *A Proclamation* (Massachusetts, 1718; Database: *ECCO*); Marcus Rediker, *Villains of All Nations: Atlantic Pirates in the Golden Age* (Boston: Beacon Press, 2004), 46, 112.

[16] Farley Grubb, "The Transatlantic Market for British Convict Labor," *The Journal of Economic History* 60.1 (2000), 108; Farley Grubb, "The Market Evaluation of Criminality: Evidence from the Auction of British Convict Labor in America, 1767-1775," *The American Economic Review* 91.1 (2001), 301; Atkinson, 101; W[illiam]Green, *The Sufferings of William Green, Being a Sorrowful Account, of His Seven Years Transportation* (London: J. Long, [undated, but after 1774]; Database: *ECCO*), 7.

[17] Gwenda Morgan and Peter Rushton, "Running Away and Returning Home: The Fate of English Convicts in the American Colonies," *Crime, Histoire & Sociétié /Crime, History & Societies* 7.2 (2003), 69-70; [Runaway Advertisement], *The Pennsylvania Gazette* (October 28, 1742; Database: *AHN*), 3.

[18] Peter Wilson Coldham, *Emigrants in Chains: A Social History of Forced Emigration to the Americas of Felons, Destitute Children, Political and Religious Non-Conformists, Vagabonds, Beggars and Other Undesirables, 1607-1776* (Baltimore, MD: Genealogical Pub. Co., 1992), 125.

[19] Kenneth Morgan, "Convict Runaways in Maryland, 1745-1775," *Journal of American Studies* 23.2 (Aug., 1989), 255; Morgan and Rushton, "Running Away," 65.

[20] [Runaway Advertisement], *The Pennsylvania Gazette* (May 21, 1752; Database: *AHN*), 3.

[21] William Eddis, *Letters from America, Historical and Descriptive, Comprising Occurrences from 1769 to 1777, Inclusive* (London: William

Eddis, 1792; Database: *ECCO*), 70-71; Morgan, "Convict Runaways" 260-262.

22 [Runaway Advertisement], *The Virginia Gazette* (Hunter) (July 3, 1752, no. 79; Database: *CWDL*), 3.

23 [Runaway Advertisement], *The Pennsylvania Gazette* (February 27, 1753, issue 1262; Database: *AHN*), 3.

24 "Philadelphia, July 16," *The Virginia Gazette* (Hunter) (August 28, 1752, no. 87; Database: *CWDL*), 3.

25 "Williamsburg, August 18," *The American Weekly Mercury* (September 7, 1738; Database: *AHN*), 2.

26 The following account is based on the following sources: "Annapolis, July 29," *The New-York Gazette, and Weekly Mercury* (August 9, 1773; Database: *AHN*), 1; "Extract of a Letter from Shippensburg, in Pennsylvania, August 6, 1773," *The New-Hampshire Gazette* (September 17, 1773; Database: *AHN*), 3; "Philadelphia, November 10," *The Boston Post-Boy* (November 15, 1773; Database: *AHN*), 2.

27 "London, Feb. 10," *The Boston News-Letter* (From Monday, April 16 to Monday, April 23, 1722; Database: *AHN*), 4.

28 "London, May 20," *The American Weekly Mercury* (From Thursday, August 31 to Thursday, September 7, 1721; Database: *AHN*), 3.

29 Jones, 54.

30 Smith, *Colonists in Bondage*, 120; Middleton, 169-170.

31 Coldham, *Emigrants in Chains*, 65; Sollers, 28-29.

32 Middleton, 170.

33 J. Thomas Scharf, *History of Maryland: From the Earliest Period to the Present Day*, 3 vols. (Baltimore: John B. Piet, 1879), vol. I: 371-372.

34 "Philadelphia, May 9," *The Pennsylvania Gazette* (May 9, 1751; Database: *AHN*), 1-2.

35 Farley Grubb, "The Market Evaluation," 303; Smith, *Colonists in Bondage*, 132.

36 Daniel Defoe, *The Fortunes and Misfortunes of the Famous Moll Flanders*, ed. G. A. Starr (New York: Oxford University Press, 1971), 88.

37 Ibid., 87.

38 Paula R. Backscheider, *Daniel Defoe: His Life* (Baltimore, MD: The Johns Hopkins University Press, 1989), 485-487.

39 For information about Moll King, see Gerald Howson, *Thief-Taker General: Jonathan Wild and the Emergence of Crime and Corruption as a Way of Life in Eighteenth-Century England* (New Brunswick, NJ: Transaction Books, 1970), 156-170. Factual information about King's transportation to America can be found in Peter Wilson Coldham, *The King's Passengers to Maryland and Virginia* (Westminster, MD: Heritage Books, 1997).

40 *Old Bailey Proceedings Online*, (www.oldbaileyonline.org, 19 May 2009) October 1693, trial of Mary King (t16931012-48).

41 *Old Bailey Proceedings Online*, (www.oldbaileyonline.org, 19 May 2009) December 1718, trial of Mary Goulston. (t17181205-19).

42 Defoe, 4.

43 Coldham, *Emigrants in Chains*, 11-12, 126; Morgan and Rushton, "Running Away," 73-74.

44 John Poulter, *The Discoveries of John Poulter, Alias Baxter*, Eleventh ed. (London: R. Goadby, 1754; Database: *ECCO*), 28.

45 Bampfylde-Moore Carew, *An Apology for the Life of Mr Bampfylde-Moore Carew*, Eighth ed. (London: Printed for R. Goadby and W. Owen, 1768. Database: *ECCO*), 103.

46 Coldham, *Emigrants in Chains*, 13, 126.

47 *Old Bailey Proceedings* (www.oldbaileyonline.org, 6 January 2011), *Ordinary of Newgate's Account*, 3 April 1721 (OA17210403).

48 *The Virginia Gazette* (Parks) (January 28, 1737; Database: *CWDL*), p. 4.

49 Morgan and Rushton, "Running Away," 72.

50 My account of Samuel Ellard is based on the following sources: *Old Bailey Proceedings Online* (www.oldbaileyonline.org, 6 January 2011) April 1741, trial of Samuel Ellard (t17410405-54); *The Ordinary of Newgate, His Account of the Behaviour, Confession, and Dying Words, of the Malefactors Who Were Executed at Tyburn, on Wednesday the 7th of November, 1744* (London: John Applebee, 1744; Database: *ECCO*); *Old Bailey Proceedings Online* (www.oldbaileyonline.org, 5 August 2009) May 1736, trial of Christopher Freeman and Samuel Ellard (t17360505-60); *Old Bailey Proceedings Online* (www.oldbaileyonline.org, 5 August 2009) October 1744, trial of Samuel Ellard (t17441017-29).

Chapter Nine: The End of Convict Transportation

1 Alan Atkinson, "The Free-Born Englishman Transported Convict Rights as a Measure of Eighteenth-Century Empire," *Past and Present* 144 (1994), 101.

2 A. Roger Ekirch, *Bound for America: The Transportation of British Convicts to the Colonies, 1718-1775* (New York: Oxford University Press, 1987), 155.

3 Marion J. Kaminkow and Jack Kaminkow, *Original Lists of Emigrants in Bondage from London to the American Colonies, 1719-1744* (Baltimore, MD: Magna Carta Book Co., 1967), ix; Allan Kulikoff, *Tobacco and Slaves: The Development of Southern Cultures in the Chesapeake, 1680-1800* (Chapel Hill, NC: The University of North Carolina Press, 1986), 76.

4 Kaminkow and Kaminkow, viii.

5 "Observations in Several Voyages and Travels in America (from *the London Magazine*, July 1746)," *William and Mary College Quarterly Historical Magazine* 16.1 (1907), 9.

6 Gary B. Nash, "Poverty and Politics in Early American History," *Down and Out in Early America*, ed. Billy G. Smith (University Park, PA: The Pennsylvania University Press, 2004), 7-8.

7 Kulikoff, 76.

8 William Eddis, *Letters from America, Historical and Descriptive, Comprising Occurrences from 1769 to 1777, Inclusive* (London: William Eddis, 1792; Database: *ECCO*), 67; "Philadelphia, May 9," *The Pennsylvania Gazette* (May 9, 1751; Database: *AHN*), 1-2.

9 Arthur Pierce Middleton, *Tobacco Coast: A Maritime History of Chesapeake Bay in the Colonial Era* (Baltimore, MD: The Johns Hopkins University Press, 1953), 172; Gwenda Morgan and Peter Rushton, "Running Away and Returning Home: The Fate of English Convicts in the American Colonies," *Crime, Histoire & Sociétiés/Crime, History & Societies* 7.2 (2003), 76.

10 "Journal of a French Traveller in the Colonies, 1765, I," *The American Historical Review* 26.4 (1921), 738.

11 Fairfax Harrison, "When the Convicts Came," *Virginia Historical Magazine of History and Biography* 30:3 (July, 1922), 252.

12 A. B., "To the Printer of the Maryland Gazette," *The Maryland Gazette* (Thursday, July 30, 1767; Database: *AM*), 2.

13 *Old Bailey Proceedings Online*, (www.oldbaileyonline.org, 25 August 2009) April 1737, trial of Jonathan Adey (t17370420-38); *Old Bailey Proceedings*, (www.oldbaileyonline.org, 26 August 2009) *Ordinary of Newgate's Account*, June 1737 (OA17370629).

14 *Old Bailey Proceedings Online*, (www.oldbaileyonline.org, 25 August 2009) May 1737, trial of Nicholas Baker (t17370526-5).

15 *Old Bailey Proceedings Online*, (www.oldbaileyonline.org, 25 August 2009) January 1737, trial of James Moulding and George Gew (t17370114-19).

16 Robert W. Barnes, *Colonial Families of Maryland: Bound and Determined to Succeed* (Baltimore, MD: Clearfield, 2007), 10, 23; Gew comes from "Pretty Patsie," *Immigrant Ships Transcribers Guild* (http://immigrantships.net/1700/prettypatsie17370902.html, 25 August 2009).

17 *Old Bailey Proceedings Online*, (www.oldbaileyonline.org, 25 August 2009) March 1726, trial of Mary Slider (t17260302-72); Barnes, 158.

18 *Old Bailey Proceedings Online*, (www.oldbaileyonline.org, 25 August 2009) April 1726, trial of Ann Ambrose (t17260420-47); Barnes, 171-173.

19 Polly Cary Mason, "More About 'Jayle Birds' in Colonial Virginia," *The Virginia Magazine of History and Biography* 53.1 (1945), 39.

20 Morgan, Gwenda and Peter Rushton, "Print Culture, Crime and Transportation in the Criminal Atlantic," *Continuity and Change* 22.1 (2007), 56; Kenneth Morgan, "Petitions against Convict Transportation, 1725-1735," *The English Historical Review* 104.410 (Jan., 1989), 112.

21 "The Lives of John Austin, a Footpad ...," *Lives of the Most Remarkable Criminals*, vol. 2 (London: John Osborn, 1735; Database: *ECCO*), 120-121.

22 "The Life of Ebenezer Ellison, a Notorious Irish Thief," *Lives of the Most Remarkable Criminals*, vol. 3 (London: John Osborn, 1735; Database: *ECCO*), 233-234.

23 George Ollyffe, *An Essay Humbly Offer'd, for an Act of Parliament to Prevent Capital Crimes* (London: Printed for J. Downing, 1731; Database: *ECCO*), 12-15.

24 Thomas Robe, "A Method Whereby Criminals Liable to Transportation ...," *Ways and Means Wherby His Majesty May Man*

His Navy with Ten Thousand Able Sailors, 2nd ed. (London: Printed for
J. Wilcox, [1726?]; Database: *ECCO*).

[25] Joshua Gee, *The Trade and Navigation of Great-Britain Considered*
(London: Printed for Sam. Buckley, 1729; Database: *ECCO*), 58-65.

[26] Gwenda Morgan and Peter Rushton, "Running Away," 62.

[27] Peter Wilson Coldham, *Emigrants in Chains: A Social History of
Forced Emigration to the Americas of Felons, Destitute Children,
Political and Religious Non-Conformists, Vagabonds, Beggars and
Other Undesirables, 1607-1776* (Baltimore, Md.: Genealogical Pub. Co.,
1992), 67.

[28] J. M. Beattie, *Crime and the Courts in England, 1660-1800*
(Princeton, NJ: Princeton University Press, 1986), 560-565.

[29] Coldham, *Emigrants in Chains*, 67-68, 82-83; Ekirch, *Bound for
America*, 74; Farley Grubb, "The Transatlantic Market for British
Convict Labor," *The Journal of Economic History* 60.1 (2000), 105.

[30] Ibid., 67-68.

[31] Ekirch, *Bound for America*, 228-229; "London, July 4," *The Virginia
Gazette* (Dixon and Hunter) (September 16, 1775; Database: *CWDL*), 3.

[32] Ekirch, *Bound for America*, 229.

[33] Coldham, *Emigrants in Chains*, 151.

[34] Qtd. James Boswell, *Life of Johnson*, ed. R. W. Chapman, Oxford
World's Classics (New York: Oxford University Press, 1970), 590.

[35] Kenneth Morgan, "The Organization of the Convict Trade to
Maryland: Stevenson, Randolph and Cheston, 1768-1775," *The William
and Mary Quarterly*, 3rd Series, 42.2 (Apr., 1985), 206.

[36] Aaron S. Fogleman, "From Slaves, Convicts, and Servants to Free
Passengers: The Transformation of Immigration in the Era of the
American Revolution," *The Journal of American History* 85.1 (1998),
45, 60.

[37] Ibid., 61.

[38] Charles Campbell, *The Intolerable Hulks: British Shipboard Confinement, 1776-1857* (Bowie, MD: Heritage Books, 1994), 2-3, 10.

[39] Ibid., 10-11.

[40] Campbell, 12; "London, May 24," *The Virginia Gazette* (Dixon and Hunter) (October 11, 1776; Database: *CWDL*), 4; Beattie, *Crime and the Courts*, 566.

[41] Patrick Colquhoun, *A Treatise on the Police of the Metropolis; Containing a Detail of the Various Crimes and Misdemeanors ... And Suggesting Remedies for Their Prevention*, 5 ed. (London: Printed by H. Fry, for C. Dilly, 1797; Database: *ECCO*), 303.

[42] Coldham, *Emigrants in Chains*, 152; Beattie, *Crime and the Courts*, 566.

[43] Eric Partridge, *A Dictionary of the Underworld* (New York: Bonanza Books, 1961), 255; Campbell, 10, 31-34; Colquhoun, 307.

[44] Beattie, *Crime and the Courts*, 592-599; A. Roger Ekirch, "Great Britain's Secret Convict Trade to America, 1783-1784," *The American Historical Review* 89.5 (1984), 1286; Thomas Keneally, *A Commonwealth of Thieves: The Improbable Birth of Australia* (New York: Nan A. Talese, 2006), 14-17.

[45] The following account is based on Ekirch, "Great Britain's Secret Convict Trade" and Campbell, 14-15.

[46] Hugh Williamson, "Hugh Williamson to Samuel Johnston [October 17, 1788]," *Letters of Delegates to Congress*, vol. 25 (March 1, 1788-December 31, 1789; Database: *AMem*), 433.

[47] Keneally, 14-18; Robert Hughes, *The Fatal Shore* (New York: Vintage, 1986), 56-67.

[48] Bruce Kercher, "Perish or Prosper: The Law and Convict Transportation in the British Empire, 1700-1850," *Law and History Review* 21.3 (2003), 541, 582.

[49] Campbell, 30.

[50] Colquhoun, 318-322.

Conclusion: Winners and Losers

[1] My account of Anthony Lamb is based on Silvio A. Bedini, "At the Sign of the Compass and Quadrant: The Life and Times of Anthony Lamb," *Transactions of the American Philosophical Society*, New Series, 74.1 (1984), 1-84; and *Old Bailey Proceedings Online*, (www.oldbaileyonline.org, 13 January 2011) July 1724, trial of Anthony Lamb (t17240708-26).

[2] Gerald Howson, *Thief-Taker General: Jonathan Wild and the Emergence of Crime and Corruption as a Way of Life in Eighteenth-Century England* (New Brunswick, NJ: Transaction Books, 1970), 208-210.

[3] *Old Bailey Proceedings Online*, (www.oldbaileyonline.org, 13 January 2011) July 1724, trial of Thomas Shepherd (t17240708-12).

[4] *Old Bailey Proceedings Online*, (www.oldbaileyonline.org, 13 January 2011) February 1725, trial of Thomas Sheppard (t17250224-39).

[5] *Commons Journals*, 28 July 1785, qtd. Dorothy M. George, *London Life in the Eighteenth Century* (Chicago: Academy Chicago Publishers, 1965), 356 n.101.

[6] For a history of the development of the modern penitentiary, see Michael Ignatieff, *A Just Measure of Pain: The Penitentiary in the Industrial Revolution, 1750-1850* (New York: Penguin Books, 1978) and Michel Foucault, *Discipline and Punish: The Birth of the Prison*, trans. Alan Sheridan (New York: Vintage Books, 1977).

7 Adam Liptak, "More Than 1 in 100 Adults Are Now in Prison in U.S.," *The New York Times* (Friday, February 29, 2008), National Report: A14.

8 The following account of Jack Sheppard and Jonathan Wild is based on Howson, 212-226.

9 Peter Linebaugh, "The Tyburn Riot Against the Surgeons," *Albion's Fatal Tree: Crime and Society in Eighteenth-Century England*, ed. Douglas Hay, et al. New York: Pantheon, 1975.

10 Capt. Alexander Smith, *Memoirs of the Life and Times of the Famous Jonathan Wild* (London: Printed for Sam Briscoe, 1726), 22; "Particular Account of the Life and Trials of Jonathan Wild," 81; Howson, 277.

11 "Particular Account of the Life and Trials of Jonathan Wild," 81; Peter Wilson Coldham, *The Complete Book of Emigrants, 1607-1776* (CD-ROM) (Baltimore, MD: Genealogical Publishing Co., 1996).

12 [Death notice], *Connecticut Journal* (December 22, 1784, issue 895; Database: *AHN*), 3.

Sources

Database Key:

AHN = America's Historical Newspapers, Readex/Newsbank.

AM = Archives of Maryland Online
(http://aomol.net/html/mdgazette.html), Maryland State
Archives.

AMem = American Memory: Library of Congress
(http://memory.loc.gov/).

CWDL = CW Digital Library
(http://research.history.org/DigitalLibrary.cfm), Colonial
Williamsburg Foundation.

ECCO = Eighteenth Century Collections Online, Gale.

IA = Internet Archive (http://www.archive.org).

ILEJ = The Internet Library of Early Journals
(http://www.bodley.ox.ac.uk/ilej/), eLib.

I. Primary sources

A. B. "To the Printer of the Maryland Gazette." *The Maryland Gazette*,
Thursday, July 30, 1767, p. 2. Database: *AM*.

"Annapolis." *The Maryland Gazette*. June 12, 1751, p. 3. Database: *AM*.

"Annapolis, April 16." *The Pennsylvania Gazette*. May 7, 1752, p. 2.
Database: *AHN*.

"Annapolis, December 6." *The Boston Post-Boy*. December 24, 1770, p.
4. Database: *AHN*.

"Annapolis, March 17." *The Boston News-Letter*. April 7, 1768, issue
3366, Supplement, p. 1. Database: *AHN*.

"Annapolis, May 3." *The Pennsylvania Gazette*. May 9, 1745, p. 2.
Database: *AHN*.

"Annapolis, in Maryland, August 14." *The New-York Gazette, or Weekly
Post-Boy*. August 26, 1751, p. 2. Database: *AHN*.

"Annapolis, in Maryland, June 26." *The New-York Gazette, or Weekly
Post-Boy*. July 15, 1751, p. 2. Database: *AHN*.

"Annapolis, July 29." *The New-York Gazette, and Weekly Mercury*,
August 9, 1773, p. 1. Database: *AHN*.

Beverley, Robert. *The History of Virginia in Four Parts*. Reprinted from
the second revised edition, 1722. Richmond, VA: J. W. Randolph,
1855.

The Bloody Register. Vol. 2. London: Printed for E. and M. Viney, 1764.
Database: *ECCO*.

Boswell, James. *Life of Johnson*. Ed. R. W. Chapman. Oxford World's
Classics. New York: Oxford University Press, 1970.

Boucher, Jonathan. "On American Education." *A View of the Causes
and Consequences of the American Revolution; in Thirteen
Discourses, Preached in North America between the Years 1763
and 1775*. London, 1797, pp. 152-201.

"Bristol, May 2." *The Maryland Gazette*. Thursday, August 20, 1752, p.
3. Database: *AM*.

Carew, Bampfylde-Moore. *An Apology for the Life of Mr Bampfylde-
Moore Carew*. 8th ed. London: Printed for R. Goadby and W.
Owen, 1768. Database: *ECCO*.

"The Chronological Diary." *The Historical Register*. Vol. 8. London: C.
Meere, 1723, p. 12. Database: *IA*.

Colquhoun, Patrick. *A Treatise on the Police of the Metropolis;
Containing a Detail of the Various Crimes and Misdemeanors ...
And Suggesting Remedies for Their Prevention*. 5 ed. London:
Printed by H. Fry, for C. Dilly, 1797. Database: *ECCO*.

*A Complete Guide to All Persons Who Have Any Trade or Concern with
the City of London and Parts Adjacent*. London: Printed for J.
Osborn, 1740. Database: *ECCO*.

The Complete Newgate Calendar. Vol. 3. London: The Navarre Society, 1926.

Creole. *The Fortunate Transport; or, the Secret History of the Life and Adventures of the Celebrated Polly Haycock.* London: T. Taylor, [1750?]. Database: *ECCO.*

[Death notice]. *Connecticut Journal.* December 22, 1784, issue 895, p. 3. Database: *AHN.*

Defoe, Daniel. *An Effectual Scheme for the Immediate Preventing of Street Robberies.* London, 1731.

---. *The Fortunes and Misfortunes of the Famous Moll Flanders, & C.* Ed. G. A. Starr. New York: Oxford University Press, 1971.

---. *The True and Genuine Account of the Life and Actions of the Late Jonathan Wild.* London, 1725. In Henry Fielding, *Jonathan Wild,* ed. David Nokes, New York: Penguin, 1982.

Eddis, William. *Letters from America, Historical and Descriptive, Comprising Occurrences from 1769 to 1777, Inclusive.* London: William Eddis, 1792.

"Eight Pounds Reward," *The Virginia Gazette* (Rind), July 26, 1770, p. 3. Database: *CWDL.*

"Extract of a Letter from a Gentleman in Waterford, to His Friend in Dublin, Dated Oct. 18," *The New-York Gazette, or Weekly Post-Boy,* February 12, 1767, issue 1258, p. 2. Database: *AHN.*

"Extract of a Letter from Capt. James Dobbins," *The Virginia Gazette* (Parks). May 29, 1746, p. 2. Database: *CWDL.*

"The Earl of Fife to George Selwyn." *George Selwyn and His Contemporaries: With Memoirs and Notes.* Ed. John Heneage Jesse. Vol. II. London: Bickers & Son, 1882, pp. 388-390.

Fielding, Henry. *An Enquiry into the Causes of the Late Increase of Robbers, &C.* Dublin: Printed for G. Faulkner, P. Wilson, R. James, and M. Williamson, 1751. Database: *ECCO.*

"From The 'Political State,' For the Month of June." *The Virginia Gazette* (Parks). Friday, November 19 to Friday, November 26, 1736, pp. 1-3. Database: *CWDL.*

Gay, John. *The Beggar's Opera.* Ed. Edgar V. Roberts. Regents
Restoration Drama Series. Lincoln, NE: University of Nebraska
Press, 1969.

Gee, Joshua. *The Trade and Navigation of Great-Britain Considered.*
London: Printed for Sam. Buckley, 1729. Database: *ECCO.*

Green, W[illiam]. *The Sufferings of William Green, Being a Sorrowful
Account, of His Seven Years Transportation.* London: J. Long,
[undated, but after 1774]. Database: *ECCO.*

Grimes, John. *The Confession of John Grimes.* 1765. Database:
Becoming American: The British Atlantic Colonies, 1690-1763:
National Humanities Center
(http://nationalhumanitiescenter.org/pds/becomingamer/).

Guthrie, James. *The Ordinary of Newgate, His Account of the
Behaviour, Confession, and Dying Words, of the Malefactors,
Who were Executed at Tyburn, on Wednesday the 18th of March,
1740.* London: John Applebee, 1740. Database: *ECCO.*

Hakluyt, Richard. *A Discourse Concerning Western Planting, Written
in the Year 1584.* Ed. Charles Deane. Cambridge: John Wilson
and Son, 1877.

Hanging, Not Punishment Enough. London: Longman, Hurst, Rees,
Orme, and Brown, 1812 [Originally published: 1701].

Harrower, John. "Diary of John Harrower, 1773-1776." *The American
Historical Review* 6.1 (1900): 65-107.

The History of the Lives and Actions of Jonathan Wild, Thief-Taker.
London: Printed for Edward Midwinter, 1725. Database: *ECCO.*

Howard, John. *The State of the Prisons in England and Wales, with
Preliminary Observations, and an Account of Some Foreign
Prisons.* Warrington: Printed by William Eyres, 1777. Database:
ECCO.

"James Dalton, for a Robbery." *Select Trials for Murders, Robberies,
Rapes, Sodomy, Coining, Frauds, and Other Offenses.* Vol. III.
London, 1735. Database: *ECCO.*

Jefferson, Thomas. *The Writings of Thomas Jefferson*. Ed. Paul
Leicester Ford. Vol. IV. New York: G. P. Putnam's Sons, 1894.

"Jonathan Wild, For Felonies." *Select Trials for Murders, Robberies,
Rapes, Sodomy, Coining, Frauds, and Other Offenses: At the
Sessions-House in the Old-Bailey*. Vol. II. London: Printed for J.
Wilford, 1735. Database: *ECCO*.

Jones, Hugh. *The Present State of Virginia*. Reprinted from the 1724
edition. New York: Joseph Sabin, 1865.

"Journal." *The Virginia Gazette* (Rind). April 14, 1768, p. 4. Database:
CWDL.

"Journal of a French Traveller in the Colonies, 1765, I." *The American
Historical Review* 26.4 (1921): 726-47.

Langley, Batty. *An Accurate Description of Newgate, with the Rights,
Privileges, Allowances, Fees, Dues, and Customs Thereof*.
London: Printed for T. Warner, 1724. Database: *ECCO*.

*The Life and Glorious Actions of the Most Heroic and Magnanimous
Jonathan Wilde*. London: Printed for H. Whitridge, 1725.
Database: *ECCO*.

"The Life of Ebenezer Ellison, a Notorious Irish Thief." *Lives of the Most
Remarkable Criminals*. Vol. 3. London: John Osborn, 1735.
Database: *ECCO*.

"The Life of James Dalton, a Thief." *Lives of the Most Remarkable
Criminals*. Vol. III. London: John Osborn, 1735. Database:
ECCO.

The Life of Jonathan Wild, from His Birth to His Death. London, 1725.
Database: *ECCO*.

"The Life of Mary Standford, Pickpocket and Thief." *Lives of the Most
Remarkable Criminals*. Vol. II. London: John Osborn, 1735,
283-290. Database: *ECCO*.

"The Life of the Famous Jonathan Wild, Thief-Taker." *Lives of the Most
Remarkable Criminals*. Vol. II. London: John Osborn, 1735.
Database: *ECCO*.

"The Lives of John Austin, a Footpad ...." *Lives of the Most Remarkable Criminals*. Vol. 2. London: John Osborn, 1735. Database: *ECCO*.

"London." *The New-York Gazette, or Weekly Post-Boy*. May 1, 1749, issue 328, p. 2; Database: *AHN*.

"London, April 10." *The Virginia Gazette* (Parks). July 13, 1739, p. 3. Database: *CWDL*.

"London, Feb. 10." *The Boston News-Letter*. From Monday, April 16 to Monday, April 23, 1722, p. 4. Database: *AHN*.

"London, January 23." *The New-York Journal*. April 23, 1767, issue 1268, p. 1. Database: *AHN*.

"London, July 4." *The Virginia Gazette* (Dixon and Hunter) September 16, 1775, p. 3. Database: *CWDL*.

"London, May 20." *The American Weekly Mercury*. From Thursday, August 31 to Thursday, September 7, 1721, p. 3. Database: *AHN*.

"London, May 24." *The Virginia Gazette* (Dixon and Hunter) October 11, 1776, p. 4. Database: *CWDL*.

Marlyn, Benjamin. *An Account Shewing the Progress of the Colony of Georgia in America from Its First Establishment*. London: 1741. Database: *ECCO*.

"Mary Young, *alias* Jenny Diver, *and* Elizabeth Davis, *alias* Catherine Huggins, *for a* Robbery, *Jan.* 17, 1741." *Select Trials for Murders, Robberies, Rapes, Sodomy, Coining, Frauds, and Other Offenses*. 2nd ed. Vol. IV. London: Printed for L. Gilliver and J. Huggonson, 1742. Database: *ECCO*.

Memoirs of an Unfortunate Young Nobleman, Return'd from a Thirteen Years Slavery in America. London: J. Freeman, 1743. Database: *ECCO*.

Mittelberger, Gottlieb. *Gottlieb Mittelberger's Journey to Pennsylvania in the Year 1750 and Return to Germany in the Year 1754*. Trans. Carl Theodor Eben. Philadelphia: John Jos. McVey, 1898.

"Monday, 10." *The Gentleman's Magazine*. 1736, p. 290. Database: *ECCO*.

"Monday, 17." *The Gentleman's Magazine*. 1736, p. 290. Database: *ECCO*.

"Observations in Several Voyages and Travels in America (From *The London Magazine*, July, 1746)." *William and Mary College Quarterly Historical Magazine* 16:1 (Jan., 1907), 1-17.

Oglethorpe, James Edward. *A New and Accurate Account of the Provinces of South-Carolina and Georgia*. London: Printed for J. Worrall, 1732. Database: *ECCO*.

Old Bailey Proceedings (www.oldbaileyonline.org, 31 March 2009), *Ordinary of Newgate's Account*, 19 September 1720 (OA17200919).

---. (www.oldbaileyonline.org, 6 January 2011), *Ordinary of Newgate's Account*, 3 April 1721 (OA17210403).

---. (www.oldbaileyonline.org, 5 November 2010), *Ordinary of Newgate's Account*, 12 May 1721 (OA17210512).

---. (www.oldbaileyonline.org, 31 March 2009), *Ordinary of Newgate's Account*, 3 April 1721 (OA17210403).

Old Bailey Proceedings Online. (www.oldbaileyonline.org, 13 January 2011) July 1724, trial of Anthony Lamb (t17240708-26).

---. (www.oldbaileyonline.org, 13 January 2011) July 1724, trial of Thomas Shepherd (t17240708-12).

---. (www.oldbaileyonline.org, 13 January 2011) February 1725, trial of Thomas Sheppard (t17250224-39).

---. (www.oldbaileyonline.org, 26 January 2009), *Ordinary of Newgate's Account*, 3 August 1726 (OA17260803).

---. (www.oldbaileyonline.org, 26 August 2009) *Ordinary of Newgate's Account*, June 1737 (OA17370629).

---. (www.oldbaileyonline.org, 22 July 2009), *Ordinary of Newgate's Account*, August 1739 (OA17390803).

Old Bailey Proceedings Online. (www.oldbaileyonline.org, 19 May 2009) October 1693, trial of Mary King (t16931012-48).

---. (www.oldbaileyonline.org, 1 February 2008), February 1718, trial of Edward Higgins (t17180227-19).

---. (www.oldbaileyonline.org, 1 February 2008), February 1718, trial of Richard Wood (t17180227-33).

---. (www.oldbaileyonline.org, 19 May 2009) December 1718, trial of Mary Goulston. (t17181205-19).

---. (www.oldbaileyonline.org, 15 April 2009) January 1720, trial of Sarah Wells (t17200115-47).

---. (www.oldbaileyonline.org, 31 March 2009) March 1720, trial of William Smith and Mary his Wife (t17200303-19).

---. (www.oldbaileyonline.org, 6 October 2008), July 1720, trial of Edward Higgins (t17200712-20).

---. (www.oldbaileyonline.org, 16 August 2010) September 1720 (17200907).

---. (www.oldbaileyonline.org, 31 March 2009) March 1721, trial of John Filewood, Henry Davis, Mary North, Charles Hinchman, Samuel Whittle, Jasper Andrews, Martin Gray, James Dalton (t17210301-61).

---. (www.oldbaileyonline.org, 7 April 2008), December 1722, trial of Charles Lynch and Morrice Lynch (t17221205-15).

---. (www.oldbaileyonline.org, 7 April 2008), December 1722, trial of Elizabeth Knight (t17221205-34).

---. (www.oldbaileyonline.org, 22 October 2009), December 1722, trial of John Flint t17221205-17).

---. (www.oldbaileyonline.org, 15 April 2009) December 1722, trial of Margaret Hayes (t17221205-19).

---. (www.oldbaileyonline.org, 15 April 2009) December 1722, trial of Sarah Nut (t17221205-12).

---. (www.oldbaileyonline.org, 7 April 2008), January 1723, trial of James Bell (t17230116-9).

---. (www.oldbaileyonline.org, 15 April 2009) January 1723, trial of John Dier (t17230116-1).

---. (www.oldbaileyonline.org, 26 March 2009) January 1723, trial of John Harris (t17230116-25).

---. (www.oldbaileyonline.org, 15 April 2009) January 1723, trial of John Watkins (t17230116-19).

---. (www.oldbaileyonline.org, 15 April 2009) January 1723, trial of Sarah Wells (t17230116-22).

---. (www.oldbaileyonline.org, 13 January 2011) July 1724, trial of Anthony Lamb (t17240708-26).

---. (www.oldbaileyonline.org, 13 January 2011) July 1724, trial of Thomas Shepherd (t17240708-12).

---. (www.oldbaileyonline.org, 13 January 2011) February 1725, trial of Thomas Sheppard (t17250224-39).

---. (www.oldbaileyonline.org, 25 August 2009) March 1726, trial of Mary Slider (t17260302-72).

---. (www.oldbaileyonline.org, 25 August 2009) April 1726, trial of Ann Ambrose (t17260420-47).

---. (www.oldbaileyonline.org, 26 January 2009), July 1726, trial of Mary Stanford (t17260711-51).

---. (www.oldbaileyonline.org, 22 January 2009), May 1727, trial of John Wilson (t17270517-1).

---. (www.oldbaileyonline.org, 22 January 2009), December 1728, trial of Elizabeth Howard (t17281204-37).

---. (www.oldbaileyonline.org, 5 August 2009) May 1736, trial of Christopher Freeman and Samuel Ellard (t17360505-60).

---. (www.oldbaileyonline.org, 29 October 2009), May 1736, trial of Henry Justice (t17360505-88).

---. (www.oldbaileyonline.org, 25 August 2009) January 1737, trial of James Moulding and George Gew (t17370114-19).

---. (www.oldbaileyonline.org, 25 August 2009) April 1737, trial of Jonathan Adey (t17370420-38).

---. (www.oldbaileyonline.org, 25 August 2009) May 1737, trial of Nicholas Baker (t17370526-5).

---. (www.oldbaileyonline.org, 6 January 2011) April 1741, trial of Samuel Ellard (t17410405-54).

---. (www.oldbaileyonline.org, 23 June 2010) October 1741, trial of
Catharine Davis (t17411014-40)

---. (www.oldbaileyonline.org, 23 June 2010) May 1744, trial of Mary
Shirley (t17440510-26).

---. (www.oldbaileyonline.org, 5 August 2009) October 1744, trial of
Samuel Ellard (t17441017-29).

Ollyffe, George. *An Essay Humbly Offer'd, for an Act of Parliament to Prevent Capital Crimes*. London: Printed for J. Downing, 1731. Database: *ECCO*.

The Ordinary of Newgate His Account, of the Behaviour, Confession, and Dying Words of the Malefactors, Who Were Executed at Tyburn, on Tuesday the 12th, of This Instant May, 1730. London: John Applebee, 1730. Database: *ECCO*.

The Ordinary of Newgate, His Account of the Behaviour, Confession, and Dying Words, of the Malefactors Who Were Executed at Tyburn, on Wednesday the 7th of November, 1744. London: John Applebee, 1744. Database: *ECCO*.

The Ordinary of Newgate: His Account of the Behaviours, Confessions, and Last Dying Words of the Malefactors That Were Executed at Tyburn on Wednesday the 8th of February, 1720-21. London: John Applebee, 1721. Database: *ECCO*.

"Particular Account of the Extraordinary Exploits of Mary Young, alias Jenny Diver, Who Was Executed for Privately Stealing." *The Malefactor's Register*. Vol. II. London: Alexander Hogg, 1779. Database: *ECCO*.

"Particular Account of the Life and Trials of Jonathan Wild." *The Malefactor's Register*. Vol. II. London: Alexander Hogg, 1779. Database: *ECCO*.

"Philadelphia, April 11." *The Pennsylvania Gazette*. April 11, 1751, p. 2. Database: *AHN*.

"Philadelphia, July 16," *The Virginia Gazette* (Hunter), August 28, 1752, no. 87, 3. Database: *CWDL*.

"Philadelphia, May 9." *The Pennsylvania Gazette.* May 9, 1751, pp. 1-2. Database: *AHN.*

"Philadelphia, November 10." *The Boston Post-Boy.* November 15, 1773, p. 2. Database: *AHN.*

Poulter, John. *The Discoveries of John Poulter, Alias Baxter.* Eleventh ed. London: R. Goadby, 1754. Database: *ECCO.*

Probing the Past: Virginia and Maryland Probate Inventories, 1740-1810. (http://chnm.gmu.edu/probateinventory/index.php) John Brice, 5/1/1767, 184-185.

"Proceedings and Acts of the General Assembly, 1769-1770." *Archives of Maryland* [Electronic Edition]. Vol. 62. Maryland State Archives, 2006, pp. 165-167. Database: *AM.*

Revel, James. *The Poor Unhappy Transported Felon's Sorrowful Account of His Fourteen Years Transportation at Virginia in America.* London, 1780. Database: *ECCO.* A later edition is also available from *Documenting the American South,* http://docsouth.unc.edu/southlit/revel/revel.html.

Robe, Thomas. "A Method Whereby Criminals Liable to Transportation ...." *Ways and Means Wherby His Majesty May Man His Navy with Ten Thousand Able Sailors.* 2nd ed. London: Printed for J. Wilcox, [1726?]. Database: *ECCO.*

[Runaway Advertisement]. *The Pennsylvania Gazette,* October 28, 1742, p. 3. Database: *AHN.*

[Runaway Advertisement]. *The Pennsylvania Gazette,* May 21, 1752, p. 3. Database: *AHN.*

[Runaway Advertisement], *The Pennsylvania Gazette,* February 27, 1753, issue 1262, p. 3. Database: *AHN.*

[Runaway Advertisement], *The Virginia Gazette* (Hunter), July 3, 1752, no. 79, 3. Database: *CWDL.*

"Saturday, 8." *The Gentleman's Magazine,* 1736, p. 290. Database: *ECCO.*

Shute, Samuel. *A Proclamation.* Massachusetts, 1718. Database: *ECCO.*

Smith, Capt. Alexander. *Memoirs of the Life and Times of the Famous Jonathan Wild*. London: Printed for Sam. Briscoe, 1726. Database: *ECCO*.

Smith, Paul H., et al., eds. "John Adams' Diary: January 1, 1777 - April 30, 1777." *Letters of Delegates to Congress, 1774-1789*. Vol. 6. Washington, D.C.: Library of Congress, 1976-2000. Database: *AMem*.

"Ten Pounds Reward," *The Virginia Gazette* (Purdie), April 21, 1775, p. 3. Database: *CWDL*.

"The Trial of Jonathan Wild, for Felony, with the Most Remarkable Passages of His Life." *The Bloody Register*. Vol. II. London: Printed for E. and M. Viney, 1764. Database: *ECCO*.

"*The Trials of* William Wreathock, Peter Chamberlain, James Ruffet, *alias* Ruf-Head, George Bird, *the Younger, and* Gilbert Campbell, *for a Robbery*." *The Tyburn Chronicle*. Vol. III. London: Printed for J. Cooke, 1768. Database: *ECCO*.

"The Tryals of James Wilson and John Homer." *A Compleat Collection of Remarkable Tryals of the Most Notorious Malefactors*. Vol. IV. London: 1721. Database: *ECCO*.

The Virginia Gazette (Parks), Friday, September 24, 1736, pp. 2-3. Database: *CWDL*.

The Virginia Gazette (Parks) January 28, 1737, p. 4. Database: *CWDL*.

The Virginia Gazette (Rind), Thursday, January 5, 1769, p. 2. Database: *CWDL*.

"Williamsburg, August 18." *The American Weekly Mercury*, September 7, 1738, p. 2. Database: *AHN*.

"Williamsburg, July 28," *The Virginia Gazette* (Rind). Thursday, July 28, 1774, *p. 3*. Database: *CWDL*.

Williamson, Hugh. "Hugh Williamson to Samuel Johnston [October 17, 1788]." *Letters of Delegates to Congress*. Vol. 25: March 1, 1788-December 31, 1789, p. 433. Database: *AMem*.

II. Secondary sources

Ackroyd, Peter. *London: The Biography*. New York: Anchor Books, 2000.

Atkinson, Alan. "The Free-Born Englishman Transported Convict Rights as a Measure of Eighteenth-Century Empire." *Past and Present* 144 (1994): 88-115.

Backscheider, Paula R. *Daniel Defoe: His Life*. Baltimore, MD: The Johns Hopkins University Press, 1989.

Barnes, Robert W. *Colonial Families of Maryland: Bound and Determined to Succeed*. Baltimore, MD: Clearfield, 2007.

Beattie, J. M. *Crime and the Courts in England, 1660-1800*. Princeton: Princeton University Press, 1986.

---. *Policing and Punishment in London, 1660-1750: Urban Crime and the Limits of Terror*. New York: Oxford University Press, 2001.

Bell, Ian A. *Literature and Crime in Augustan England*. New York: Routledge, 1991.

Bedini, Silvio A. "At the Sign of the Compass and Quadrant: The Life and Times of Anthony Lamb." *Transactions of the American Philosophical Society*, New Series, 74.1 (1984): 1-84.

Bender, John. *Imagining the Penitentiary: Fiction and the Architecture of Mind in Eighteenth-Century England*. Chicago: The University of Chicago Press, 1987.

Benton, Jr., J. H. *Early Census Making in Massachusetts, 1643-1765*. Boston: Charles E. Goodspeed, 1905.

Breen, T. H. *Tobacco Culture: The Mentality of the Great Tidewater Planters on the Eve of the Revolution*. Princeton, NJ: Princeton University Press, 1985.

Butler, James Davie. "British Convicts Shipped to American Colonies." *American Historical Review* 2.1 (1896): 12-33.

Campbell, Charles. *The Intolerable Hulks: British Shipboard Confinement, 1776-1857*. Bowie, MD: Heritage Books, 1994.

Clemens, Paul G. E. "The Operation of an Eighteenth-Century
Chesapeake Tobacco Plantation." *Agricultural History* 49:3
(July, 1975): 517-531.

Coldham, Peter Wilson. *The Complete Book of Emigrants, 1607-1776*
(CD-ROM). Baltimore, MD: Genealogical Publishing Co., 1996.

---. *Emigrants in Chains: A Social History of Forced Emigration to the
Americas of Felons, Destitute Children, Political and Religious
Non-Conformists, Vagabonds, Beggars and Other Undesirables,
1607-1776*. Baltimore, MD: Genealogical Pub. Co., 1992.

---. *The King's Passengers to Maryland and Virginia*. Westminster,
MD: Heritage Books, 1997.

Dexter, Franklin Bowdith. *Estimates of Population in the American
Colonies*. Worcester, MA: Press of Charles Hamilton, 1887, p. 20.

Ekirch, A. Roger. *At Day's Close: Night in Times Past*. New York: W. W.
Norton, 2005.

---. "Bound for America: A Profile of British Convicts Transported to the
Colonies." *The William and Mary Quarterly* 42.2 (1985): 184-
200.

---. *Bound for America: The Transportation of British Convicts to the
Colonies, 1718-1775*. New York: Oxford University Press, 1987.

---. "Great Britain's Secret Convict Trade to America, 1783-1784." *The
American Historical Review* 89.5 (1984): 1285-91.

---. "The Transportation of Scottish Criminals to America During the
Eighteenth Century." *The Journal of British Studies* 24.3 (1985):
366-74.

Faller, Lincoln B. *Turned to Account: The Forms and Functions of
Criminal Biography in Late Seventeenth- and Early Eighteenth-
Century England*. New York: Cambridge UP, 1987.

Fogleman, Aaron S. "From Slaves, Convicts, and Servants to Free
Passengers: The Transformation of Immigration in the Era of the
American Revolution." *The Journal of American History* 85.1
(1998): 43-76.

Ford, Worthington Chauncey. *Washington as an Employer and Importer of Labor*. Brooklyn, NY: Privately printed, 1889.

Foss, Edward. *The Judges of England; with Sketches of Their Lives*. Vol. VIII. London: John Murray, 1864.

Foucault, Michel. *Discipline and Punish: The Birth of the Prison*. Trans. Alan Sheridan. New York: Vintage Books, 1977.

George, M. Dorothy. *London Life in the Eighteenth Century*. Chicago: Academy Chicago Publishers, 1965.

Gilliam, Charles Edgar. "Jail Bird Immigrants to Virginia." *The Virginia Magazine of History and Biography* 52.3 (July, 1944): 180-182.

Grubb, Farley. "The Market Evaluation of Criminality: Evidence from the Auction of British Convict Labor in America, 1767-1775." *The American Economic Review* 91.1 (2001): 295-304.

---. "The Transatlantic Market for British Convict Labor." *The Journal of Economic History* 60.1 (2000): 94-122.

Harrison, Fairfax. "When the Convicts Came." *Virginia Historical Magazine of History and Biography* 30:3 (July, 1922): 250-260.

Hendricks, George and Louis De Vorsey. "United States of America: Georgia." *The New Encyclopaedia Britannica*. Ed. Philip W. Goetz. 15th ed. Vol. 29: 322. Chicago: Encyclopaedia Britannica, Inc., 1991.

Hibbert, Ben Weinreb and Christopher, ed. *London Encyclopaedia*. London: Macmillan, 1983.

Hill, Christopher. *The Pelican Economic History of Britain: Volume 2: 1530-1780, Reformation to Industrial Revolution*. New York: Pelican Books, 1969.

Hitchcock, Tim and Robert Shoemaker. "Crimes Tried at the Old Bailey: Explanations of Types and Categories of Indictable Offences." *Old Bailey Proceedings Online* (www.oldbaileyonline.org, 1 February 2008).

---. *Tales from the Hanging Court*. London: Hodder Arnold, 2006.

Hoffman, Ronald, in collaboration with Sally D. Mason. *Princes of Ireland, Planters of Maryland: A Carroll Saga, 1500-1782.* Chapel Hill, NC: The University of North Carolina Press, 2000.

Howson, Gerald. *Thief-Taker General: Jonathan Wild and the Emergence of Crime and Corruption as a Way of Life in Eighteenth-Century England.* New Brunswick, NJ: Transaction Books, 1970.

Hughes, Robert. *The Fatal Shore.* New York: Vintage, 1986.

Ignatieff, Michael. *A Just Measure of Pain: The Penitentiary in the Industrial Revolution, 1750-1850.* New York: Penguin Books, 1978.

Introduction. *Proceedings of the Maryland Court of Appeals, 1695-1729.* Vol. 77, xlii-xliv. Database: *AM.*

Jordon, Don and Michael Walsh. *White Cargo: The Forgotten History of Britain's White Slaves in America.* New York: New York University Press, 2007.

Kaminkow, Marion J., and Jack Kaminkow. *Original Lists of Emigrants in Bondage from London to the American Colonies, 1719-1744.* Baltimore, MD: Magna Carta Book Co., 1967.

Kamoie, Laura Croghan. *Irons in the Fire: The Business History of the Tayloe Family and Virginia's Gentry, 1700-1860.* Charlottesville, VA: University of Virginia Press, 2007.

Keneally, Thomas. *A Commonwealth of Thieves: The Improbable Birth of Australia.* New York: Nan A. Talese, 2006.

Kercher, Bruce. "Perish or Prosper: The Law and Convict Transportation in the British Empire, 1700-1850." *Law and History Review* 21.3 (2003): 527-84.

Kramnick, Isaac. *Bolingbroke and His Circle: The Politics of Nostalgia in the Age of Walpole.* Ithaca, NY: Cornell University Press, 1968.

Kulikoff, Allan. *Tobacco and Slaves: The Development of Southern Cultures in the Chesapeake, 1680-1800.* Chapel Hill, NC: The University of North Carolina Press, 1986.

Land, Aubrey. "The Tobacco Staple and the Planter's Problems: Technology, Labor, and Crops." *Agricultural History* 43:1 (Jan., 1969): 69-82.

Lewis, Ronald L. "Slavery on Chesapeake Iron Plantations Before the American Revolution." *The Journal of Negro History* 59:3 (July, 1974): 242-254.

Linebaugh, Peter. *The London Hanged: Crime and Civil Society in the Eighteenth Century*. New York: Cambridge University Press, 1992.

---. "The Tyburn Riot against the Surgeons." *Albion's Fatal Tree: Crime and Society in Eighteenth-Century England*. Ed. Douglas Hay, et al. New York: Pantheon Books, 1975.

Liptak, Adam. "More Than 1 in 100 Adults Are Now in Prison in U.S." *The New York Times* Friday, February 29, 2008, National Report: A14.

Mantoux, Paul. *The Industrial Revolution in the Eighteenth Century: An Outline of the Beginnings of the Modern Factory System in England*. Chicago: The University of Chicago Press, 1983.

Marks, Alfred. *Tyburn Tree: Its History and Annals*. London: Brown, Langham, 1908. Database: IA.

Mason, Polly Cary. "More About 'Jayle Birds' in Colonial Virginia." *The Virginia Magazine of History and Biography* 53.1 (1945): 37-41.

McLynn, Frank. *Crime and Punishment in Eighteenth-Century England*. New York: Oxford University Press, 1991.

Middleton, Arthur Pierce. *Tobacco Coast: A Maritime History of Chesapeake Bay in the Colonial Era*. Baltimore, MD: The Johns Hopkins University Press, 1953.

Morgan, Gwenda and Peter Rushton. "Print Culture, Crime and Transportation in the Criminal Atlantic." *Continuity and Change* 22.1 (2007): 49-71.

---. "Running Away and Returning Home: The Fate of English Convicts in the American Colonies." *Crime, Histoire & Sociétés/Crime, History & Societies* 7.2 (2003): 61-80.

Morgan, Kenneth. "Convict Runaways in Maryland, 1745-1775." *Journal of American Studies* 23.2 (Aug., 1989): 253-268.

---. "Convict Transportation to Colonial America (Review of A. Roger Ekirch, *Bound for America: The Transportation of British Convicts to the Colonies, 1718-1775*)." *Reviews in American History* 17.1 (1989): 29-34.

---. "The Organization of the Convict Trade to Maryland: Stevenson, Randolph and Cheston, 1768-1775." *The William and Mary Quarterly* 42.2 (1985): 201-27.

---. "Petitions against Convict Transportation, 1725-1735." *The English Historical Review* 104.410 (1989): 110-13.

Nash, Gary B. "Poverty and Politics in Early American History." *Down and Out in Early America*. Ed. Billy G. Smith. University Park, PA: The Pennsylvania University Press, 2004.

Neill, Edward D. *Terra Mariæ; or, Threads of Maryland Colonial History*. Philadelphia: J. B. Lippincott, 1867. Database: *Making of America*, University of Michigan Library (http://name.umdl.umich.edu/AAV9753.0001.001).

Nokes, David. Introduction. *Jonathan Wild* by Henry Fielding. Ed. David Nokes. New York: Penguin, 1982.

"Oglethorpe, James Edward." *The New Encyclopaedia Britannica*. Ed. Philip W. Goetz. 15th ed. Vol. 8: 886. Chicago: Encyclopaedia Britannica, Inc., 1991.

Partridge, Eric. *A Dictionary of the Underworld, British and American*. New York: Bonanza Books, 1961.

Picard, Liza. *Dr. Johnson's London: Coffee-Houses and Climbing Boys, Medicine, Toothpaste and Gin, Poverty and Press-Gangs, Freakshows and Female Education*. New York: St. Martin's Griffin, 2000.

Pocock, J. G. A. *Virtue, Commerce, and History: Essays on Political Thought and History, Chiefly in the Eighteenth Century*. New York: Cambridge University Press, 1985.

Porter, Roy. *English Society in the Eighteenth Century.* Revised edition. New York: Penguin Books, 1990.

"Pretty Patsie." *Immigrant Ships Transcribers Guild.* (http://immigrantships.net/1700/prettypatsie17370902.html, 25 August 2009).

Rediker, Marcus. *The Slave Ship: A Human History.* New York: Viking, 2007.

---. *Villains of All Nations: Atlantic Pirates in the Golden Age.* Boston: Beacon Press, 2004.

Scharf, J. Thomas. *History of Maryland: From the Earliest Period to the Present Day.* 3 vols. Baltimore: John B. Piet, 1879.

Schwartz, Richard B. *Daily Life in Johnson's London.* Madison, WI: The University of Wisconsin Press, 1983.

Shaw, A. G. L. *Convicts and the Colonies: A Study of Penal Transportation from Great Britain and Ireland to Australia and Other Parts of the British Empire.* London: Faber and Faber, 1966.

Smith, Abbot Emerson. *Colonists in Bondage: White Servitude and Convict Labor in America, 1607-1776.* New York: Norton, 1971.

---. "The Transportation of Convicts to the American Colonies in the Seventeenth Century." *The American Historical Review* 39.2 (1934): 232-49.

Sollers, Basil. "Transported Convict Laborers in Maryland during the Colonial Period." *Maryland Historical Magazine* (Mar., 1907): 17-47.

Stillé, Charles J. "American Colonies as Penal Settlements," *The Pennsylvania Magazine of History and Biography* 12.4 (Jan. 1889): 457-464.

Thompson, E. P. *Whigs and Hunters: The Origin of the Black Act.* New York: Pantheon, 1975.

"Thompson or Thomson, Sir William (1678-1739)." *Dictionary of National Biography.* Vol. XIX. Sidney Lee, ed. New York: The Macmillan Company, 1909, pp. 706-707.

Vaver, Anthony Theodore. *Reading Criminals/Criminal Readings: Early Eighteenth-Century English Constructions of Criminality.* Doctoral dissertation. Stony Brook, NY: The State University of New York at Stony Brook, 1994.

Weinreb, Ben and Christopher Hibbert, eds. *The London Encyclopaedia.* London: Macmillan, 1983.

Wells, Camille. "The Planter's Prospect: Houses, Outbuildings, and Rural Landscapes in Eighteenth-Century Virginia." *Winterthur Portfolio* 28:1 (Spring, 1993): 1-31.

Whitfield, Peter. *London: A Life in Maps.* London: The British Library, 2006.

Index

About the Author

Anthony Vaver is the author and publisher of Early American Crime (http://www.EarlyAmericanCrime.com), a website that explores crime, criminals, and punishments from America's past. He holds a B.A. from Cornell College, a Ph.D. from the State University of New York at Stony Brook, and an M.L.S. from Rutgers University. He is currently working on a new book about early American criminals. He has never spent a night in jail, but he was once falsely accused of shoplifting.

To see pictures of the author at various historic sites mentioned in this book, visit www.PickpocketPublishing.com.

Made in the USA
Lexington, KY
03 November 2011